THE CATHOLIC NOVEL

GARLAND REFERENCE LIBRARY
OF THE HUMANITIES
(Vol. 690)

THE CATHOLIC NOVEL
An Annotated Bibliography

Albert J. Menendez

GARLAND PUBLISHING, INC. • NEW YORK & LONDON
1988

Library of Congress Cataloging-in-Publication Data

Menendez, Albert J.
    The Catholic Novel: An Annotated Bibliography / Albert J.
Menendez
        p.   cm — (Garland reference library of the humanities; v.
690)
    Includes Indexes
    ISBN 0–8240–8534–5 (alk. paper)
    1. Christian fiction—Catholic authors—Bibliography.
2. Christian fiction—Catholic authors—Stories, plots, etc.
3. Bibliography—Best books—Fiction. I. Title.   II. Series:
Garland reference library of the humanities; v. 690.
Z5917.C47M46   1988   [PN3448.C48]   016.80883'9382—dc19
88-1718   CIP

Printed on acid-free, 250-year-life paper
Manufactured in the United States of America

For Shirley

CONTENTS

Introduction................................. ix

Religious Novels: Criticism................. 3

The Catholic Novel: Criticism.............. 9

Individual Authors: Criticism.............. 23

The Novels.................................. 49

The 100 Best Catholic Novels............... 283

Subject Index............................... 289

Title Index of Novels...................... 301

THE CATHOLIC NOVEL: INTRODUCTION

The earliest Catholic novels were generally instruments of propaganda in a hostile society. They explored permanent Catholic truths and values in ways calculated to strengthen the faithful but also to attract sympathetic and well meaning non-Catholics. They were often heavy on doctrine and dogma, light on personality and character development. Rarely did they explore complexity or the grey areas of ethics and competing values. The early nineteenth century Catholic novelists preferred to delineate the black areas of sin and rebellion and the white areas of grace and truth.

One authority, Willard Thorp, in his study of Catholic novels published between 1829 and 1865, says, "In the main these novels are exemplary, written to show how good Catholics lived and practiced their religion. In the beginning they were directed to Catholics themselves, particularly young people, so that they might be instructed while being delighted."

David S. Reynolds argues, "Unlike Protestant novelists, who wished to find diverting, sentimental replacements for the rigorous theology of the Puritan past, Roman Catholics generally devoted their novels to attacking what they saw as Protestant divisiveness, theological evasion, and lack of logic. The free Biblical interpretation and privately formed faith that Protestant novels increasingly extolled were ultimate heresy for the Catholic writer, who tried to validate the authority of the historical True Church as a cure for contemporary Protestant corruption. While

ix

Protestant fiction was generally nontheoretical,
much Catholic fiction before 1850 attempted to be
intellectual and polemical."

By the 1840s, though, the Catholic novelist,
according to Reynolds, "faced a uniquely difficult
task: to win the sympathy of predominantly
Protestant readers who were apt to dislike not
only Catholicism but authoritarian religion of any
sort." In order to compete in the marketplace,
Catholic novelists were forced to move toward
sentimental fiction in the two decades preceding
the Civil War.

The poisonous anti-Catholic crusade that
began with the Nativists and Know Nothings and
culminated in church burnings and riots shocked
and dismayed the entire Catholic community,
immigrant and old-timer alike. Anti-Catholic
works dominated the Protestant and secular
publishing lists during this era. To survive, "A
new tone of defensive vindictiveness" characterized much of the new Catholic fiction, according
to Reynolds.

Reynolds also argues that Catholic novelists
did not indulge in "sheer emotionalism" but
"presented their novels as reasoned refutations of
unreasonable Protestant slander." Catholic
fiction was still highly anecdotal and illustrative. While still argumentative and intellectual
in tone, the Catholic novel became more down to
earth. Conversion to Catholicism was a common
literary device and was presented as a dramatic
climax worthy of all respect and calling for the
greatest literary skill an author could muster.

One early Catholic novelist, Jedidiah
Huntington, asked openly, "Can romantic fiction be
imbued with Catholic faith and morality, so as to
serve the interest of religion?" Then he answered
his own question by defining the ideal Catholic
novel: "I define a Catholic novel as one that
represents human life in the present or in past
ages as interpreted by the supernatural element

imparted to it by the Catholic faith."

One dissenter in this period was the prominent convert Orestes Brownson, who repeatedly
called for adherence to strict logic.   He
condemned novelists who "secularized the spiritual
and spiritualized the secular." He wrote frequent
essays and reviews and also contributed four
novels of his own to the debate, in which he
continued the tradition of didactic intellec-
tualism in fiction. In one of his late essays
Brownson still maintained that a Catholic novelist
was "not to paint actual life but to idealize it
and raise it as far as possible to the Christian
standard."

After the Civil War and Reconstruction
Catholic fiction writers turned toward strengthen-
ing the growing Catholic community, holding up
what were perceived to be its consistent and
eternal values. This was the era of women
novelists like Anna Dorsey, Mary Ann Sadlier, Mary
Agnes Tinckner, and Christian Reid. Several were
romantics and converts to the church. Their
efforts were supported by new Catholic literary
journals and scholarly magazines which sought to
enlighten and inform the Catholic community of the
importance of good literature.

This was the era of optimism in American
Catholic fiction. In his admirable study of
Catholic writers from 1880 to 1915, James A. White
says that these novelists "revealed to their
readers the beauties of their Faith and shared
their advice regarding contemporary social
problems." Opposition to divorce and secular
education were recurring themes. White affirms
that Catholic writers of that era were "well
intentioned men and women in an age of do-gooders"
who "desired to lead their fellow Americans and
co-religionists to a finer appreciation of
culture, education and religion."

This was the time when F. Marion Crawford's
novels were consistent best sellers. Often

steeped in Catholicism they were superior to most
Catholic oriented fiction of previous decades.
The charming southern Catholic novelist Christian
Reid was immensely popular among Catholic readers.
Henry Harland's The Cardinal's Snuff Box, a
charming but inconsequential romance set in Italy,
was a best seller which allegedly produced many
conversions.   The first Catholic book to become a
best seller was Ludovic Halevy's The Abbe
Constantin in 1882.   Paul Messbarger claims this
"was the first truly popular and sympathetic
presentation of Catholicism in American history."
While these novels were mostly read by Catholics,
many readers of other faiths obviously enjoyed
them also.   Catholics were now producing a body of
writers both praised and respected by the reading
public and critics alike.   If they were not of the
first rank, they were at least making a real
contribution to letters.

Paul Messbarger has argued that most American
Catholic fiction of this era had a parochial
purpose.   He says, "Catholic fiction served a
purpose, a crucial one: As an instrument of
cultural adjustment.   It gave American Catholics a
special identity, anchored to the unique circum-
stances of American life.   It filled their minds
with images of a glorious past which each could
claim as a personal legacy, and with models of
success that spoke to each one's immediate needs."

By the 1920s American Catholic fiction had an
exuberant, self-confident quality, even though the
secular world was characterized by post-war
disillusionment and exhaustion.   Catholic fiction
did not embark on new directions as yet but
tended, Arnold Sparr argues, to "promote, defend
and redeem."

These were the twilight years of Catholic
didactic tradition, which was polemical,
moralistic and provincial.   Sparr continues, "Its
underlying premise was that fiction was a highly
affected medium for promoting and defending the

church while transmitting lessons of faith to both
Catholic and non-Catholic alike....More than any
other cultural group between 1920 and 1950,
Catholics regarded literature as a significant
cultural force capable of shaping the conscious-
ness of society for good or evil. Through the
novel Catholics would penetrate and change
culture, leavening it with Christian truth."

Catholic novelists defended the church's
position on birth control and divorce, on the
redemptive value of suffering, the shallowness of
materialism, and the transitory nature of worldly
success. Catholic novelists remained, as they had
always been, antimodern, antisecular, often
antirational. Sparr emphasizes this point: "An
overriding message in Catholic fiction of this
period was that Catholics were different. They
were a people set apart and it was their philosophy of life and the demands of their faith that
made them so. Most non-Catholics in these stories
are uncertain about first principles. They are
without a theology of birth, death and marriage,
and lack objective standards of right and wrong.
Catholics, in contrast, are ruled by a fixed body
of religious truths, and a firm moral philosophy."

Defense of tradition and reverence for order
and authority characterize many of the great
novels of the English Catholic writer Robert Hugh
Benson, who drew on the rich historical heritage
of the church, of the philisophical novelist Owen
Dudley Edwards, and the romanticist Montgomery
Carmichael.

While Catholics still gloried in their own
faith and traditions, changes within Catholicism
would produce changes in the Catholic novel.

As the depression days grew dimmer and more
seemingly hopeless, Catholic novelists began to
grow restive. They began to apply critical
insights to the problems and failures of their own
hallowed community.

Catholics now began to show the warts in the Catholic community, the failure of many individual Catholics to live up to the high calling that faith and commitment implied. Not all Catholic characters were seen as noble. Catholics could be villainous and hypocritical. Even priests were subjected to the new cricitism. Non-Catholics often appear as more genuinely Christian and worthy of respect than Catholics in the Catholic fiction of 1935 to 1960.

Catholic novelists, in particular Harry Sylvester, turned a critical eye to social and political problems and often castigated the church and its people for failure to build a just, compassionate social order. Sylvester condemned racism in Catholic southern Maryland, in <u>Dearly Beloved</u> and blasted political corruption and anti-Semitism among Catholic New Yorkers in <u>Moon Gaffney</u>.

The Catholic laity emerge as a social and cultural force in the new Catholic fiction. Leo Brady's novels "clearly prefer the outcast and the sinner over the comfortably saved," says Arnold Sparr. Indeed, self-criticism had become so essential that Sparr could write that "this new group of American writers tended to be angry young men alienated from significant dimensions of Catholic life and the institutional church." Joe Dever and J.F. Powers are representative of this new breed.

Still, the American critics saw their role as that of the loyal opposition, a corrective force within the household of faith. Sparr, for example, is able to say, "Catholic fiction affirmed Catholic life between 1935 and 1950. A remarkable number of American Catholic intellectuals and writers - and fictional heroes and heroines - broke with the Catholic ghetto during this period, but they did not break with their identities as Christians. Their faith was still their premise for action."

But above all else the novels of Graham
Greene, George Bernanos, Leon Bloy, and Francois
Mauriac revolutionized Catholic fiction. They
explored the seminal themes of Christian faith in
a complex, paradoxical world where darkness and
light, faith and doubt, holiness and despair seem
almost interchangeable. The great themes of
pride, hypocrisy and self-deception among the
outwardly pious have never been so fully explored
as in the continental Catholic literary renais-
sance of the 20th century.

The popularity of these Cathlic novelists in
America testifies to their abiding influence in
both Catholic and secular intellectual life.
Their unpopularity among traditional Catholics
also showed the tensions that such realism
produces.

Frank Kellogg believes that Catholic novels
were sterile aesthetically and intellectually
"until the Catholic artists transformed the
established and chronic Catholic spirit of opposition to the secular world into opposition to their
own tradition also, and began their criticism of
their own community." He concludes, "When the
Catholic novelists turned to scrutinize what was
most sensitively their own, they touched for the
first time the developing thought of a great
creative tradition."

It goes without saying that Catholic fiction
reflected the status and self-identity of the
religious community. Self-criticism is impossible
when hostile forces sought to repress Catholic
participation in public life and to circumscribe
Catholics into a ghetto. Only as Catholicism
became more comfortable in and more respected by
the whole society was it possible for its writers
to probe critically the institution itself.

Catholic fiction, pronounced dead in the
turmoil of the late 1960s, has made a great
comeback. The "parables" of Andrew Greeley have
soared to the best-seller lists. The works of
Brian Moore, Mary Gordon and David Lodge are
highly praised, and deservedly so. The literary
imagination derived from the Catholic experience

is alive and well in the 1980s, even if many of
the leading exponents no longer practice the faith
in the way ecclesiastical authorities prefer.

An indication of the increasing importance of
the Catholic novel was the publication of a
special issue (the Spring/Summer number for 1987)
of U.S. Catholic Historian devoted exclusively to
"American Fiction and Catholic Culture." This
excellent journal is published by the U.S.
Catholic Historical Society.

This guide has been prepared to assist those
who are interested in religious novels, specifically those of the Catholic tradition.

One of the more perplexing aspects of
producing this book was deciding what to include,
and what to exclude. Hence the need for a definition. No one has yet developed a completely
satisfactory definition of the Catholic novel.
Not only does no adequate definition exist but no
one really knows when the Catholic novel began.
Sister Marietta Gable argues convincingly in the
Catholic Bookman's Guide that Allessandro
Manzoni's The Betrothed, published in English in
1828, was the first.

But back to the definition. Two scholars of
the field offered these definitions. Paul
Messbarger says Catholic novels are works by
Catholics for a Catholic audience, "employing
specifically Catholic materials from a Catholic
point of view." Frank Kellogg limits the concept
to only those novels "whose mainspring of dramatic
action depends upon Roman Catholic theology, or
upon the history of thought within one of the
world's large Roman Catholic communities."

I offer this working definition: A Catholic
novel is one which reflects the values, culture
and conflicts of the Roman Catholic faith and its
community. This may seem slightly unecumenical,
but it is necessary to establish some parameters
to differentiate the Catholic novel from other
kinds of religious fiction. This means, for
example, that Iris Murdoch's The Bell and Rumer
Godden's Black Narcissus are necessarily excluded

since they deal with Anglican convent life, not Roman Catholic.

Some readers will no doubt be disappointed by the exclusion of Flannery O'Connor, that remarkable Southern Catholic writer, the interpretation of whose writings has become a virtual cottage industry of late. Miss O'Connor is primarily a short story writer, and short stories are outside the scope of this bibliography. Furthermore, both of O'Connor's superb novels draw upon the fundamentalist Protestant heritage of her native Georgia. Novels must deal with the Catholic subculture to be included in this volume.

Another problem was whether to include novels which are primarily critical of Catholicism. I chose to do so in most cases, since criticism is essential to literary integrity. Anticlerical novels have a long and honorable heritage in Continental European literature, and many practicing Catholic authors have criticized church policies and spiritual imperfections at crucial periods in church history. The critical spirit has become an increasingly important facet of Catholic fiction since World War II.

But so-called "anti-Catholic" fiction does not belong here - There has been enough of this kind of material published since the early 19th century to fill another bibliography. But fiction designed solely to slander Catholics and Catholicism belongs to another category of fiction altogether. Most of it was subliterary and puerile, based almost completely on misrepresentation and ignorance. Most of these novels have long been forgotten and with good reason.

Several interesting subcategories are included: the Catholic historical novel, the Vatican thriller, and the Catholic murder mystery. The last-named is a particularly felicitous category in which is probed the nature of theological evil in a suspenseful setting. In each of these categories outstanding novels have been produced.

I have also included many ethnic novels reflecting the vitality of the many nationalist groups which have contributed to the mosaic of American Catholicism, though only those novels which reflect a strong religious emphasis are included.

One does not have to be Catholic to write a Catholic novel. Some of the best authors are lapsed, like Brian Moore, while some others, like Harry Sylvester, broke with the church completely. Many were Protestant. Frederick Buechner is a Presbyterian minister. John Rathbone Oliver was an Episcopal priest. Franz Werfel was Jewish. But the majority have been practicing Catholics, and an extraordinary number have been converts to the Old Faith.

Locating the obscure Catholic novels has been a task, though a joyous and exciting one. Quite a number are not found in the Library of Congress. But I have scoured the secondhand bookstores far and wide. Hundreds of these were located in that veritable mecca of Catholica, the Christian Classics bookstore in the placid little town of Westminster, Maryland. There are no more knowledgeable or helpful booksellers left in this country than John and Kitty McHale of Christian Classics. John Prosser in Chicago and the fine folks at Acres of Books in Long Beach, California have also been unfailingly helpful.

Most of the novels annotated here have been examined by me. The few that are not annotated have been unobtainable thus far, but I have included those which appeared in such authoritative sources as the University of London's Cumulated Fiction Index for the years 1945 to 1979, and Stephen J. Brown's Fiction and Tales by Catholic Authors, published by the Central Catholic Library in Dublin in 1945.

As a final lagniappe to the reader, I have offered my nominations for the "100 Greatest Catholic Novels." The selection is mine, but I have of course taken into account the judgment of many critics. A few of the entries may seem idiosyncratic but I stand by them!

A word about format: This bibliography cites 1703 novels and 489 critical works illustrative of the Catholic novel.   The earliest titles date from the 1820s, when the genre seems to have emerged. All periods of church history, except the biblical and early apostolic ones, are included.   (Novels of this inchoate period of Christianity deserve a separate volume.)   All nations and times are included, as the Subject Index will indicate.

The first chapter includes references to religious fiction in general followed by a chapter citing references to Catholic novels in particu- lar.   The third chapter recommends critical and biographical material about the major authors included in the main portion of the text - the annotated guide to representative Catholic novels. A list of the "100 Best," a Subject Index, and a Title Index follow.

Albert J. Menendez
Gaithersburg, Maryland
January 1988

THE CATHOLIC NOVEL

RELIGIOUS NOVELS: CRITICISM

1. Anker, Roy M. "Doubt and Faith in Late
    Nineteenth Century Fiction." Ph.D. disser-
    tation. Michigan State University, 1974.

2. Barkowsky, Edward R. "The Popular Christian
    Novel in America 1918-1953." Ph.D. disser-
    tation. Ball State University, 1975.

3. Barrett, E. Boyd. "Modern Writers and
    Religion." Thinker 3 (May 1931): 32-38.

4. Beary, Thomas John. "Religion and the Modern
    Novel." Catholic World, 166 (December
    1947), 203-211.

5. Bennett, Eugene Ernest. "The Image of the
    Christian Clergyman in Modern Fiction."
    Ph.D. dissertation. Vanderbilt Divinity
    School, 1970.

6. Brooke, Stopford A. Religion in Literature
    and Religion in Life. New York: Crowell,
    1901.

7. Bunting, John J., Jr. "Religion Among the
    Novelists." Religion in Life 24 (Spring
    1955): 208-218.

8. Burnett, Ernest. "The Image of the Clergyman
    in Modern Fiction." Ph.D. dissertation.
    Vanderbilt University, 1960.

9. Carey, R.A. "Bestselling Religion." Ph.D.
    dissertation. Michigan State University,
    1971.

10. Davies, Horton. The Image of the Ministry in
    Fiction. New York: Oxford University
    Press, 1959.

11. Davies, W.E. "Religious Issues in Late
     Nineteenth-Century American Novels."
     Commonweal 35 (July 1963): 34-42.

12. Dillistone, F.W. The Novelist and the
     Passion Story. New York: Sheed & Ward,
     1960.

13. Exman, Eugene. "Reading, Writing and
     Religion." Harper's 206 (May 1953): 84-90.

14. Fitt, Frank. "The Saint As a Best-Seller."
     Christian Century 58 (September 3, 1941):
     1081-1082.

15. Flood, Ethelbert. "Christian Language in
     Modern Literature." Culture 22 (March
     1961): 28-42.

16. Frederick, John T. The Darkened Sky:
     Nineteenth Century American Novelists and
     Religion. Notre Dame, IN: Notre Dame
     University Press, 1969.

17. Gerlach, John C. "The Kingdom of God and
     Nineteenth Century American Fiction."
     Ph.D. dissertation. Arizona State
     University, 1969.

18. Hart, James D. "Platitudes of Piety: Relgion
     and the Popular Modern Novel." American
     Quarterly 6 (Winter 1954): 311-322.

19. Hawkins, Maude Miller. "Religious Aspects of
     Modern American Fiction." M.A. Thesis.
     University of South Carolina, 1932.

20. Hawkins, Peter S. The Language of Grace.
     Cambridge, MA: Cowley Publications, 1983.

21. Hurley, Leonard B. "The American Novel
     1830-1850: Its Reflections of Contemporary
     Religious Conditions." Ph.D. dissertation.
     University of North Carolina, 1932.

22. Keller, Arnold F., Jr. "The Clergyman in
     Recent Fiction." Lutheran Church Quarterly
     20 (April 1947): 193-198.

23. Maison, Margaret M. The Victorian Vision:
    Studies in the Religious Novel. New York:
    Sheed & Ward, 1961.

24. Mooney, Harry J., Jr. and Thomas F. Staley,
    eds. The Shapeless God: Essays on Modern
    Fiction. Pittsburgh: University of
    Pittsburgh Press, 1968.

25. Murchland, Bernard G. "Theology and
    Literature." Commonweal 71 (October 16,
    1959): 63-66.

26. Noon, William T. "God and Man in Twentieth
    Century Fiction." Thought 37 (Spring
    1962): 35-56.

27. O'Connor, Leo F. "The Image of Religion in
    Selected American Novels 1860-1920." Ph.D.
    dissertation. New York University, 1972.

28. Panichas, George A., ed. Mansions of the
    Spirit: Essays in Literature and Religion.
    New York: Hawthorn Books, 1967.

29. Reinhardt, Kurt F. The Theological Novel of
    Modern Europe. New York: Frederick Ungar,
    1969.

30. Reynolds, David S. Faith in Fiction: The
    Emergence of Religious Literature in
    America. Cambridge: Harvard University
    Press, 1981.

31. Sampson, Ashley. "Religion in Modern
    Literature." Contemporary Review 147
    (April 1935): 462-470.

32. Scott, Nathan A., Jr. ed. Adversity and
    Grace: Studies in Recent American
    Literature. Chicago: University of Chicago
    Press, 1968.

33. ————. The Broken Center: Studies in the
    Theological Horizon of Modern Literature.
    New Haven: Yale University Press, 1966.

34. ————. Craters of the Spirit. Washington,
    D.C.: Corpus Books, 1968.

35.   ————. Modern Literature and the Religious
       Frontier. New York: Harper, 1958.

36.   ————. Negative Capability: Studies in the
       Religious Situation. New Haven: Yale
       University Press, 1969.

37.   ————, ed. The New Orpheus: Essays Toward a
       Christian Poetic. New York: Sheed & Ward,
       1964.

38.   Shuck, Emerson C. "Clergymen in
       Representative American Fiction 1830-1930."
       Ph.D. dissertation. University of
       Wisconsin, 1943.

39.   Suderman, Elmer F. "Religion in the American
       Novel, 1870-1900." Ph.D. dissertation.
       University of Kansas, 1960.

40.   Thompson, James J., Jr. Christian Classics
       Revisited. San Francisco: Ignatius Press,
       1983.

41.   Thorp, Willard. "The Religious Novel As Best
       Seller in America." Religious Perspectives
       in American Culture. Edited by James Ward
       Smith and Leland Jamison. Princeton:
       Princeton University Press, 1961, pp. 195-
       242.

42.   Turnell, Martin. "Belief and the Writer."
       Commonweal 62 (May 13, 1955): 143-146.

43.   ————. Modern Literature and Christian
       Faith. Westminster, MD: Newman Press,
       1961.

44.   ————. "The Religious Novel." Commonweal
       55 (October 26, 1951): 55-57.

45.   Ulbrich, Armand Henry. "The Trend Toward
       Religion in the Modern American Novel,
       1925-1951." Ph.D. dissertation.
       University of Michigan, 1953.

46.   Voigt, Gilbert P. "The Spiritual Aspect of
       Recent American Literature." Lutheran
       Church Quarterly 17 (January 1944): 3-13.

47. Williams, Virginia. "Religion and Church as
     Motifs in American Fiction." Ph.D.
     dissertation. Vanderbilt University,
     1930.

48. Wolff, Robert Lee. Gains and Losses: Novels
     of Faith and Doubt in Victorian England.
     New York: Garland, 1977.

THE CATHOLIC NOVEL: CRITICISM

49. Antush, John V. "Realism in the Catholic Novel." Catholic World 185 (July 1957): 276-279.

50. Barth, Hilary Leighton. "The Catholic Writer of Tomorrow." Catholic School Editor 9 (January 1940): 4-5, 14.

51. Bateman, May. "The Catholic View in Modern Fiction." Catholic World 102 (February 1916): 577-589.

52. Belvedere, Joseph. "Catholic Fiction: Achilles' Heel." America 65 (August 23, 1941): 550-551.

53. Bergonzi, Bernard. "A Conspicious Absentee: The Decline and Fall of the Catholic Novel." Encounter 55 (August-September, 1980): 44-56.

54. Boland, Allen. "Catholic English Literature in America." Franciscan Educational Conference - Reports 22 (December 1940): 123-169.

55. Brady, Charles A. "A Brief Survey of Catholic Fiction." Books on Trial 12 (January-February 1954): 159-160, 190-191.

56. ———. "Catholic Fiction: Lifting Fog?" America 65 (August 30, 1941): 579-580.

57. ———. "Priests in the New Novel." Lamp 61 (August 1963): 10-11, 30-31.

58. Brady, Ignatius. "Catholic English Literature in the British Isles in the Twentieth Century." Franciscan Educational Conference - Reports. 22 (December 1940): 103-120.

59. Braybrooke, Neville. "Catholics and the
     Novel." Renascence 5 (Autumn 1952):
     22-32.

60. ———. "The Continuity of Catholic
     Literature." Clergy Review 41 (May 1956):
     257-274.

61. ———. "The Priest in Contemporary
     Fiction." Christus Rex 12 (July 1958):
     215-219.

62. Braybrooke, Patrick. Some Catholic
     Novelists: Their Art and Outlook. London:
     Burns & Oates, 1931.

63. Bregy, Katherine. "Priests in Recent
     Literature." America 66 (November 8,
     1941): 129-130

64. ———. "Religion Comes Back to Our
     Fiction." America 62 (December 7, 1929):
     211-212.

65. Brennan, Joseph X. "The American Catholic
     and American Literature." Emerson
     Quarterly 39 (1965): 85-93.

66. Brinkmeyer, Robert H., Jr. Three Catholic
     Writers of the Modern South. Jackson:
     University Press of Mississippi, 1985.

67. Broderick, Robert C. "The Position of the
     Catholic Fictionist." Ave Maria 49
     (February 4, 1939): 129-133.

68. Brown, Stephen J. "The Catholic Novelist and
     His Themes." Irish Monthly 63 (July 1935):
     432-444.

69. Brown, Stephen J. and Thomas McDermott. A
     Survey of Catholic Literature. Milwaukee:
     Bruce, 1945.

70. Butler, Robert Olen. "On the Role of the
     Catholic Novelist." National Catholic
     Register 23 (June 9, 1985): 1, 6.

71. Carey, Charles M. "Catholic Novel Writing." *Ave Maria* 47 (March 5, 1938): 298-300.

72. "The Catholic Novel." *Commonweal* 19 (January 19, 1934): 312.

73. "Catholic Novels and Reprobates." *Catholic World* 168 (March 1949): 417-421.

74. Cavanaugh, Sister Mary Stephana. "Catholic Book Publishing in the United States, 1784-1850." Master's thesis. University of Illinois, 1937.

75. Chen, Josephine Ti Ti. "A Survey of Catholic Americana and Catholic Book Publishing in the United States, 1891-1895." Master's thesis. Catholic University of America, 1956.

76. Connolly, Francis X. "Catholic Fiction: Two Reactions." *America* 65 (September 13, 1941): 634-635.

77. ————. "The Catholic Theme." *America* 50 (December 9, 1933): 233-235.

78. ————. "The Catholic Writer and Contemporary Culture." *Thought* 14 (September 1939): 373-383.

79. Connolly, Peter R. "The Priest in Modern Irish Fiction." *Furrow* 9 (December 1958): 782-797.

80. Cunningham, Lawrence. "Catholic Sensibility and Southern Writers." *Bulletin of the Center for the Study of Southern Culture and Religion* 2 (1978): 7-10.

81. Curley, Thomas F. "Catholic Novels and American Culture." *Commentary* 36 (July 1963): 34-42.

82. Dawson, Avelina. "A Survey of Catholic Americana and Catholic Book Publishing in the United States, 1881-1885." Master's thesis. Catholic University of America, 1951.

83. Dever, Joseph. "The Catholic Novel." <u>Today</u>
    1 (October 1947): 15-16.

84. ————. "Yes, We Have No Bernanos." <u>Books
    On Trial</u> 9 (March 1951): 248-250.

85. Dooley, D.J. "The Strategy of the Catholic
    Novelist." <u>Catholic World</u> 189 (July 1959):
    300-304.

86. Dooley, Roger Burke. "The Catholic in the
    Eighteenth Century Novel." Ph.D.
    dissertation. Catholic University, 1956.

87. Doyle, Brian. "Morals and Novels." <u>Ave
    Maria</u> 77 (April 25, 1953): 532-533.

88. Driscoll, Annette S. <u>Literary Convert Women</u>.
    Manchester, NH: Magnificat Press, 1928.

89. Egan, Maurice F. "The Basis of the Catholic
    Novel." <u>Catholic World</u> 76 (1902): 316-327.

90. English, Jack. "Can a Catholic Write a
    Novel?" <u>American Mercury</u> 31 (January
    1934): 90-95.

91. Evans, Fallon. "The Convent Wall and the
    Connubial Bed (A Literary History)." <u>New
    Catholic World</u> 228 (July/August 1985):
    153-156.

92. Ewens, Mary. <u>The Role of the Nun in
    Nineteenth Century America</u>. New York:
    Arno Press, 1978.

93. Fahey, Margaret Ann. "A Survey of Catholic
    Americana and Catholic Book Publishing in
    the United States, 1876-1880." Master's
    thesis. Catholic University of America,
    1954.

94. Farrell, T. "The Priest and the Novel."
    <u>America</u> 89 (August 8, 1953): 460-461.

95. Fecher, Charles A. "Literary Freedom and the
    Catholic Novelist." <u>Catholic World</u> 184
    (February 1957): 340-344.

96. Feiten, Patricia. "A Survey of Catholic
     Americana and Catholic Book Publishing in
     the United States, 1896-1900." Master's
     thesis. Catholic University of America,
     1958.

97. Fischer, Edward. "How Realistic Can a
     Catholic Writer Be?" Catholic Library
     World 21 (December 1949): 73-74.

98. Fitzmorris, Thomas J. "Formula For the Great
     American Catholic Novel." America 53
     (August 19, 1935): 425-426.

99. Folk, Barbara Nauer. "Fiction: A Problem For
     the Catholic Writer." Catholic World 188
     (November 1958): 105-109.

100. Gable, Sister Mariella. "Arrows at the
     Center." Catholic Library World 18 (April
     1947): 219-224.

101. ————. "Catholic Fiction." Catholic World
     151 (December 1940): 296-302.

102. ————. "Catholic Fiction Arrives in
     America." Today 1 (April 30, 1947): 12-13.

103. ————. "Prose Satire and the Modern
     Christian Temper." American Benedictine
     Review 11 (March-June 1960): 21-34.

104. ————. This Is Catholic Fiction. New York:
     Sheed & Ward, 1948.

105. Gandolfo, Anita. "The Demise of Father
     O'Malley: Reflections on Recent American
     Catholic Fiction." U.S. Catholic Historian
     6 (Spring/Summer 1987): 231-240.

106. Gardiner, Harold C. "The Catholic Novel:
     Two Important Statements." America 94
     (December 17, 1955): 333-334.

107. ————. "The Direction of Catholic Writing."
     Books On Trial 15 (April-May 1957): 379,
     418-419.

108. Gavigan, Walter V. "Nuns in Novels." Catholic World 140 (November 1934): 186-195.

109. Gilman, Richard. "Salvation, Damnation and the Religious Novel." New York Times Book Review (December 2, 1984): 7, 58, 60.

110. Graef, Hilda. "Marriage and Our Catholic Novelists." Catholic World 189 (June 1959): 185-190.

111. Graham, John E. "As the Novelist Sees the Priest." Truth 33 (February 1919): 10-12.

112. Grande, Luke M. "Renegade Priests in Recent Fiction." Catholic Library World 32 (April 1961): 407-410.

113. Guinan, J.W. "The Catholic and the Novel." Catholic Churchman 5 (March/April 1942): 112-114.

114. Guiney, Louise Imogen. "Catholic Writers and Their Handicaps." Catholic World 90 (November 1909): 204-215.

115. Hassard, J.R.G. "Catholic Literature and the Catholic Public." Catholic World 7 (1870): 399-407.

116. Hazo, Samuel J. "Belief and the [Catholic] Critic." Renascence 13 (Summer 1961): 187-199.

117. Healey, Robert C. A Catholic Book Chronicle. New York: Kenedy, 1951.

118. Hebblethwaite, Peter. "How Catholic Is the Catholic Novel?" Times Literary Supplement (July 27, 1967): 678-679.

119. Heppenstall, Rayner. The Double Image: Mutations of Christian Mythology in the Work of Four French Catholic Writers of Today and Yesterday. London: Secker, 1947.

120. Hertzel, Leo J. "Brother Juniper, Father Urban and the Unworldly Tradition." Renascence 17 (Summer 1965): 207-210.

121. Hickey, Emily. Our Catholic Heritage in English Literature. London: Sands, 1910.

122. Holzhauer, Jean. "The Nun in Literature." Commonweal 65 (February 22, 1957): 527-529.

123. Hope, Felix. "Modern Catholic Literature." Blackfriars 16 (August 1935): 600-611.

124. Hughes, Catharine. "The Priest in Current Fiction." Ave Maria 93 (May 6, 1961): 24-29.

125. Hurley, Doran. "Catholic Fiction: For the Defense." America 65 (September 20, 1941): 662-663.

126. Hurley, Neil. "The Priest in Literature." America 102 (January 23, 1960): 496-98.

127. Immaculate, Sister Joseph. "The Catholic Novelist as Apostle." Catholic Library World 23 (May 1952): 247-251.

128. "Is There a Catholic Novel?" Commonweal 19 (March 30, 1934): 593-594.

129. Jacobsen, Josephine. "A Catholic Quartet." Christian Scholar 47 (Summer 1964): 139-154.

130. Kellogg, Gene. "The Catholic Novel in Convergence." Thought 45 (1970): 265-296.

131. ———. The Vital Tradition: The Catholic Novel in a Period of Convergence. Chicago: Loyola University Press, 1970.

132. Kennedy, John S. "The Catholic Novel." Sign 22 (April 1943): 551-553.

133. ———. "Fifteen Years of Catholic Writing." Books On Trial 15 (April-May 1957): 369-371, 425-428.

134.   Kerngan, W.J. "Opposed Modalities - Pitfalls
       For Catholic Writers." Renascence 5
       (Autumn 1952): 15-21.

135.   Kevin, Neil. "Fiction Priests." Irish
       Ecclesiastical Record 60 (October 1942):
       253-257.

136.   Kissel, Susan Steves. "For a Hostile
       Audience: A Study of the Fiction of
       Flannery O'Connor, Walker Percy and J.F.
       Powers." Ph.D. dissertation. University
       of Cincinnati, 1975.

137.   Kuenelt-Leddihn, Eric Von. "The Failure of
       Catholic Literature." Catholic World 165
       (May 1947): 116-122.

138.   Kunkel, Francis L. "The Priest as Scapegoat
       in the Modern Catholic Novel." Ramparts 1
       (May 1962): 72-78.

139.   Lacoste, Andre Pierre. "Mercy, Grace, Sin in
       the Religious Vision of Graham Greene,
       Flannery O'Connor and Walker Percy." Ph.D.
       dissertation. Tulane University, 1982.

140.   Larnen, Brendan. "Novels of Catholicism."
       Dominicana 20 (September 1935): 159-162.

141.   Lathrop, George and Rose Hawthorne. "The
       Catholic Tendency in American Literature."
       American Catholic Quarterly Review 18
       (1893): 372-392.

142.   Lavelle, Francis. "Novels and Novel Writing."
       Catholic World 43 (1886): 521-522.

143.   Lonergan, Joan Mary. "Publishing Trends
       Reflected in Works of Academy Members of
       the Gallery of Living Catholic Authors."
       Master's thesis. Catholic University of
       America, 1955.

144.   Luker, Ralph E. "To Be Southern, To Be
       Catholic: An Interpretation of the Thought
       of Five American Writers." Southern
       Studies 23 (1984): 3-7.

145. Maison, Margaret M. "Anglican Agony; conver-
     sion Novels of the Victorian Age." Month
     15 (June 1956): 344-354.

146. Marshall, Bruce. "The Responsibilities of
     the Catholic Novelist." Commonweal 50 (May
     27, 1949): 169-171.

147. Mason, Herbert. "Two Catholic Traditions:
     France and America." Commonweal 74
     (September 22, 1961): 516-518.

148. McDermott, William A. Down at Caxton's.
     Baltimore: Murphy, 1895.

149. McDonnell, Lawrence V. "The Priest-Hero in
     the Modern Novel." Catholic World 146
     (February 1963): 306-311.

150. McMillan, Thomas. "The Growth of Catholic
     Reading Circles." Catholic World 61
     (1895): 709-712.

151. McNamara, Eugene. "Prospects of the Catholic
     Novel." America 97 (August 17, 1957):
     505-506, 508.

152. McNamara, R. "Phases of American Religion in
     Thornton Wilder and Willa Cather."
     Catholic World 135 (September 1932):
     641-649.

153. Meath, Gerard. "Catholic Writing."
     Blackfriars 32 (December 1951): 602-609.

154. Meehan, Thomas. "Catholic Literary New York,
     1800-1840." Catholic Historical Review 4
     (1918): 399-414.

155. ———. "The Centenary of American Catholic
     Fiction." Historical Records and Studies
     19 (1929): 52-72.

156. ———. "The House of Sadlier." America 47
     (1932): 214-215.

157.   Merrill, William S. Catholic Authorship in
       the American Colonies Before 1774.
       Washington, DC: Catholic University of
       America Press, 1917.

158.   Messbarger, Paul Robert. Fiction With a
       Parochial Purpose: Catholic Fiction
       1884-1900. Boston: Boston University
       Press, 1971.

159.   Mohler, Edward F. "Priests and Nuns of
       Modern Fiction." Ave Maria 56 (September
       5, 1942): 310-312.

160.   Morse, Charles A. "The Priest in Fiction."
       Catholic World 65 (May 1897): 145-153.

161.   Neame, A.J. "Black and Blue - A Study in the
       Catholic Novel." The European 2 (April
       1953): 26-36.

162.   O'Brien, Conor Cruise. Maria Cross:
       Imaginative Patterns in a Group of Modern
       Catholic Writers. New York: Oxford
       University Press, 1952.

163.   O'Connor, Flannery. "The Church and the
       Fiction Writer." America 96 (March 30,
       1957): 733-735.

164.   ————. "The Role of the Catholic Novelist."
       Greyfriar 7 (1964): 5-12.

165.   O'Connor, John J. "Catholic Writing Today."
       Catholic Action 31 (February 1949): 8-9.

166.   O'Neill, James L. Catholic Literature in
       Catholic Homes. New York: P. O'Shea,
       1894.

167.   O'Rourke, William. "Catholics Coming of Age:
       The Literary Consequences." Catholic World
       228 (July/August 1985): 148-152.

168.   Parsons, Wilfred A. "Catholic Literature's
       Dilemma." America 42 (January 11, 1930):
       337-340.

169. Pick, John. "Survey of United States
      Catholic Letters in the Twentieth Century."
      Journal of the Faculty of Arts, Royal
      University of Malta (March 1957): 58-74.

170. Powers, J.F. "The Catholic and Creativity."
      American Benedictine Review 15 (March
      1964): 63-80.

171. "Problems of the Catholic Writer." Catholic
      World 161 (March 1948): 481-486.

172. Quillin, Michael. "Since Blue Died: American
      Catholic Novels Since 1961." Critic 34
      (Fall, 1975): 25-35.

173. Rago, Henry. "Catholics and Literature."
      Commonweal 59 (October 30, 1953): 81-84.

174. Rank, Hugh D. "The Image of the Priest in
      American Catholic Fiction, 1945-1965."
      Ph.D. dissertation. University of Notre
      Dame, 1969.

175. Repplier, Agnes. "Catholic Letters and the
      Catholic World." Catholic World 101 (April
      1915): 31-37.

176. Ribalow, Harold U. "Catholic Literature to
      an Outsider." Catholic World 181 (May
      1955): 120-124.

177. Roche, Stephen J. "Priest-Workers in
      Fiction." Tablet 202 (July 11, 1953):
      31-35.

178. Ruskin, Mary Patricia. "A Survey of Catholic
      Americana and Catholic Book Publishing in
      the United States, 1886-1890." Master's
      thesis. Catholic University of America,
      1952.

179. Ryan, John Julian. "Catholic Romanticism - A
      Diagnosis of the Aches and Pains of
      Catholic Fiction Writers." Books On Trial
      9 (October 1950): 121-122, 153.

180.   Ryan, Stephen P. "The Catholic Novelist in
       the U.S.A." Catholic World 188 (February
       1959): 388-393.

181.   Sandra, Sister Mary. "The Priest-Hero in
       Modern Fiction." Personalist 46 (Autumn
       1965): 527-542.

182.   Shaw, James. "The Paper Priest." Books On
       Trial 10 (May 1952): 311-312, 338.

183.   Sheed, Wilfrid. "The Catholic as Writer:
       Enemies of Catholic Promise." Commonweal
       77 (February 22, 1963): 560-563.

184.   Sheerin, John B. "Catholic Novels and
       Reprobates." Catholic World 168 (March
       1949): 417-421.

185.   Shuster, George N. The Catholic Spirit in
       Modern English Literature. New York:
       Macmillan, 1925.

186.   Simons, John W. "The Catholic and the
       Novel." Four Quarters 9 (November 1959):
       15-20.

187.   Sisk, John P. "The Confessional Hero."
       Commonweal 72 (May 13, 1960): 167-170.

188.   Slavick, William H. "The Priest in Modern
       Fiction." Today 9 (January 1954): 12-13.

189.   Smith, Larry. "Catholics, Catholics
       Everywhere, A Flood of Catholic Novels."
       Critic 37 (December 1978): 3-8.

190.   Sonnenfeld, Albert. "The Catholic Novelist
       and the Supernatural." French Studies 22
       (October 1968): 307-319.

191.   ————. "Twentieth Century Gothic: Reflec-
       tions on the Catholic Novel." Southern
       Review n.s. 1 (April 1965): 388-405.

192.   Sparr, Arnold J. "The Catholic Literary
       Revival in America, 1920-1960." Ph.D.
       dissertation. University of Wisconsin,
       1985.

193. ———. "From Self-Congratulation to
     Self-Criticism: Main Currents in American
     Catholic Fiction, 1900-1960." U.S.
     Catholic Historian 6 (Spring/Summer 1987):
     213-230.

194. Spearman, Frank H. "The Catholic Novelist."
     America 34 (January 30, 1926): 381-383.

195. Sullivan, Richard. "A Definition of Catholic
     Fiction." Books On Trial 12 (January-
     February 1954): 157-181.

196. Sylvester, Harry. "Problems of the Catholic
     Writer." Atlantic 181 (January 1948):
     109-113.

197. Talbot, Francis X., ed. Fiction by Its
     Makers. New York: America Press, 1928.

198. ———. "Novelists and Critics, Both
     Catholic." America 42 (November 2, 1929):
     91-93.

199. Tarr, Sister Mary Muriel. Catholicism in
     Gothic Fiction. Washington, DC: Catholic
     University Press, 1946.

200. Thorp, Willard. Catholic Novelists in
     Defense of Their Faith, 1829-1865. New
     York: Arno Press, 1978.

201. Valentine, Mary Hester. "Novel Nuns."
     Critic 40 (Winter 1985): 43-58.

202. White, James A. The Era of Good Intentions:
     A Survey of American Catholic Writing
     1880-1915. New York: Arno Press, 1978.

203. Williams, Michael. "The Catholic Spirit in
     American Literature." Forum 80 (September
     1928): 441-449.

204. Wills, Garry. "Catholic Faith and Fiction."
     New York Times Book Review (January 16,
     1972): 1-2, 16-18.

INDIVIDUAL AUTHORS: CRITICISM

John Ayscough

205.   Downey, John J.   "The Inspiration of John
       Ayscough."   Commonweal 8 (August 1, 1928):
       330-331.

206.   Keller, Leo W.   "John Ayscough, Novelist."
       Catholic World 111 (May 1920): 164-173.

207.   Talbot, Francis X.   "In the Name of John
       Ayscough."   America 39 (August 11, 1928):
       428-429.

       See also Item 62, pp. 75-110.

Maurice Baring

208.   Lovat, Laura.   Maurice Baring, a Postscript.
       London: Hollis & Carter, 1947.

209.   Smyth, Ethel.   Maurice Baring.   London:
       Heinemann, 1938.

Rene Bazin

210.   Gosse, Edmund.   "The Novels of Rene Bazin."
       Contemporary Review 79 (1901): 264-277.

211.   Ryan, Mary.   "Rene Bazin."   Studies 21
       (1932): 627-635.

Robert Hugh Benson

212.   Benson, A.C.   Hugh: Memories of a Brother.
       London: Murray, 1915.

213.   Cornish, Blanche Ware.   Memories of Robert
       Hugh Benson.   New York: P.J. Kenedy, 1915.

23

214.   Martindale, C.C. The Life of Robert Hugh
        Benson. 2 vols. New York: Longmans, 1916

215.   Parr, Olive Katharine. Robert Hugh Benson:
        An Appreciation. New York: Hutchinson,
        1915.

216.   Reynolds, E.E. "The Historical Novels of
        Robert Hugh Benson." Dublin Review 233
        (Autumn, 1959): 272-278.

217.   Watt, Reginald. Robert Hugh Benson: Captain
        in God's Army. London: Burns & Oates,
        1918.

        See also Item 62, pp. 113-144.

Georges Bernanos

218.   Coles, Robert. "The Pilgrimage of Georges
        Bernanos." New York Times Book Review
        (June 8, 1986): 3, 35.

219.   Hebblethwaite, Peter. Bernanos. New York:
        Hillary House, 1965.

220.   McCarthy, Abigail Quigley. "The Novels of
        Bernanos." Today 1 (October 15, 1947): 14.

        See also Item 29, pp. 93-129
                 Item 40, pp. 26-30.

Leon Bloy

221.   Beguin, Albert. Leon Bloy. London: Sheed &
        Ward, 1947.

222.   Dubois, Elfriede Theresa. Portrait of Leon
        Bloy. New York: Sheed & Ward, 1951.

223.   Heppenstall, Rayner. Leon Bloy. New Haven:
        Yale University Press, 1954.

224.   Polimeni, Emmanuela. Leon Bloy: The Pauper
        Prophet. New York: Philosophical Library,
        1951.

        See also: Item 29, pp. 74-92
                  Item 40, pp. 128-132

Heinrich Boll

225. Conrad, Robert C. Heinrich Boll. Boston:
      Twayne, 1984.

Henry Bordeaux

226. Crawford, Virginia. "Henry Bordeaux."
      Studies 16 (1927): 306-316.

227. Scheifley, William H. "Henry Bordeaux."
      Catholic World 110 (January 1920): 471-475.

Lucille Papin Borden

228. Mary Louise, Sister. "Lucille Papin Borden,
      American Novelist of the Great Tradition."
      Catholic Literary World 14 (March 1943):
      163-169.

Paul Bourget

229. Dimnet, Ernest. Paul Bourget. Boston:
      Houghton, Mifflin, 1913.

Orestes A. Brownson

230. Maynard, Theodore. Orestes Brownson: Yankee,
      Radical, Catholic. New York: Macmillan,
      1943.

231. Schlesinger, Arthur M., Jr. A Pilgrim's
      Progress: Orestes A. Brownson. Boston:
      Little, Brown, 1939.

232. Sveino, Per. Orestes A. Brownson's Road to
      Catholicism. New York: Humanities Presse,
      1970.

233. Whalen, Doran. Granite for God's House: The
      Life of Orestes Brownson. New York: Sheed
      & Ward, 1941.

Morley Callaghan

234. Higgins, Michael W. and Douglas R. Letson.
      "Morley Callaghan." Portraits of Canadian
      Catholicism. Toronto: Griffin House,
      1986, pp. 86-96.

Montgomery Carmichael

235.   Kelly, Blanche. "Montgomery Carmichael,
       Humanist." Catholic World 144 (December
       1936): 328-333.

236.   Wager, Charles. "The Writings of Montgomery
       Carmichael." Catholic World 103 (June
       1916): 360-364.

Gilbert Keith Chesterton

237.   Barker, Dudley. G.K. Chesterton. New York:
       Stein & Day, 1973.

238.   Dale, Alzina Stone. The Outline of Sanity: A
       Life of G.K. Chesterton. Grand Rapids:
       Erdmans, 1982.

239.   Las Vergnas, Raymond, Chesterton, Belloc,
       Baring. London: Sheed & Ward, 1938.

240.   Ward, Maisie. Gilbert Keith Chesterton. New
       York: Sheed & Ward, 1943.

241.   ———. Return to Chesterton. New York:
       Sheed & Ward, 1952.

       See also Item 62, pp. 3-33.

Isabel Clarke

242.   Brickel, Alfred G. "The Novels of Isabel
       Clarke." America 20 (November 30, 1918):
       187-188.

Katherine E. Conway

243.   Driscoll, Arnette S. "Katherine E. Conway."
       Ave Maria 36 (October 8, 1932): 449-454.

Baron Corvo

244.   Devine, Susan. "Corvo the Enigma." Catholic
       World 140 (November 1934): 138-142.

245.   Symons, A.J.A. The Quest for Corvo. New
       York: Macmillan, 1934.

246. Weeks, Donald. Corvo: Saint or Madman? New
      York: McGraw-Hill, 1971.

Francis Marion Crawford

247. Moran, John C. An F. Marion Crawford
      Companion. Westport, CT: Greenwood Press,
      1981.

248. Pilkington, John, Jr. Francis Marion
      Crawford. New York: Twayne, 1964.

A.J. Cronin

249. Frederick, John T. "A.J. Cronin." College
      English 3 (November 1941): 121-129.

250. Fytton, Francis. "Dr. Cronin: An Essay in
      Victoriana." Catholic World 183 (August
      1956): 356-362.

251. Salwak, Dale. A.J. Cronin. Boston: Twayne,
      1985.

Enid Dinnis

252. Meagher, Charlotte. "Enid Dinnis."
      Magnificat 77 (July 1943): 130-135.

253. Talbot, Francis X. "The World of Enid
      Dinnis." America 38 (November 12, 1927):
      115-116.

254. Wheaton, L. "The Books of Enid Dinnis."
      America. 29 (May 5, 1923): 64-65.

Andre Dubus

255. Feeney, Joseph J. "Andre Dubus at Fifty."
      America 154 (November 15, 1986): 296-301.

Owen Francis Dudley

256. LeFevre, Alice Louise. "Owen Francis Dudley
      and the Philosophical Novel." Catholic
      Library World 14 (April 1943): 195-200.

257. Willmann, Dorothy J. "Owen Francis Dudley –
     Priest and Novelist." Queens Work 23
     (January 1931): 1.

Michael Earls

258. Egan, Maurice F. "The Books of Michael
     Earls." America 27 (June 24, 1922):
     232-234.

Maurice F. Egan

259. Egan, Maurice F. Recollections of a Happy
     Life. New York: Doran, 1924.

Ronald Firbank

260. Merritt, James Douglas. Ronald Firbank. New
     York: Knopf, 1969.

F. Scott Fitzgerald

261. Allen, Joan M. Residual Catholicism in
     Selected Works of F. Scott Fitzgerald.
     Ph.D. dissertation. University of
     Massachusetts, 1973.

Lady Georgianna Fullerton

262. Craven, Mrs. Augustus. Life of Lady
     Georgianna Fullerton. London: Richard
     Bentley & Son, 1888.

Caroline Gordon

263. Cheney, Brainard. "Caroline Gordon's The
     Malefactors." Sewanee Review 79 (1971):
     360-372.

264. ―――. "Caroline Gordon's Ontological
     Quest." Renascence 16 (1963): 3-12.

265. Cowan, Louise. "Nature and Grace in Caroline
     Gordon." Critique 1 (Winter 1956): 11-27.

266. Fraistat, Rose Ann. Caroline Gordon as
     Novelist and Woman of Letters. Baton
     Rouge: Louisiana State University Press,
     1984.

267. Griscom, Joan. "Bibliography of Caroline
      Gordon." Critique 1 (1956): 74-78.

268. King, Lawrence T. "The Novels of Caroline
      Gordon." Catholic World 181 (1955):
      274-279.

269. Rocks, James E. "The Christian Myth as
      Salvation: Caroline Gordon's The Strange
      Children." Tulane Studies in English 16
      (1968): 149-160.

270. Stuckey, William J. Caroline Gordon. New
      York: Twayne, 1972.

271. Waldron, Ann. Close Connections: Caroline
      Gordon and the Southern Renaissance. New
      York: Putnam, 1987.

      See also Item 66, pp. 73-117.

Mary Gordon

272. Iannone, Carol. "The Secret of Mary Gordon's
      Success." Commentary 79 (June 1985):
      62-66.

273. Tookey, Christopher. "The Gospel According
      to Mary." Books & Bookmen 364 (February
      1986): 24-26.

Dorothy Fremont Grant

274. Grant, Dorothy Fremont. What Other Answer?
      Milwaukee: Bruce, 1943.

275. ————. Born Again, Milwaukee: Bruce,
      1950.

John Gray

276. Cevasco, G.A. John Gray. New York: Twayne,
      1982.

277. Sewell, Brocord. In the Dorian Mode: A Life
      of John Gray 1866-1934. Padstow, England:
      1983.

Andrew M. Greeley

278. Barr, Donald. "Sin and Salvation: The Novels
      of Andrew M. Greeley." New York Times Book
      Review (June 17, 1984): 12-13.

279. Greeley, Andrew. Confessions of a Parish
      Priest. New York: Simon & Schuster, 1986.

280. Shafer, Ingrid H. Eros and the Womanliness
      of God: Andrew Greeley's Romances of
      Renewal. Chicago: Loyola University Press,
      1987.

281. Stange, Mary Zeiss. "Little Shop of Horrors:
      Women in the Fiction of Andrew Greeley."
      Commonweal 114 (July 17, 1987): 412-417.

Graham Greene

282. Allain, Marie-Grancoise. The Other Man:
      Conversations with Graham Greene. New
      York: Simon & Schuster, 1983.

283. Allott, Kenneth and Mariam Farris. The Art
      of Graham Greene. New York: Russell,
      1963.

284. Atkins, John. Graham Greene. London:
      Calder & Boyars, 1957.

285. Boardman, Gwenn R. Graham Greene: The
      Aesthetics of Exploration. Gainesville:
      University of Florida Press, 1971.

286. Boyle, Alexander. "Graham Greene." Irish
      Monthly 77 (November 1949): 519-525.

287. Connolly, Francis X. "Inside Modern Man: The
      Spiritual Adventures of Graham Greene."
      Renascence 1 (Spring 1949): 16-24.

288. Costello, Donald P. "Greene and the Catholic
      Press." Renascence 12 (Autumn 1959): 3-28.

289. DeVitis, A.A. Graham Greene. Boston:
      Twayne, 1986.

290. Evans, Robert O., ed. Graham Greene: Some Critical Considerations. Lexington: University Press of Kentucky, 1963.

291. Gardiner, Harold C. "Graham Greene, Catholic Shocker." Renascence 1 (Spring 1949): 12-15.

292. Hynes, Samuel L., ed. Graham Greene: A Collection of Critical Essays. Englewood Cliffs, NJ: Prentice-Hall, 1973.

293. Kelly, Richard. Graham Greene. New York: Ungar, 1984.

294. Kunkel, Francis. The Labyrinthine Ways of Graham Greene. New York: Sheed & Ward, 1959.

295. Kurismmotil, K.C. Heaven and Hell. Chicago: Loyola University Press, 1982.

296. Lerner, Lawrence. "Graham Greene." Critical Quarterly 5 (Autumn 1963): 217-231.

297. Lewis, R.W.B. "Graham Greene: The Religious Affair." The Picaresque Saint. Philadelphia: Lippincott, 1959, pp. 220-274.

298. Lodge, David. Graham Greene. New York: Columbia University Press, 1966.

299. Marshall, Bruce. "Graham Greene and Evelyn Waugh." Commonweal 51 (March 3, 1950): 551-553.

300. Mesnet, Marie-Beatrice. Graham Greene and the Heart of the Matter. London: Cresset, 1954.

301. Miller, Robert H. Graham Greene, a Descriptive Catalog. Lexington: University Press of Kentucky, 1979.

302. Pryce-Jones, David. Graham Greene. London: Bodley Head, 1961.

303.   Sharrock, Roger. Saints, Sinners and
        Comedians: The Novels of Graham Greene.
        Notre Dame, IN: University of Notre Dame
        Press, 1984.

304.   Smith, Graheme. The Achievement of Graham
        Greene. London: Harvester Press, 1986.

305.   Spurling, John. Graham Greene. London:
        Methuen, 1983.

306.   Stratford, Philip. Faith and Fiction:
        Creative Process in Greene and Mauriac.
        Notre Dame, IN: University of Notre Dame, 1964.

307.   Sullivan, Kevin K. "Graham Greene Gets to
        the Heart of the Matter." Georgetown
        Magazine (Winter 1985): 12-13.

308.   Turnell, Martin. Graham Greene: A Critical
        Essay. Grand Rapids: Eerdmans, 1967.

309.   Wassmer, Thomas A. "The Problem and the
        Mystery of Sin in the Works of Graham
        Greene." The Christian Scholar 43 (Winter
        1960): 309-315.

310.   Waugh, Evelyn. "Felix Culpa?" Commonweal 48
        (July 16, 1948): 322-325.

311.   Wobbe, R.A. Graham Greene: A Bibliography
        and Guide to Research. New York: Garland,
        1979.

312.   Wolfe, Peter. Graham Greene, the Entertainer.
        Carbondale, IL: Southern Illinois Univer-
        sity Press, 1972.

313.   Wyndham, Francis. Graham Greene. London:
        Longmans, Green, 1955.

       See also: Item 29, pp. 170-202
                   Item 40, pp. 15-20
                   Item 129

John Howard Griffin

314.   Campbell, Jeff H. John Howard Griffin.
        Austin: Steck-Vaughn Company, 1970.

Louise Imogen Guiney

315. Brown, Alice. Louise Imogen Guiney.
      New York: Macmillan, 1921.

316. Fairbanks, Henry G. Louise Imogen Guiney:
      Laureate of the Lost. Albany, NY: Magi
      Books, 1972.

317. Hart, Mary Adorita. Soul Ordained To Fail.
      New York: Pageant Press, 1962.

318. Tenison, Eva Mabel. Louise Imogen Guiney:
      Her Life and Works. London: Macmillan,
      1923.

Cecily Hallack

319. Murphy, J.P. "Miss Cecily Hallac." Tablet
      172 (October 29, 1938): 570-572.

Pete Hamill

320. McInerny, Ralph. "Hamill, Breslin &
      Flaherty, Inc." Commonweal 99 (February 1,
      1974): 439-441.

Henry Harland

321. Burke, John J. "Henry Harland's Novels."
      Catholic World 75 (June 1902): 398-403.

322. Clarke, John James. "Henry Harland, a
      Critical Biography." Ph.D. dissertation.
      Brown University, 1957.

323. Parry, A. "Henry Harland, Expatriate."
      Bookman 76 (January 1933): 1-10.

324. Roberts, Donald A. "Henry Harland and His
      World." Commonweal 7 (February 8, 1928):
      1039-1040.

Emily Hickey

325. Dinnis, Enid. "Emily Hickey." Catholic
      World 120 (March 1925): 732-736.

John Oliver Hobbes

326.   Clarke, Isabel. "John Oliver Hobbes."
       Thought 6 (September 1931): 282-295.

Caryle Houselander

327.   Ward, Maisie. Caryle Houselander. New York:
       Sheed & Ward, 1962.

J.V. Huntington

328.   Walsh, J.J. "Doctor J.V. Huntington and the
       Oxford Movement in America." Records of
       American Catholic Historical Society 16
       (1905): 241-267, 416-442.

J.K. Huysmans

329.   Laver, James. The First Decadent: The
       Strange Life of J.K. Huysmans. New York:
       Citadel Press, 1955.

330.   Shuster, George N. "Joris Huymans: Egoist
       and Mystic." Catholic World 113 (July
       1921): 452-464.

Elizabeth Jordan

331.   Jordan, Elizabeth. Three Rousing Cheers.
       New York: Appleton, 1938.

332.   Leavey, Lawrence Andres. "Elizabeth Jordan."
       Catholic Library World 14 (February 1943):
       131-135.

James Joyce

333.   Morse, J. Mitchell. The Sympathetic Alien:
       James Joyce and Catholicism. London:
       Peter Owen, 1959.

Sheila Kaye-Smith

334.   Allen, W. Gore. "Sheila Kaye-Smith: Convert
       Novelist." Irish Ecclesiastical Record,
       5th series, 69 (June 1947): 518-528.

335. Davis, Margaret. "The Catholic Chord in the
      Art of Sheila Kaye-Smith." Magnificat 52
      (October 1933): 272-276.

336. Kaye-Smith, Sheila. Three Ways Home. New
      York: Harper, 1937.

337. Stack, Mary. "Sheila Kaye-Smith, Novelist."
      Commonweal 21 (January 8, 1935): 335-336.

      See also Item 62, pp. 179-206.

Francis Clement Kelley

338. Gaffey, James P. Francis Clement Kelley and
      the American Catholic Dream. Bersenville,
      IL: Heritage Foundation, 1980.

Gertrud von LeFort

339. Hilton, Inez. "Gertrud von LeFort: A
      Christian Writer." German Life and Letters
      15 n.s. (1962): 300-307.

340. O'Boyle, Ita. Gertrude von LeFort. New
      York: Fordham University Press, 1964.

      See also Item 29, pp. 217-234.

Compton Mackenzie

341. Dooley, D.J. Compton Mackenzie. New York:
      Twayne, 1974.

342. Linklater, Andro. Compton Mackenzie: A Life.
      London: Chatto & Windus, 1987.

343. Robertson, Leo. Compton Mackenzie: An
      Appraisal. Folcroft, PA: Folcroft
      Library, 1979.

344. Young, Kenneth. Compton Mackenzie. New
      York: Longmans, 1968.

Bruce Marshall

345. Fytton, Francis. "The Bite of Bruce
      Marshall." Catholic World 180 (February
      1955): 354-358.

John McGahern

346. Lynch, Audrey L. "An Interview with John
      McGahern." Books Ireland 88 (November
      1984): 213.

Francois Mauriac

347. Brown, J.L. "Francois Mauriac and the
      Catholic Novel." Catholic World 149 (April
      1939): 36-41.

348. Caspary, Sister A.M. Francois Mauriac. St.
      Louis: Herder, 1968.

349. Dunlea, William. "A Genius for Passion and
      Purity." Commonweal (May 23, 1986):
      297-300.

350. Jarrett-Kerr, Martin. Francois Mauriac.
      Cambridge, England: Bowes and Bowes,
      1954.

351. Jenkins, Cecil. Mauriac. London: Oliver &
      Boyd, 1965.

352. Moloney, Michael F. Francois Mauriac, A
      Critical Study. Denver: Swallow, 1958.

353. ————. "Francois Mauriac: The Way of
      Pascal." Thought 32 (1957): 398-408.

354. Pell, Elsie. Francois Mauriac: In Search of
      the Infinite. New York: Philosophical
      Library, 1947.

355. Rubin, Louis D., Jr. "Francois Mauriac and
      the Freedom of the Religious Novelist."
      Southern Review 2, n.s. (1966): 17-39.

356. Shuster, George N. "Francois Mauriac."
      Bookman 72 (1931): 466-475.

357. Stratford, Paul. "Francois Mauriac and His
      Critics." Tamarack Review 3 (Spring 1957):
      64-77.

358. ————. "One Meeting With Mauriac." Kenyon
      Review 21 (1959): 611-622.

359. Vial, Frances. "Francois Mauriac Criticism:
      A Bibliography." Thought 27 (1952):
      235-260.

      See also Item 29, pp. 130-154.
                Item 306

George H. Miles

360. Kenny, Thomas W. "Sketch of the Life of
      George H. Miles." Records of American
      Catholic Historical Society of
      Philadelphia, 10 (1899): 423-447.

Brian Moore

361. Bray, Richard T. "A Conversation with Brian
      Moore." Critic 35 (Fall 1976): 42-48.

362. Cooper, Stephen. "The Faithless Faith of
      Brian Moore." Critic 41 (Summer 1987):
      59-67.

363. Dahlie, Hallvard. Brian Moore. New York:
      Twayne, 1981.

364. Dorenkamp, J.H. "Finishing the Day: Nature
      and Grace in Two Novels by Brian Moore."
      Eire-Ireland 13 (Spring 1978): 103-112.

365. Flood, Jeanne. Brian Moore. Lewisburg, PA:
      Bucknell University Press, 1974.

366. Farrell, Michael J. "The Lonely Passion of
      Brian Moore." Nathional Catholic Reporter
      21 (September 13, 1985): 9, 17-18.

George Moore

367. Brown, Malcolm. George Moore: A Reconsider-
      ation. Seattle: University of Washington
      Press, 1955.

368. Dunleavy, Janet Egleson. George Moore.
      Lewisburg, PA: Bucknell University Press,
      1973.

369. Farrow, Anthony. George Moore. New York:
      Twayne, 1978.

370. Freeman, John. <u>A Portrait of George Moore in
      a Study of His Work</u>. London: Werner
      Laurie, 1922.

371. Gilcher, Edwin. <u>A Bibliography of George
      Moore</u>. DeKalb, IL: Northern Illinois
      University Press, 1970.

372. Hone, Joseph. <u>The Life of George Moore</u>. New
      York: Macmillan, 1936.

373. Hughes, Douglas A. <u>The Man of Wax: Critical
      Essays on George Moore</u>. New York: New
      York University Press, 1971.

374. Mitchell, Susan. <u>George Moore</u>. Dublin:
      Maunsel, 1916.

375. Moore, Maurice. <u>An Irish Gentleman: George
      Henry Moore</u>. London: Werner Laurie, 1913.

376. Morgan, Charles. <u>Epitaph on George Moore</u>.
      New York: Macmillan, 1935.

377. Owens, Graham, ed. <u>George Moore's Mind and
      Art</u>. New York: Barnes & Noble, 1970.

378. Wolfe, Humbert. <u>George Moore</u>. New York:
      Oxford University Press, 1932.

Iris Murdoch

379. Dipple, Elizabeth. <u>Iris Murdoch: Work for
      the Spirit</u>. Chicago: University of
      Chicago Press, 1982.

380. Johnson, Deborah. <u>Iris Murdoch</u>.
      Bloomington: Indiana University Press,
      1987.

      See also Item 20, pp. 87-127.

Edward F. Murphy

381. Murphy, Edward F. <u>Yankee Priest</u>. New York:
      Doubleday, 1952.

John Henry Newman

382. Griffin, John R., comp. Newman: A Bibliography of Secondary Studies. Front Royal, VA: Christendom College Press, 1985.

Kathleen Norris

383. Mohler, Edward F. "Kathleen Norris." America 15 (September 23, 1916): 573.

Edwin O'Connor

384. Dooley, Roger B. "The Womanless World of Edwin O'Connor." Saturday Review 47 (March 21, 1964): 34-36.

385. Rank, Hugh. "O'Connor's Image of the Priest." New England Quarterly 41 (1968): 3-29.

Walker Percy

386. Allen, William R. Walker Percy: A Southern Wayfarer. Jackson: University Press of Mississippi, 1986.

387. Atkins, Anselm. "Walker Percy and Post-Christian Search." Centennial Review 12 (1968): 73-95.

388. Coles, Robert. Walker Percy: An American Search. Boston: Little, Brown, 1978.

389. Daniel, Robert D. "Walker Percy's Lancelot: Secular Raving and Religious Salience." Southern Review 14 (1978): 186-194.

390. Gaston, Paul L. "The Revelation of Walker Percy." Colorado Quarterly 20 (1972): 459-470.

391. Godshalk, William L. "Walker Percy's Christian Vision." Louisiana Studies 13 (1974): 130-141.

392. Hardy, John Edward. The Fiction of Walker Percy. Champaign, IL: University of Illinois Press, 1987.

393. Jones, John Griffin. "A Conversation with
      Walker Percy." Critic 40 (Spring 1986):
      19-32.

394. Kazin, Alfred. "The Pilgrimage of Walker
      Percy." Harper 242 (June 1972): 81-86.

395. Lauder, R.E. "The Catholic Novel and the
      Insider God." Commonweal 51 (October 25,
      1974): 78-81.

396. Lawson, Lewis A. and Victor A. Kramer, eds.
      Conversations with Walker Percy. Oxford,
      MS: University Press of Mississippi,
      1985.

397. Leclair, Thomas. "The Eschatological Vision
      of Walker Percy." Renascence 26 (1974):
      1115-1122.

398. ————. "Walker Percy's Devil." Southern
      Literary Journal 10 (1977): 3-13.

399. Lehun, Richard. "The Way Back: Redemption in
      the Novels of Walker Percy." Sewanee
      Review, n.s. 4 (1968): 306-319.

400. Mullen, Jane Ann. "Novelist as Philosopher."
      Christian Science Monitor (July 5, 1985):
      B4.

401. Percy, Walker. "Interview." National
      Catholic Register 62 (January 5, 1986): 1,
      7, 9.

402. Samway, Patrick H. "An Interview with Walker
      Percy." America (February 15, 1986):
      121-123.

403. Sweeny, Mary K. Walker Percy and the
      Postmodern World. Chicago: Loyola Univer-
      sity Press, 1987.

404. Tharpe, Jac. Walker Percy. New York:
      Twayne, 1985.

      See also: Item 20, pp. 51-85.
                 Item 66, pp. 119-168.

Ellis Peters

405. Greeley, Andrew M. "Ellis Peters: Another
      Umberto Eco?" The Armchair Detective 18
      (Summer 1985): 238-245.

406. Harriott, John F.X. "Detective Extraordi-
      nary." Tablet 240 (October 10, 1986):
      1066.

Charles Constantine Pise

407. Moffatts, Sister Eulalia Teresa. "Charles
      Constantine Pise." Historical Records and
      Studies 20 (1931): 64-98.

J.F. Powers

408. Bates, Barclay W. "Flares of Special Grace:
      The Orthodoxy of J.F. Powers." Midwest
      Quarterly 11 (October 1969): 91-106.

409. Colligan, Joseph P. "Powers' Morte d'Urban:
      A Layman's Indictment." Renascence, 16
      (Fall 1963): 20-21, 51-52.

410. Dolan, Paul J. "God's Crooked Line: Powers'
      Morte d'Urban." Renascence, 21 (Winter
      1969): 95-102.

411. Dufner, Angeline. "The Sainting of Father
      Urban." American Benedictine Review 24
      September 1973): 327-341.

412. Hagopian, John V. J.F. Powers. New York:
      Twayne, 1968.

413. Henault, Marie J. "The Saving of Father
      Urban. America 108 (March 2, 1963):
      290-292.

414. Hinchliffe, Arnold P. "Nightmare of Grace: A
      Note on Morte d'Urban." Blackfriar's 45
      (February 1964): 61-69.

415. McCorry, Vincent P. "Urban in the Lion's
      Den." America 108 (March 2, 1963):
      292-294.

416.   Malloy, Suster M. Kristin. "The Catholic and
       Creativity: J.F. Powers." American
       Benedictine Review 15 (March 1964): 63-80.

417.   Merton, Thomas. "Morte d'Urban: Two
       Celebrations." Worship 36 (November 1962):
       645-650.

418.   O'Brien, Charles F. "Morte d'Urban and the
       Catholic Church in America." Discourse 12
       (Summer 1969): 324-328.

419.   Preston, Thomas. "Christian Folly in the
       Fiction of J.F. Powers." Critique 16
       (1974): 91-107.

420.   Shannon, J.P. "J.F. Powers on the Priest-
       hood." Catholic World 174 (September
       1952): 432-437.

421.   Sisk, John P. "The Complex Moral Vision of
       J.F. Powers." Critique 2 (Fall 1958):
       28-40.

422.   Steichen, Donna M. "J.F. Powers and the
       Noonday Devil." American Benedictine
       Review 20 (December 1969): 528-551.

423.   Wymard, Eleanor B. "J.F. Powers: His
       Christian Comic Vision." Ph.D. disser-
       tation. University of Pittsburgh, 1968.

       See also Item 129

Christian Reid

424.   Becker, Kate Harbes. Christian Reid.
       Belmont, NC: privately printed, 1941.

425.   Egan, Maurice F. "About Christian Reid." Ave
       Maria 47 (May 14, 1898): 304-306.

426.   ─────. "Christian Reid: A Southern Lady."
       America 23 (April 24, 1920): 18-19.

427.   Sadlier, Anna T. "Christian Reid." Ave
       Maria 11 (1880): 688-691.

Canon Sheehan

428. Boyle, Francis. Canon Sheehan. Dublin:
     Gill, 1927.

429. Braybrooke, Patrick. "Canon Sheehan." Some
     Victorian and Georgian Catholics. London:
     Burns & Oates, 1932, pp. 103-133.

430. Heuser, Herman J. Canon Sheehan of
     Doneraile. New York: Longmans, 1918.

Ignazio Silone

431. Gaffney, John. "Silone and the Pope."
     Commonweal 89 (1968): 112-115.

John Talbot Smith

432. Cavanaugh, John William. The Reverend John
     Talbot Smith. Notre Dame, IN: Ave Maria
     Press, 1924.

433. McMillan, Thomas. "John Talbot Smith."
     Catholic World 118 (November 1923):
     218-220.

434. Whalen, W.W. "Reminiscences of John Talbot
     Smith." Fortnightly Review 37 (October
     1930): 226-228.

Muriel Spark

435. Boyd, Alan. Muriel Spark. New York:
     Methuen, 1986.

436. Bold, Alan, ed. Muriel Spark: An Odd
     Capacity for Vision. Totowa, NJ: Barnes &
     Noble, 1984.

437. Greene, Graham. "Reading of Muriel Spark."
     Thought 43 (1968): 393-407.

438. Kemp, Peter. Muriel Spark. London: Elek,
     1974.

439. Malkoff, Karl. Muriel Spark. New York:
     Columbia University Press, 1968.

440.   Massie, Allan. Muriel Spark. Edinburgh:
       Ramsay Head, 1979.

441.   Richmond, Velma Bourgeois. Muriel Spark.
       New York: Ungar, 1984.

442.   Schneider, H.W. "The Fiction of Muriel
       Spark." Critique 5 (1962): 28-45.

443.   Spark, Muriel. "My Conversion." Twentieth
       Century 170 (Autumn 1961): 60-62.

444.   Stanford, Derek. Muriel Spark. London:
       Centaur, 1963.

445.   Stubbs, Patricia. Muriel Spark: A Biogra-
       phical and Critical Study. Harlow,
       England: Longmans, 1973.

446.   Whittaker, Ruth. The Faith and Fiction of
       Muriel Spark. New York: St. Martin's,
       1982.

       See also Item 129.

Sigrid Undset

447.   Bayerschmidt, Carl F. Sigrid Undset. New
       York: Twayne, 1970.

448.   Cransen, Carl. "The Triumph of Sigrid
       Undset." Commonweal 3 (March 10, 1926):
       492-494.

449.   Gustafson, Alrik. "Christian Ethics in a
       Pagan World: Sigrid Undset." Six
       Scandinavian Novelists. Minneapolis:
       University of Minnesota Press, 1968, pp.
       286-361.

450.   Hoeck, Kees van. "Sigrid Undset." America
       40 (January 12, 1929): 340-341.

451.   James, S.B. "The Significance of Sigrid
       Undset." Irish Monthly 59 (June 1931):
       351-357.

452.   ———. "Sigrid Undset." Missionary 44
       (November 1930): 369-371.

453. ————. "Sigrid Undset Rediscovers the
Past." Ave Maria 33 (June 13, 1931):
737-740.

454. MacKenzie, Michael. "Sigrid Undset, Catholic
Novelist." Month 155 (June 1930): 548-550.

455. Maynard, Theodore. "Sigrid Undset."
Catholic World 147 (April 1938): 20-30.

456. Schuster, George N. "Sigrid Undset and the
Nobel Prize." Commonweal 9 (December 26,
1928): 227-229.

457. Undset, Sigrid. The Longest Years. New
York: Knopf, 1935.

458. ————. Return to the Future. New York:
Knopf, 1942.

459. ————. Stages on the Road. New York:
Knopf, 1934.

460. Vinde, Victor. Sigrid Undset, a Nordic
Moralist. Seattle: University of
Washington Bookstore, 1930.

461. Winsnes, Andreas H. Sigrid Undset, a Study
of Christian Realism. New York: Sheed &
Ward, 1953.

Wilfred Ward

462. Crawford, Virginia. "Mrs. Wilfred Ward's
Novels." Catholic World 137 (May 1933): 14,
152-157.

Evelyn Waugh

463. Allen, W. Gore. "Evelyn Waugh and Graham
Greene." Irish Monthly 77 (January 1949):
16-22.

464. Bradbury, Malcolm. Evelyn Waugh. Edinburgh:
Oliver & Boyd, 1964.

465. Carens, James F. The Satiric Art of Evelyn
Waugh. Seattle: University of Washington
Press, 1966.

466.   Cook, William J., Jr. "Modes, Masks and
       Morals: The Art of Evelyn Waugh." Teaneck,
       NJ: Fairleigh Dickinson University Press,
       1971.

467.   Corr, Peter. "Evelyn Waugh: Sanity and
       Catholicism." Studies 51 (1966): 388-399.

468.   Cossman, M. "The Nature and Work of Evelyn
       Waugh." Colorado Quarterly 4 (1956):
       428-441.

469.   Crabbe, Katharyn W. Evelyn Waugh. New York:
       Ungar, 1987.

470.   Davis, Robert Murray. Evelyn Waugh. St.
       Louis: Herder, 1969.

471.   DeVitis, A.A. Roman Holiday: The Catholic
       Novels of Evelyn Waugh. New York: Bookman
       Associates, 1956.

472.   Doyle, Paul A. "The Church, History and
       Evelyn Waugh." American Benedictine Review
       9 (1958-1959): 202-208.

473.   ———. Evelyn Waugh. Grand Rapids:
       Eerdmans, 1969.

474.   Hollis, Christopher. Evelyn Waugh. New
       York: Longmans, 1954 (1966 rev.ed.).

475.   Lane, Calvin W. Evelyn Waugh. Boston:
       Twayne, 1981.

476.   Lodge, David. Evelyn Waugh. New York:
       Columbia University Press, 1971.

477.   Macaulay, Rose. "Evelyn Waugh." Horizon 14
       (December 1946): 360-376.

478.   Morriss, Margaret and D.J. Dooley. Evelyn
       Waugh. Boston: G.K. Hall, 1984.

479.   Phillips, Gene D. Evelyn Waugh's Officers,
       Gentlemen and Rogues. Chicago: Nelson-
       Hall, 1975.

480. Pryce-Jones, David. <u>Evelyn Waugh and His</u>
      <u>World</u>. New York: Norton, 1973.

481. Rolo, Charles, ed. <u>The World of Evelyn</u>
      <u>Waugh</u>. Boston: Little, Brown, 1958.

482. Stannard, Martin. <u>Evelyn Waugh: The Early</u>
      <u>Years, 1903-1939.</u> New York: Norton, 1987.

483. Stopp, Frederick J. <u>Evelyn Waugh: Portrait</u>
      <u>of an Artist</u>. London: Chapman & Hall,
      1958.

484. Sykes, Christopher. <u>Evelyn Waugh</u>. Boston:
      Little, Brown, 1975.

      See also: Item 29, pp. 203-216.
                 Item 299.

Franz Werfel

485. Goldstein, David. "Franz Werfel, Jewish
      Author." <u>Catholic Mind</u> 43 (May 1945):
      285-289.

Antonia White

486. Chitty, Susan. <u>Now To My Mother: A Very</u>
      <u>Personal Memoir of Antonia White</u>. London:
      Weidenfeld & Nicholson, 1985.

487. White, Antonia. <u>The Hound and the Falcon:</u>
      <u>The Story of a Reconversion to the Catholic</u>
      <u>Faith</u>. London: Longmans, 1965.

Shusaku Endo

487a. Higgins, Jean. "East-West Encounter."
      <u>Dialogue and Alliance</u>. (Fall 1987): 12-21.

487b. Mathy, Francis. "Shusaku Endo: Japanese
      Catholic Novelist." <u>Thought</u> 42 (1967):
      595-601.

THE NOVELS

488. Aasheim, Ashley. _The Apostate_. New York:
      Critic's Choice, 1987.

      A man excommunicated from the Order of the
      Knights of St. John fights for the Huguenots
      against the Catholics in the 16th Century
      religious wars. Then he fights for
      Christians against the Muslims.

489. Abdullah, Achmed. _Deliver Us From Evil_.
      New York: Putnam, 1939.

      Many different kinds of people bring their
      hopes and fears to St. Patrick's Cathedral
      during Holy Week.

490. Abelson, Ann. _Angel's Metal_. New York:
      Harcourt, 1947.

      A young woman at a Catholic woman's college
      in the early 1940s discovers a challenging
      intellectual life and marries the college
      physician.

491. Agnew, Emily C. _Geraldine, A Tale of
      Conscience_. London: Burns & Oates, 1839.

492. ————. _Rome and the Abbey_. London: Burns
      & Oates, 1849.

493. ————. _The Merchant Prince and His Heir_.
      Dublin: Duffy, 1863.

      Three mediocre conversion tales.

494. Ainsworth, W. Harrison. _Guy Fawkes_. New
      York: Dutton, 1841.

      The Gunpowder Plot.

495. Aird, Catherine. <u>The Religious Body</u>. New
      York: Doubleday, 1966.

      A delightfully well-told tale of a murder
      in an English convent.

496. Alarcon, Pedro Antonio de. <u>Child of the</u>
      <u>Ball</u>. New York: Serrano, 1892.

      A good priest fights the forces of evil to
      win the soul of a young friend.

497. Aldridge, James. <u>My Brother Tom</u>. Boston:
      Little, Brown, 1966.

      In a small town in Australia in the 1930s
      an English Protestant boy falls in love with
      an Irish Catholic girl. Religious and
      cultural differences between their families
      threaten to destroy their relationship. To
      the Protestants "all Roman Catholics were
      untrustworthy, disloyal and self-seeking;
      they were moral outsiders."

498. Allen, Mabel E. <u>Murder at the Flood</u>.
      London: Stanley Paul, 1957.

      A murder mystery set in a convent.

499. Allen, Steve. <u>Not All of Your Laughter, Not</u>
      <u>All of Your Tears</u>. New York: Geis, 1962.

      A successful, married Catholic songwriter
      in Hollywood falls hopelessly in love with
      another woman. His wife is Protestant and he
      feels he cannot seek a divorce.

500. Allison, E.M.A. <u>Through the Valley of</u>
      <u>Death</u>. New York: Doubleday, 1983.

      Someone has murdered Brother Anselm, a
      Cistercian monk. Brother Barnabas, a monk
      gifted in logic, searches for the killer. A
      thriller set in 14th century England.

501. Allyn, Marjory. <u>The Sound of Anthems</u>. New
      York: St. Martin's, 1983.

      A young girl growing up in Northern Ireland

in the 1940s becomes painfully aware of
Protestant-Catholic animosity and
separateness.

502. Almedingen, Edith Martha. A Candle at Dusk.
      New York: Farrar, Straus, 1969.

      An eighth century Frankish boy lives at an
      abbey to learn how to read, though his father
      is a religious skeptic.

503. ————. The Ladies of St. Hedwigs. New
      York: Vanguard, 1967.

      A community of Polish nuns living in
      Czarist Russia is threatened by political
      upheaval during the 1863 Polish mutiny.
      Their undaunted Mother Superior must decide
      whether to flee or to remain faithful to the
      path of grace and face possible arrest. They
      are all hanged at the end.

504. ————. Stephen's Light. New York: Holt,
      1969.

      After being jilted by her fiancé, a young
      woman decides to enter the business world,
      not a convent as her father had wished.

505. ————. The Winter in the Heart. New York:
      Appleton, 1960. (British title – The
      Little Stairway. London: Hutchinson,
      1960.)

      A character study of a young priest, set in
      Russia and Finland during World War I and the
      Bolshevik Revolution. Louis Terrin, a
      brilliant scholar, is sent to a primitive
      Finnish villa whose residents are German
      peasants. He begins to realize his own
      coldness and smugness. He soon becomes a
      whole man with a radiant spirituality. He
      elects to stay despite the political terror
      and other dangers.

506. Ames, F.S.D. Marion Howard. Philadelphia:
      Cunningham, 1872.

      A light-hearted "exposition of Catholic
      truth" aimed at Evangelical Protestants.

507.   Andersen, Richard. <u>Straight Cut Ditch</u>. Port
       Washington, New York: Ashley, 1979.

       A funny and obscure novel about a beginning
       teacher's problems in a Catholic high school
       staffed mainly by gay priests.

508.   Andres, Stefan Paul. <u>We Are Utopia</u>. London:
       Gollancz, 1955.

       Paco, a defrocked priest who has lived
       twenty years away from the church, is
       imprisoned during the Spanish Civil War. The
       prison guard learns that Paco is a priest and
       asks to go to confession, after which he
       offers to let the priest escape. But Paco,
       now reconciled to the faith, chooses to stay
       and console the two hundred other prisoners,
       and he dies with them.

509.   Andrew, Prudence. <u>Ordeal By Silence</u>. New
       York: Putnam, 1961.

       Portrait of a thirteenth century English
       saint.

510.   ————. <u>A Question of Choice</u>. New York:
       Putnam, 1962.

       A monastery comes under siege during the
       Wars of the Roses.

511.   Armour, John <u>Run With the Killer</u>. London:
       Hale, 1969.

       A priest helps solve a murder in a small
       Nebraska town.

512.   Ardizzone, Tony. <u>In the Name of the Father</u>.
       New York: Doubleday, 1978.

       A "growing up" novel about Tonto Schwartz,
       an improbable Catholic who matures in
       Catholic schools on Chicago's tough North
       Side. The schools are satirized delight-
       fully, especially the nuns' lessons about
       martyrdom and "the will of God."

513. Armstrong, Ann Seidel. <u>Remember No More</u>.
      Milwaukee: Bruce, 1963.

      A biographical novel about Saints Perpetua
      and Felicity.

514. Armstrong, April Oursler. <u>Water in the Wine</u>.
      New York: McGraw-Hill, 1963.

      A devoutly Catholic family faces a crisis
      after the wife, mother of six children, is
      told that any future pregnancy will likely
      cause her death. She and her husband try
      continence for many months but it nearly
      destroys their marriage, despite heroic
      efforts. Then the long-feared tragedy
      occurs. The bleak and somber ending will
      disappoint many readers but emphasis on
      loving God and placing the spiritual life
      above all else makes this an uncommonly
      moving novel. It is also a richly revealing
      picture of Catholic life in the suburbs
      around 1960 when solidarity and unquestioning
      loyalty to the church and its teachings (even
      on birth control) were hallmarks.

515. Armstrong, Thomas. <u>The Face of a Madonna</u>.
      Bath: Chivers, 1973.

516. Arnold, Lewis. <u>Valley of Sound</u>. London:
      Evans, 1949.

      A war-blinded English airman rebuilds his
      life with the help of a Dominican priest.

517. Arnothy, Christine. <u>The Captive Cardinal</u>.
      New York: Doubleday, 1964.

      Cardinal Mindszenty of Hungary.

518. Arpino, Giovanni. <u>The Novice</u>. New York:
      Braziller, 1962.

      Written in diary format, a story of a
      middle-aged accountant's growing love for a
      young novice. While this book won a prize in
      Italy, it was called "sacrilegious and
      anti-clerical" by <u>Ave Maria</u>.

519.   Artajo, Javier Martin. The Embattled.
       Westminster, MD: Newman, 1956.

       A frankly partisan pro-Franco account of
       the Spanish Civil War in novel format. A
       devout priest gives his life for a schoolmate
       and fellow prisoner. Years later, the
       survivor's son becomes a priest.

520.   Arthur, Frederick. The Accuser. New York:
       Nash & Grayson, 1927.

       Titus Oates and the Popish Plot.

521.   Asch, Sholem. East River. New York:
       Putnam, 1946.

       When a Jewish man deserts his Catholic wife
       and daughter, his father takes them in.

522.   Ashton, Mary Grace. Shackles of the Free.
       New York: Stokes, 1929.

       A blundering woman tries to break down the
       religious convictions of others but fails.

523.   Atteridge, Helen. At the Sign of the Silver
       Cup. New York: P.J. Kenedy, 1926.

       A love story set in the days of the Popish
       Plot.

524.   Atwell, Lester. Life With Its Sorrow, Life
       With Its Fear. New York: Simon &
       Schuster, 1971.

       An orphan goes to live with his Irish
       Catholic relatives in a big house in suburban
       New York in the 1930s.

525.   Austin, Mary. Isidro. Boston: Houghton,
       Mifflin, 1905.

       A romantic tale of Old Spanish California.
       Isidro was "promised" to the church by his
       brother on his way to join the Franciscans.
       Young Isidro encounters handships and a love
       affair. The relationship between the
       missions and their converts is accurately
       depicted.

526. Aycott, Bob. <u>Cry for Tomorrow</u>. London:
     Everest, 1974.

     A British Protestant soldier marries an
     Ulster girl but the IRA hunts them down and
     kills them.

527. Ayscough, John. <u>Abbotscourt</u>. New York:
     P.J. Kenedy, 1920.

     A Catholic girl disarms the prejudices of
     her Protestant kinfolk.

528. ———. <u>Dobachi</u>. New York: Macmillan,
     1923.

     A tiny fishing village on a bleak New
     England coast forms the background to a
     contrast between an emasculated, grim
     Protestant sect and a warm, vital
     Catholicism. The heroine is the last
     adherent of a Puritanical sect. Her boy-
     friend's conversion to Catholicism changes
     both their lives.

529. ———. <u>Faustula</u>. New York: Benziger,
     1912.

     In 4th century Rome Christianity struggles
     to survive during the reign of Julian the
     Apostate.

530. ———. <u>Fernando</u>. New York: P.J. Kenedy,
     1919.

     The spiritual development of a young
     English convert.

531. ———. <u>Jacqueline</u>. New York: P.J. Kenedy,
     1918.

     Jacqueline enters a convent but leaves and
     enters into a poor marriage. After her
     husband dies, she returns home to devote
     herself to her mother and to seek happiness.

532. ———. <u>Mariquita</u>. New York: Benziger,
     1922.

Portrait of an intensely spiritual girl,
daughter of a wealthy Texas rancher, who
rejects worldly love for the Divine and
becomes a contemplative nun. The New York
Evening Post called it "as refreshing as an
oasis in a fiery desert." Catholic World
described the author's work as an "intimate
story of a crystalline spirituality made
fascinating and lovely by his artistry."

533.   ———. Mezzogiorno. St. Louis: Herder,
        1911.

The spiritual awakening of a woman and her
slow progress towards Catholicism.

534.   ———. San Celestino. New York: Putnam,
        1909.

The hermit Pope Celestine V.

535.   Babson, Marian. Untimely Guest. New York:
        St. Martin's, 1987.

When the daughter of a strict Irish
Catholic family leaves the convent, her
return home stirs up old hates which lead to
murder.

536.   Bailey, H.C. The Plot. London: Methuen,
        1922.

Popish Plot of 1678.

537.   Baker, Frank. Teresa. New York: Coward
        McCann, 1961.

An 85-year-old woman in a convent home
looks back on a life full of sadness and
disappointments. Religious faith is a major
concern.

538.   Baker, Gladys. Our Hearts Are Restless.
        New York: Putnam, 1955.

A successful young novelist and alcoholic
dries out in a Swiss sanitarium. She
continues to wander aimlessly until Mother
Mary, at a nearby contemplative community,

intervenes and helps her find spiritual reality.

539. Baldy, Alice Montgomery. The Romance of a Spanish Nun. Philadelphia: Lippincott, 1891.

Disappointment in love leads a beautiful Spanish girl to the cloister. She had loved a poet and a priest.

540. Baldy, Mary Elizabeth. Beautiful Lady. Boston: Christopher, 1950.

Historical novella of romance and marriage of Elise Patterson to the son of Napoleon Bonaparte. The union is complicated by the Catholic prohibition on divorce.

541. Ballinger, W.A. The Green Grassy Slopes. London: Corgi, 1969.

Based on the career of Ulster's fiery Reverend Ian Paisley, this novel depicts the beginning of the anti-Catholic crusade in Northern Ireland in the late 1960s.

542. Banim, John. The Denounced. New York: Harper, 1830.

Protestant persecution of Irish Catholics after the Williamite Wars.

543. Banim, Michael. Father Connell. London: Bow, 1840.

A saintly Irish priest dies trying to save the life of an orphan boy.

544. Baldwin, Monica. The Called and the Chosen. New York: Farrar, Straus, 1957.

Written by the author of the non-fiction I Leap Over the Wall, this is the story of a nun who leaves the convent after many years.

545. Ballesteros, Mercedes. Nothing Is Impossible. London: Harvill, 1956.

Whimsical story of a schoolboy who is in league with the saints.

546.   Banning, Margaret Culkin. The Convert. New York: Harper, 1957.

A young engineer converts to the Catholic faith but in so doing loses his wife.

547.   ————. Fallen Away. New York: Harper, 1951.

Barbara, a devout, sincere Catholic, divorces her worthless first husband and weds a Protestant. She loses her faith but finds it again.

548.   ————. Mixed Marriage. New York: Harper, 1930.

A Catholic-Protestant marriage in Minnesota is riven over the birth control question. Fair-minded presentation.

549.   ————. The Vine and the Olive. New York: Harper, 1964.

The birth control controversy.

550.   Barclay, Daphne. Amedeo. New York: Dutton, 1958.

The poignant story of a 12-year-old boy's search for the mother he never knew. America called it "a lovely story of simple, sensible deeply-Catholic principled people."

551.   Barclay, Florence L. The White Ladies of Worcester. New York: Putnam, 1917.

A romance of the 12th century in which nuns are central characters.

552.   Baring, Maurice. C. New York: Harper, 1924.

553.   ————. Cat's Cradle. New York: Harper, 1925.

554. ————. <u>Daphne Adeane</u>. New York: Harper,
      1927.

      A trilogy by the "Catholic Henry James."
      A lengthy, leisurely look at Catholic
      aristocrats and their lives in which
      conversion plays a major role.

555. ————. <u>In My End Is My Beginning</u>.
      New York: Harper, 1931.

      Catholics in Tudor England must choose
      between faith and nation. Paul Horgan said
      of this work, "It is Baring's triumph that,
      in a literary world generally oriented to
      skepticism, he is able to make religion a
      matter of reality and importance in his
      writing."

556. ————. <u>Robert Peckham</u>. New York: Knopf,
      1930.

      A Catholic gentleman and scholar in the
      England of Henry VIII and Elizabeth I
      voluntarily exiled himself and dies in Rome.

557. Barlow, James. <u>Both Your Houses</u>. London:
      Hamish Hamilton, 1971.

      A British army private falls in love with a
      Belfast Catholic girl whose family supports
      the IRA.

558. Barnes, Maurice. <u>The Sacred Hill</u>. New York:
      Macaulay, 1929.

      Three French brothers, who are priests,
      allow their greed and love of power to
      corrupt them. They leave the church and set
      up a new religion, but their fanaticism
      proves their ruination.

559. Barrett, James Francis. <u>The Loyalist</u>. New
      York: P.J. Kenedy, 1920.

      Several Catholic families support the
      Revolution of 1776.

560.   ————. The Winter of Discontent. New York:
        P.J. Kenedy, 1923.

        An anti-divorce novel set in Hartford.

561.   Barrett, William E. The Empty Shrine. New
            York: Doubleday, 1958.

        Did the Virgin Mary appear to a little girl
        in a small French Canadian community on an
        island in the St. Lawrence River? Twelve
        years later an embittered American writer,
        Keller Barkley, arrives to prove the whole
        thing a hoax. He is surprised both by what
        he learns about Valerie Ruard, now a young
        woman, and himself.

562.   ————. The Left Hand of God. New York:
            Doubleday, 1951.

        An American flyer in China impersonates a
        priest.

563.   ————. The Lillies of the Field. New York:
            Doubleday, 1962.

        A black sergeant helps German nuns build a
        church in Arizona.

564.   ————. The Shadows of the Images. New
            York: Doubleday, 1971.

        A vigorous and moving novel about the
        meaning of religious faith in personal
        experience. One character, a devout Catholic,
        is passionately in love with a girl who
        scorns his faith and buys an image of Satan
        to mock him. He marries her outside the
        church but their love endures. "A novel of
        temptation," the characters wrestle with
        concepts of good and evil.

565.   ————. The Wine and the Music. New York:
            Doubleday, 1968.

        A priest falls in love with a divorced
        Protestant woman and marries her.

566.   ————. A Woman in the House. New York:
            Doubleday, 1971.

A young monk escapes from East Germany and
falls in love with a woman in Munich.

567. Barry, Charles. The Corpse on the Bridge.
      New York: Dutton, 1928.

      Several lay brothers at a Benedictine Abbey
      disappear at about the same time a mysterious
      body is found on Waterloo Bridge. An in-
      triguing tale presided over by a detective
      inspector who once studied for the priest-
      hood.

568. Barry, William F. The New Antigone. London:
      Macmillan, 1887.

      A "fallen woman" and unabashed seductress
      repents and becomes a nun.

569. ————. The Two Standards. London: Unwin,
      1898.

      A Catholic hero in love with a married
      woman. After many tribulations, a pat ending
      unites them legally. The title comes from
      the meditations of St. Ignatius Loyola - "the
      standard of Christ vs. the standard of
      Lucifer."

570. Barth, Hilary Leighton. Flesh Is Not Life.
      Milwaukee: Bruce, 1938.

      A lapsed Catholic labor organizer clashes
      with a conservative hierarchy and priests. A
      social-minded Catholic liberal shows the way
      to true social justice that the institutional
      church has avoided. A beautiful radical girl
      becomes a Catholic in a subplot.

571. Bartlett, Barbara. The Shiksa. New York:
      Morrow, 1987.

      A Catholic woman's rebellious obsession
      with Jewish men fails to bring happiness.

572. Bates, Herbert Ernest. The Scarlet Sword.
      Boston: Little, Brown, 1951.

      A priest defends his mission from Indian
      attacks.

573.   Bausch, Richard.   Real Presence.   New York:
          Dial, 1980.

          A monsignor, recovering from a heart attack
          and a nervous breakdown, retreats to a
          Virginia estate.   His hope for peace is
          shattered by the arrival of a family of ne'er-
          do-wells who upset his life.   Time said,
          "This is Flannery O'Connor country, where
          souls are tormented and agony seems the only
          common measure of humanity....The doctrine of
          the Real Presence becomes a metaphor for the
          world beyond the sanctuary, where the Real
          Presence must be sought among the lowliest of
          people and the darkest of hearts."

574.   Bazin, Herve.   A Tribe of Women.   London:
          Hamish Hamilton, 1958.

575.   Bazin, Rene.   The Barrier.   New York:
          Benziger, 1909.

          Story of three friends.   A young Englishman
          embraces the Catholic faith, while his French
          friend renounces it.   A deeply religious
          French girl is a friend to both.

576.   ————.   The Coming Harvest.   New York:
          Scribners, 1908.

          An honest pagan finds peace in religion.

577.   ————.   Davidee Birot.   New York:
          Scribners, 1912.

          A young French teacher moves from atheism
          to faith.

578.   ————.   Magnificat.   New York: Macmillan,
          1932.

          Story of a vocation to priesthood in
          Catholic Brittany.   Gildas gives up the girl
          he loves, and his faith gives Anna the
          strength to endure.

579.   ————.   The Nun.   New York: Scribner,
          1908.

Five nuns disband their community and
return to the world. The young and pretty
Pascale is betrayed and is cast low in sin
and suffering.

580.   ———. Redemption. New York: Scribners,
          1908.

A saintly woman gives herself in complete
love and self sacrifice to all whom she
encounters, especially the sin-burdened and
misery-stricken.

581.   ———. This, My Son. New York: Scribners,
          1909.

Pierre studies for the priesthood in order
to receive a superior education though he
knows he will never be ordained. He goes to
Paris to pursue a literary calling but lives
a dissolute life. He returns home, the
prodigal son.

582.   ———. Those of His Own Household. New
          York: Devin Adair, 1914.

A husband and wife, separated for ten
years, decide to reunite.

583.   Beahn, John Edward. A Man Born Again.
          Milwaukee: Bruce, 1954.

St. Thomas More.

584.   ———. A Man Cleansed By God. Westminster,
          MD: Newman, 1959.

A novel about St. Patrick's early days,
when he prepares for his great mission to
Ireland.

585.   ———. A Man of Good Zeal. Westminster,
          MD: Newman, 1958.

Biographical novel about St. Francis de
Sales, the charming, gentle holy bishop of
Geneva.

586.   ———.   A Rich Young Man.   Milwaukee:
        Bruce, 1953.

        St. Anthony of Padua.

587.   Beck, Beatrix.   The Passionate Heart.   New
        York: Messner, 1953.   (British title - The
        Priest)

        A priest tries to bring an erring woman
        back to the church and discovers a love for
        her.

588.   Becker, Kate Harbes.   Was It Worth While?
        Belmont, NC: Outline Co., 1947.

        Autobiographical novel of a teaching nun
        who reflects on her training and commitment
        and decides she made the right choice.

589.   Belair, Richard.   The Road Less Traveled.
        New York: Doubleday, 1965.

        A young man's journey to the priesthood.

590.   Bell, Gerard.   White Lion.   London:
        Hutchinson, 1958.

591.   Bell, Josephine.   Tudor Pilgrimage.   London:
        Bles, 1967.

592.   Benard, Robert.   A Catholic Education.   New
        York: Holt, 1982.

        Explores a young seminarian's relationship
        with his parents, his desire for priesthood
        and his affection for a fellow student.
        Publishers Weekly reviewed it as "a most
        unusual and sensitive first novel, exploring
        religious and personal conflicts with
        understanding and compassion."

593.   Benedict, Isobel.   Prelude and Spring.   New
        York: Exposition, 1951.

        A serious and sensitive young girl spends
        time in a convent school.

594. Benson, Robert Hugh. <u>An Average Man</u>. New
      York: Dodd, Mead, 1913.

      A clerk alternately dreams of philandering
      and of an emotional conversion. When he
      inherits a fortune, he becomes an apostate
      and a renegade in love.

595. ————. <u>By What Authority?</u> New York:
      Benziger, 1905.

      Elizabethan England - persecution of
      Catholics - heavy theological discussions.

596. ————. <u>Come Rack! Come Rope!</u> New York:
      Dodd, Mead, 1912.

      Persecution of Catholics in Elizabethan
      England as seen by the heroism of a priest-
      martyr, Robin Audrey. His father renounces
      the faith to avoid fines. Robin leaves his
      home and his lady love and goes to Rheims to
      become a priest. He returns to England and
      death.

597. ————. <u>The Conventionalists</u>. London:
      Burns & Oates, 1908.

      A young English convert desires to become a
      monk despite family opposition.

598. ————. <u>Dawn of All</u>. London: Hutchinson,
      1911.

      Another futuristic fantasy, this is set in
      an almost entirely Catholic world in 1973.
      The Church rules everywhere except Berlin and
      Boston (!). The Pope journeys to Berlin,
      where he threatens to obliterate the
      socialist malcontents unless they conform.
      Then he goes to England in triumph. A
      bizarre bit of Catholic triumphalism, perhaps
      written to counter the pessimism and triumph
      of evil in <u>Lord of the World</u>.

599. ————. <u>Initiation</u>. New York: Dodd, Mead,
      1914.

Sir Nevill, a young man who suffers from a
hereditary disease, learns the meaning of
suffering and sacrifice from a lovely girl.

600.   ———. The King's Achievements. New York:
        Dodd, Mead, 1913.

Henry VIII and dissolution of monasteries.

601.   ———. Loneliness? New York: Dodd, Mead,
        1915.

An opera singer, a Catholic, drifts away
from her faith. She plans to wed a
Protestant. Then she loses her voice and her
best friend. Her fiancé seems to fail her.
Then she discovers her faith.

602.   ———. Lord of the World. New York: Dodd,
        Mead, 1908.

An apocalyptic novel set at the end of the
world. The final struggle between Humanism
and Catholicism.

603.   ———. Necromancers. St. Louis: Herder,
        1909.

An attack on spiritualism. A young
lukewarm Catholic takes up spiritualism
after his lover's death.

604.   ———. None Other Gods. St. Louis: Herder,
        1911.

A young man becomes a tramp after his
father's conversion to Catholicism.

605.   ———. Oddsfish! New York: Dodd, Mead,
        1914.

In days of Charles II, Roger Mallock is
sent home by the Pope to act as a secret,
unofficial representative at Royal Court. He
gets involved in court intrigues and in the
Popish Plot. He loves his Dorothy, who dies
tragically.

606. ————. Papers of a Pariah. New York:
      Longmans, 1907.

      An actor slowly arrives at Catholic truth.

607. ————. The Queen's Tragedy. St. Louis:
      Herder, 1906.

      Fictionalized portrait of Queen Mary.

608. ————. A Winnowing. St. Louis: Herder,
      1910.

      Jack Weston, a ritualistic, nominal
      Catholic, becomes sincerely devout after a
      brush with death. When he eventually dies,
      his wife becomes a nun.

609. Bentley, Charles S. The Fifth of November.
      New York: Rand, McNally, 1898.

      A romantic story of the Gunpowder Plot and
      the Protestant-Catholic antagonisms
      engendered by it.

610. Bergengruen, Werner. A Matter of Conscience.
      New York: Vanguard, 1954.

      In Renaissance Italy a poor but devout man
      confesses to a crime he did not commit in
      order to lead his neighbors to a more
      Christ-like existence.

611. Berkley, Cora. The Hamiltons. New York:
      Dunigan, 1856.

      A pious Catholic woman survives in a
      worldly, amoral Cincinnati milieu.

612. Berlin, Ellin. Lace Curtain. New York:
      Doubleday, 1948.

      A mixed Catholic-Protestant marriage in
      high society crowd on Long Island. The Irish
      Catholic wife's parents are snubbed by the
      WASPs, who refuse to recognize the Irish as
      equals. The heroine cherishes Catholicism
      for its security, its sense of order and
      ritual and soon feels herself an outsider.

613.   Bernanos, Georges. The Diary of a Country
        Priest. New York: Macmillan, 1937.

        The story of a French pastor's encounter
        with divine grace and human love.

614.   ————. Joy. New York: Pantheon, 1946.

        A seventeen-year-old mystic disrupts a
        spiritually dead middle-class household,
        precipitating a tragedy. A brilliant novel
        about the mystery of grace.

615.   ————. Night is Darkest. London: Bodley
        Head, 1953.

        A priest discovers the identity of a
        murderess, who has no remorse. His arrival
        on the scene symbolizes the triumph of
        spirituality over evil.

616.   ————. The Open Mind. London: Lane,
        1945.

        Evil under the peaceful facade of French
        provincial life.

617.   ————. The Star of Satan. New York:
        Macmillan, 1940.

        An awkward provincial priest may be a
        mystic and saint. He tries to free a liber-
        tine woman from Satan's clutches. The priest
        nearly violates the seal of confession.

618.   Bernier, Paul. Fire in the Bush. New York:
        P.J. Kenedy, 1958.

        A French missionary priest in West Africa.

619.   Bessiere, Gerard. Where Is the Pope?
        London: Burns & Oates, 1974.

        A charming fable of a Pope who absconds
        from the Vatican to become a taxi driver in
        Paris and experiences life in a different
        realm.

620. Beste, Henry Digby. <u>Poverty and the</u>
      <u>Baronet's Family: A Catholic Novel</u>.
      London: Colburn, 1845.

      A convert tale.

621. Bianchi, Martha Gilbert. <u>Modern Prometheus</u>.
      New York: Duffield, 1908.

      A Jesuit priest tries to induce an
      unhappily married American girl to enter a
      convent in Italy.

622. Bickham, Jack M. <u>The Padre Must Die</u>. New
      York: Doubleday, 1967.

      Father John searches for the murderers of
      his brother in a sleepy Texas border town.

623. ————. <u>The Shadowed Faith</u>. New York:
      Doubleday, 1968.

      Factions in the church battle for control
      of the diocesan newspaper. Sam Kinkaid, the
      lay editor, is caught in the middle, though
      he is a liberal. A good portrait of a church
      in the turmoil of change. One flaw is the
      one-dimensional characterization.

624. Billington, Rachel. <u>The Garish Day</u>. New
      York: Morrow, 1985.

      A worldly and successful man abruptly
      enounters the spiritual dimension of life.

624a. ————. <u>Occasion of Sin</u>. New York: Summit
      Books, 1983.

      A devoutly Catholic and happily married
      woman becomes obsessed with another man.

625. Bird, Kenneth. <u>Bishop Must Move</u>. London:
      Cassell, 1967.

626. Bishop, Constance E. <u>Flame of the Forest</u>.
      New York: Benziger, 1921.

      An unattractive portrait of India. The
      heroine refuses to marry an agnostic biolo-
      gist and converts to Catholicism at the end.

627. Bishop, Maria C. <u>Elizabeth Eden</u>. London:
      Bow, 1878.

      An unbelieving widow marries a Catholic
      millionaire and is eventually converted in
      this unrealistic novel.

628. Bishop, Sheila Glencairn. <u>The Second
      Husband</u>. London: Jarrolds, 1964.

629. Black, Veronica. <u>Minstrel's Leap</u>. London:
      Hale, 1973.

      A mystery with nuns in the central role.

630. Blackstock, Charity. <u>A House Possessed</u>.
      Philadelphia: Lippincott, 1962.

      An Irish spinster's small hotel in the
      Scottish Highlands is haunted by the ghost of
      a long-dead girl who protects a priceless
      necklace. When she decides to have the house
      exorcised, a more earthly problem surfaces.
      The local Presbyterians are more terrified by
      Popery than by spectral apparitions.

631. Blair, Clay, Jr. <u>The Archbishop</u>. New York:
      World, 1970.

      The birth control controversy splits the
      archdiocese of Washington apart. A mother of
      nine children rebels. So do "new breed"
      priests and nuns. But the brick and mortar
      Archbishop (modeled on Cardinal O'Boyle)
      tries to hold off the forces of change. Race
      and antiwar protests also abound.

632. Blais, Marie Claire. <u>The Manuscripts of
      Pauline Archange</u>. New York: Farrar,
      Straus, 1970.

      Pauline's childhood in Catholic French
      Canada. She struggles to find joy in a harsh
      environment surrounded by illness, death,
      drunkenness and corruption. <u>Publishers
      Weekly</u> reviewed it as a "tender, heart-
      breaking story, beautifully told."

633. Blake, Forrester. The Franciscan. New York: Doubleday, 1963.

A Franciscan missionary among the Pueblo Indians in 17th century New Mexico is confronted by many problems.

634. Blakeston, Oswell. Ever Singing Die Oh! Die. London: Hutchinson, 1970.

635. Blasco-Ibanez, Vincent. The Pope of the Sea. New York: Dutton, 1927.

A strange fantasy novel shifting from the 14th to 20th centuries, with an interesting Papal character. Ultimately unsuccessful.

636. _____. The Shadow of the Cathedral. New York: Dutton, 1909.

An epic portrait of life in the Cathedral town of Toledo, Spain. Anticlerical in tone, it shows the intensity of feelings about religion. The theme is church wealth, and much of the plot revolves around the theft of jewels from a sacred statue in the Cathedral.

637. Blatty, William Peter. The Exorcist. New York: Harper, 1971.

The classic horror tale of a little girl who becomes the vehicle of Satan. A priest nearly loses his life and sanity when performing the ancient rite of exorcism.

638. _____. Legion. New York: Simon & Schuster, 1983.

A supernatural mystery set in the Georgetown quarter of Washington, featuring Jesuit-related Georgetown University. A detective is perplexed by horrible killings that may have a supernatural origin. Since several priests are slain, Georgetown clergy assist in combatting the horror.

639. Bloom, Ursula. The Abiding City. London: Hutchinson, 1958.

640. Bloy, Leon. The Woman Who Was Poor. New
      York: Sheed & Ward, 1947. (1897 original
      published in France)

      A woman discovers that only in poverty and
      suffering does she truly encounter God. A
      bleak parable but one that challenges the
      smug materialism of western Christianity.

641. Blum, Carol O'Brien. Anne's Head. New York:
      Dial, 1982.

      Turn-of-the-century St. Louis. An Irish
      Catholic girl's tragic love affair brings
      dishonor and disaster to her family. Her
      death turns the novel into a first-rate
      suspense tale.

642. Blundell, Mary Elizabeth. Dark Rosaleen.
      New York: P.J. Kenedy, 1917.

      A Catholic-Protestant love story set in
      Ireland.

643. ———. Manor Farm. New York: Longmans,
      1902.

      English Catholics struggle to survive in
      hostile rural England.

644. ———. Tyler's Lass. St. Louis: Herder,
      1928.

      Catholic cotton mill workers in Lancashire.
      Powerfully written with genuine emotion and
      good local color.

645. Boll, Heinrich. The Clown. New York:
      McGraw-Hill, 1965.

      A philosophical novel. How can anyone
      believe in Christianity after Nazism? A
      27-year-old clown is losing faith in the
      meaning of life.

646. ———. The End of a Mission. London:
      Weidenfeld, 1968.

      A young soldier and his father set fire to
      an army jeep by chanting the Litany of the

Saints. At their trial the eccentricities of the locals, mostly Catholics, are revealed. A good portrait of an old priest who exhales ecumenism with every pipe.

647. Bonn, John Louis. And Down the Days. New York: Macmillan, 1942.

Anti-Catholicism in 19th century America. Based on the life of the daughter of Maria Monk and her conversion to Catholicism.

648. ———. House on the Sands. New York: Doubleday, 1950.

Biographical novel of the colorful life of Francis MacNutt, an American who became chamberlain to several Popes and an accomplished diplomat.

649. ———. The Lively Arts of Sister Gervase. New York: P.J. Kenedy, 1957.

A lively drama teacher (nun) has her ups and downs at St. Rita's High School. Good-natured, light-hearted, little plot. Characters lack depth.

650. ———. So Falls the Elm Tree. New York: Macmillan, 1940.

Novelized biography of a nun who founded a hospital.

651. Bonanno, Margaret. A Certain Slant of Light. New York: Seaview, 1979.

A professor at a Catholic college loses her ability to read after a stroke. A student shows compassion and tries to save the woman's job.

652. ———. Ember Days. New York: Seaview, 1980.

A four-generation Irish Catholic family novel. The role of the church is treated critically but respectfully. Ethnic family saga shows changes in religious practice since the 1940s.

653.   Book, John William. <u>Mollie's Mistake</u>.
       Cannelton, IN: privately printed, 1894.

       A plea against Catholic-Protestant
       marriage.

654.   Bordeaux, Henry. <u>Awakening</u>. New York:
       Dutton, 1914.

       A husband returns to his wife through the
       influence of a devoutly Catholic mother-in-
       law.

655.   ———. <u>Footprints Beneath the Snow</u>. New
       York: Duffield, 1913.

       A woman seeks her husband's forgiveness for
       her adultery.

656.   ———. <u>Gardens of Omar</u>. New York: Dutton,
       1924.

       A Christian woman's love for a Muslim man
       in Lebanon ends in tragedy.

657.   ———. <u>The House</u>. New York: Duffield,
       1914.

       The hero cannot make up his mind between
       Catholicism and agnosticism.

658.   ———. <u>The Lost Sheep</u>. New York:
       Macmillan, 1955.

       An unfaithful wife, abandoned by her lover,
       and eventually contrite, is taken back and
       forgiven by her husband.

659.   ———. <u>A Pathway to Heaven</u>. New York:
       Pellegrini & Cudahy, 1952.

       A naive parish priest gets into all kinds
       of trouble because of his painting and his
       kind disposition.

660.   Borden, Lucille. <u>The Candlestick Makers</u>.
       New York: Macmillan, 1932.

       A Catholic architect's life is unhappy
       because his modern wife wants no children.

661.   ———.   From Out Magdala. New York:
        Macmillan, 1927.

        A woman devotes herself to charity after
        the death of her husband.

662.   ———.   The Gates of Olivet. New York:
        Macmillan, 1922.

        An American woman in Lourdes struggles
        between spiritual and earthly love.

663.   ———.   Gentleman Riches. New York:
        Macmillan, 1925.

        A man steeped in naturalistic materialism
        also succeeds in extinguishing the spiritual
        life of a weak woman. He mends his ways and
        becomes a Franciscan monk.

664.   ———.   King's Highway. New York:
        Macmillan, 1941.

        Catholic refugees from Elizabethan England
        seek religious freedom in the New World.

665.   ———.   Silver Trumpets Calling. New York:
        Macmillan, 1931.

        A Russian princess tries to rescue children
        from the Soviet state. "A book to stir the
        heart of every Catholic," said Catholic
        World.

666.   ———.   Sing to the Sun. New York:
        Macmillan, 1934.

        The story of St. Francis.

667.   ———.   Starforth. New York: Macmillan,
        1937.

        A Catholic view of Elizabethan England.

668.   ———.   Star Trail to Bethlehem. New York:
        Macmillan, 1933.

        A Christmas story of love and faith between
        a husband and wife.

669. ————. The White Hawthorn. New York:
         Macmillan, 1935.

      A romantic Catholic Italy in the days of
      Petrarch and Boccaccio.

670. Boucher,Anthony. Nine Times Nine. New York:
         Duell, 1940

      Sister Ursula, a Los Angeles nun, helps the
      police solve the murder of a critic of a
      religious cult.

671. ————. Rocket to the Morgue. New York:
         Duell, 1942.

      Sister Ursula is involved in a bizarre
      crime among science fiction writers.

672. Bourget, Paul. Divorce. New York:
         Scribner, 1905.

      A divorcee is guilt-ridden when she marries
      again.

673. Bourquin, Paul. The Cockpit. London:
         Faber, 1965.

      The Reformation in the Low Countries.

674. ————. The Land of Delight. London:
         Faber, 1967.

      Early Christian Ireland.

675. ————. The Seven Reductions. London:
         Faber, 1966.

      Spanish missionaries in Paraguay.

676. Bowen, Robert O. The Weight of the Cross.
         New York: Knopf, 1951.

      A guilt-ridden rebellious Catholic sailor
      finds peace with God and himself in a
      Japanese POW camp. A powerful novel of
      redemption.

677. Boyce, John. <u>Shandy McGuire</u>. New York:
      Dunigan, 1848.

      Irish Catholic peasants struggle to
      maintain their religion and their civil
      rights in the face of Protestant oppression
      in the North of Ireland. McGuire is a Robin
      Hood-like figure.

678. ————. <u>The Spaewife; or The Queen's Secret</u>.
      Baltimore: Murphy, 1853.

      A critical portrait of Queen Elizabeth and
      her persecution of Catholics. Elizabeth is
      portrayed as having given up her child to a
      spaewife, a term for a female fortune-teller.

679. Boyd, Catherine Bradshaw. <u>Revenge in the</u>
      <u>Convent</u>. New York: Exposition, 1955.

      A mediocre mystery featuring a priest-
      detective.

680. Boyd, Neil. <u>Bless Me Father</u>. New York:
      Morrow, 1977.

681. ————. <u>Father Before Christmas</u>. London:
      Corgi, 1979.

682. ————. <u>Father in a Fix</u>. New York: Morrow,
      1980.

683. ————. <u>Father Under Fire</u>. New York:
      Morrow, 1980.

      A delightfully witty saga of a young priest
      who is tormented by a wily, irascible pastor
      in a London parish in the 1950s. Made into a
      television series in Britain and shown on PBS
      in this country as "Bless Me Father."

684. Boylan, Clare. <u>Holy Pictures</u>. New York:
      Summit, 1983.

      Two sheltered school girls in Dublin in the
      1920s begin to discover that life is more
      complicated, varied and magical than they had
      been led to believe.

685.   Boylan, Malcolm Stuart. The Passion of
       Gabrielle. New York: Crown, 1961.

       A Haitian priest comes up against a voodoo
       priestess who is determined to seduce him.

686.   Brackel, Frederick von. The Circus Rider's
       Daughter. New York: Benziger, 1896.

       An equestrienne enters a convent after
       losing a lover.

687.   Brady, Charles Andres. Stage of Fools. New
       York: Dutton, 1953.

       An extraordinary novel about St. Thomas
       More about which the New York Times said, "He
       succeeds in the doubly difficult task of
       blending truth with advocacy and fact with
       fiction."

688.   ————. This Land Fulfilled. New York:
       Dutton, 1958.

       An old priest reminisces about his days
       with Leif Erickson.

689.   Brady, James. Holy Wars. New York: Simon &
       Schuster, 1983.

       A brilliant, young American Jesuit, search-
       ing for faith and social justice from Vietnam
       to Central America, goes to the Vatican and
       becomes a personal friend of the Pope.

690.   Brady, Joseph. In Monavalla. Dublin: Gill,
       1963.

       The adventures of a young Irish priest in
       Brooklyn around World War I.

691.   Brady, Leo. The Edge of Doom. New York:
       Dutton, 1949.

       A priest is brutally murdered when he is
       called to perform a funeral service for a
       poor woman who loved and served the church.
       A young priest suspects the woman's disturbed
       son.

692. ————. Signs and Wonders. New York:
      Dutton, 1953.

      A critical view of the "prominent Catholic
      layman" whose pride and legalism harm his
      family and friends.

693. Braine, John. The Crying Game. Boston:
      Houghton, Mifflin, 1968.

      A Catholic journalist is caught in a web of
      corruption until rescued by his values.

694. ————. The Jealous God. Boston: Houghton,
      Mifflin, 1965.

      A Catholic schoolteacher falls in love with
      a beautiful, divorced non-Catholic librarian.
      He struggles between his passionate love for
      her and his desire to become a priest.

695. ————. The Pious Agent. New York:
      Atheneum, 1976.

      An espionage thriller starring a ruthless
      killer and womanizer who still considers
      himself a devout Catholic. He leaps in and
      out of bed with abandon but always says an
      Act of Contrition.

696. Breslin, Jimmy. World Without End, Amen.
      New York: Viking, 1973.

      A neurotic and racist New York City
      policeman, a product of parochial schools in
      Queens, goes to Northern Ireland. When he
      sees how Catholics are treated there he
      becomes a changed person.

697. Brete, Jean de la. My Uncle and the Cure.
      New York: Vanguard, 1958.

      A charming French classic about a country
      girl who turns to the local curate to help
      her face a romantic crisis.

698. Breton, Thierry. The Pentecost Project. New
      York: Holt, 1987.

The Vatican plans to establish a vast
satellite communications network to broadcast
the Pope's messages, but the Soviet Union and
Libya threaten to sabotage it.

699.   Brisbane, Abbott Hall.   Ralphton, the Young
       Carolinian of 1776.   Charleston: Burgess
       and James, 1848.

A Jesuit priest ministers secretly to a few
Catholics in Charleston in the days when the
Catholic faith was prohibited by law.   He is
a benevolent man who guides his flock wisely
and supports wise economic and political
policies.

700.   Broderick, John.   An Apology for Roses.
       London: Calder, 1973.

Materialism versus stern religion.

701.   ————.   The Chameleons.   New York:
       Obolensky, 1961.

Religious faith conflicts with material and
sensual values even in the west of Ireland.

702.   ————.   Pilgrimage.   London: Weidenfeld,
       1961.

703.   ————.   The Pride of Summer.   London:
       Harrap, 1976.

During the great hunger of the 1840s many
Protestants opened soup kitchens for the
relief of the starving, but they also sought
to convert the Catholics.

704.   ————.   The Waking of Willie Ryan.   London:
       Weidenfeld, 1965.

An old man escapes from a lunatic asylum to
which he had been wrongly committed 25 years
before.   His family tries to bring about his
reconciliation with the church, which he
hated because a priest was involved in his
original sentencing.

705. Broderick, Robert Carlton. <u>Wreath of Song</u>.
      Milwaukee: Bruce, 1948.

      The life of the tortured poet Francis
      Thompson.

706. Bromfield, Louis. <u>The Strange Case of Miss
      Annie Spragg</u>. New York: Stokes, 1928.

      A strange tale of religious fanaticism and
      the miracle of the stigmata.

707. Brookfield, Frances M. <u>A Friar Observant</u>.
      St. Louis: Herder, 1909.

      A historical novel of the Counter-
      Reformation.

708. Brooks, Winfield Sears. <u>The Shining Tides</u>.
      New York: Morrow, 1952.

      A priest on Cape Cod seeks to catch a great
      striped bass.

709. Brosia, D.M. <u>A Place of Coolness</u>. New York:
      P.J. Kenedy, 1955.

      A young schoolmaster returns from a holiday
      in Italy with a new knowledge of his moral
      defects.

710. Brownell, Henrietta. <u>God's Way, Man's Way</u>.
      New York: Catholic Publication Society,
      1885.

      Romance, renunciation, and conversion.

711. Brownson, Orestes. <u>Charles Elwood; or The
      Infidel Converted</u>. New York: Marlier,
      1840.

712. ———. <u>The Spirit Wrapper</u>. Boston:
      Little, Brown, 1854.

      A satire on spiritualism.

713. Brownson, Sarah. <u>Marian Elwood</u>. New York:
      Dunigan, 1859.

      See item 2050.

714.   Bruce, David. <u>The Valley Under the Cross</u>.
        London: Constable, 1950.

        Staunchly Catholic villagers in Bavaria try
        to stage a passion play despite Nazi
        opposition.

715.   Brunini, John Gilland. <u>Days of a Hireling</u>.
        Philadelphia: Lippincott, 1951.

        A sensitive, intellectual Catholic
        struggles to preserve his integrity and faith
        after his wife leaves him. An understanding
        priest helps him find some answers.

716.   Bryant, John Delavan. <u>Pauline Seward</u>.
        Baltimore, Murphy, 1848.

        A conversion tale.

717.   Buchanan, Rosemary. <u>This Bread</u>. Milwaukee:
        Bruce, 1945.

        An Episcopalian curate and his church
        organist fall in love but her conversion to
        Catholicism separates them for a while. Then
        he sees the light and all is well.

718.   Buechner, Frederick. <u>Brendan</u>. New York:
        Atheneum, 1987.

        An artistic re-creation of the life of St.
        Brendan the Navigator.

719.   ———. <u>Godric</u>. New York: Atheneum, 1980.

        The life and adventures of a 12th century
        English monk who was blessed with a second
        sight and the power to heal.

720.   Buell, John. <u>The Pyx</u>. New York: Farrar,
        Straus, 1959.

        "A theological thriller of great import,"
        said <u>Catholic World</u> about this novel of
        diabolism and murder.

721.   Bugg, Lelia Hardin. <u>Orchids</u>. St. Louis:
        Herder, 1894.

A young woman enters a convent to show her
freedom from the worldly success ethic.

722. Bulger, Helen M. Inviolable. New York:
      Benziger, 1932.

A woman divorces her husband because of his
cruelty. She falls in love with a Presbyterian doctor who has saved her from a mental
breakdown, but her Catholic principles
prevent their marriage.

723. Burgess, Anthony. Tremor of Intent. New
      York: Norton, 1966.

Called "an eschatological spy novel," this
is a meditation on the morality of espionage.
The two major characters are disillusioned
agents who cannot quite forget their Catholic
school upbringing.

724. Burmeister, Jon. The Darkling Plain.
      London: Sphere, 1977.

725. Burnand, F.C. My Time and What I've Done
      With It. London, 1874.

A satire on conversion.

726. Burrough, Loretta. Sister Clare. Boston:
      Houghton, Mifflin, 1960.

A joyful, sympathetic account of forty years
of a nun's life.

727. Bushell, O.A. Molokai. London: Secker,
      1964.

The life of Father Damien, the lepers'
champion.

728. Butler, Charles Edward. Follow Me Ever.
      New York: Pantheon, 1950.

An American army sergeant in World War II
refuses the stigmata, but does not understand
the significance and tries to hide the
evidence.

729.   Butler, William. <u>A Danish Gambit</u>. London:
        Owen, 1966.

730.   Byrne, Beverly. <u>Come Sunrise</u>. New York:
        Fawcett, 1987.

        A woman loves a man who becomes a priest.
        She turns to his brother instead, but her
        love for the priest never dies.

731.   ———. <u>Women's Rites</u>. New York: Villard,
        1985.

        A Boston girl enters a convent, aided by
        her youthful parish priest, but leaves years
        later to become a best-selling author. Her
        Jewish girlfriend later has an affair with
        the priest and bears his child. The ex-nun
        and now embittered fallen priest are swept
        into a healing vortex that washes away pain
        and doubt. A stunning achievement.

732.   Byrne, Robert. <u>Always a Catholic</u>. New York:
        Pinnacle, 1981.

        The sequel to <u>Memories</u>, this continues a
        young man's saga to manhood, concentrating on
        his sexual coming of age. Hilarious, if
        irreverent.

733.   ———. <u>Memories of a Non-Jewish Childhood</u>.
        New York: Lyle Stuart, 1970.

        A humorous novel about an Irish Catholic
        boy growing up in Dubuque, Iowa in the 1940s.
        (Pinnacle published a paperback edition
        called <u>Once a Catholic</u> in 1982.)

734.   Caddell, Cecilia M. <u>Blind Agnese</u>. New York:
        P.J. Kenedy, 1856.

735.   ———. <u>Home and the Homeless</u>. New York:
        P.J. Kenedy, 1858.

736.   ———. <u>Never Forgotten</u>. New York: P.J.
        Kenedy, 1871.

        The above three are examples of the Mary
        Magdalene conversion story popular in
        Victorian days.

737. ————. <u>Wild Times</u>. London: Burns & Oates,
      1872.

      The suffering of Catholics in Elizabethan
      England.

738. Caddell, Elizabeth. <u>Mixed Marriage</u>. London:
      Hodder, 1963.

      A good-humored account of the engagement
      and marriage of an English Protestant girl to
      a Portuguese Catholic aristocrat.

739. Caldecott, Moyra. <u>Ethelreda</u>. New York:
      Methuen, 1987.

      The holy life of a 7th century English
      saint.

740. Caldwell, Cyril Cassidy. <u>Speak the Sin
      Softly</u>. New York: Messner, 1946.

      An Italian missionary priest in Equador
      encounters a Machiavellian hierarchy and
      aloof, distant priests who ally themselves
      with the ruling powers against the poor and
      oppressed. A prophetic novel.

741. Caldwell, Janet Taylor. <u>Arm and the
      Darkness</u>. New York: Scribner, 1963.

      Catholics versus Huguenots in France.

742. ————. <u>Grandmother and the Priests</u>. New
      York: Doubleday, 1963.

      A deliciously wicked English widow
      befriends eleven priests who tell her
      extraordinary tales of their lives. A
      drawing room comedy.

743. ————. <u>The Wide House</u>. New York:
      Scribner, 1945.

      A small New York town is torn by Catholic-
      Protestant conflict in the 1850s.

744. Calitri, Charles. <u>Father</u>. New York: Crown,
      1962.

The narrator goes to a small mountain
village in Italy to dedicate a school to his
father's memory. His father was once a
priest who fled to New York and married a Jew
and raised his family Jewish. The son tries
to discover why his father left the priesthood.

745. Callado, Antonio. <u>Quarup</u>. New York: Knopf,
      1970.

A politically conscious Brazilian priest
battles the authorities, but leaves the
priesthood to struggle against injustice.

746. Callaghan, Morley. <u>A Passion in Rome</u>. New
      York: Coward-McCann, 1961.

A love story set in Rome, with the death
and funeral of the Pope as a superbly
dramatic counterpoint.

747. ————. <u>Such Is My Beloved</u>. New York:
      Scribner, 1934.

A young priest tries to save the souls of
prostitutes. But he succeeds only in
bringing down the law on them and causing
scandal to himself and the church.

748. Callender, Julian. <u>St. Dingan's Bones</u>. New
      York: Vanguard, 1958.

In an Irish village two precocious children
claim to have seen the vision of St. Brigid
and to have discovered the bones of St.
Dingan. Journalists and crackpots descend on
the town. Both the benevolent parish priest
and an affable Protest rector are disturbed
by these events. A reverent, charming,
whimsical satire.

749. Calvin, Henry. <u>Take Two Popes</u>. London:
      Hutchinson, 1972.

750. Cammaerts, Emile. <u>The Devil Takes the Chair</u>.
      London: Cresset, 1949.

751. Cannon, Charles James. <u>Bickerton</u>. New York: O'Shea, 1855.

    A town is dominated by anti-Catholic Know-Nothings who try to tar and feather priests and burn churches. A rip-roaring satire.

752. ————. <u>Father Felix</u>. New York: Dunigan, 1845.

    A devoted priest radiates joy and love as he converts others. He had once been a Protestant who had been disinherited upon his conversion.

753. ————. <u>Harry Layden</u>. New York: Boyle, 1842.

    A Catholic orphan prospers and maintains his faith. Another family suffers because the wife's parents disinherit her when she marries a Catholic.

754. ————. <u>Mora Carmody</u>. New York: Dunigan, 1844.

    A young Protestant falls in love with a Catholic girl, but she will not marry him until he converts. He goes away, studies the faith, and is converted. When he returns for Mora she is gone. Years later he is stricken with yellow fever and is nursed by the Sisters of Charity. From them he learns that Mora had become a nun and had died in an epidemic years before.

755. ————. <u>Scenes and Characters from a Comedy of Life</u>. New York: Dunigan, 1847.

    A young Catholic journalist exposes the bigotry of many priest haters.

756. ————. <u>Tighe Lifford</u>. New York: Miller, 1859.

    A humble but lapsed Catholic consorts with upper-class Protestants.

757. Capes, H.M. <u>Gold or God</u>. St. Louis: Herder, 1932.

Problems arise when a Catholic girl becomes
a tutor in a non-Catholic home.

758.   ———. Pardon and Peace. St. Louis:
         Herder, 1921.

Anti-Catholic prejudice causes a great
tragedy, but the perpetrator, now penitent,
dies before righting the wrong.

759.   Capp, Richard. Crown of Thorns. Port
         Washington, NY: Ashley, 1978.

A trashy, poorly written portrait of an
idealistic rebel priest who gets involved in
sex, abortion, and a bombing in a small
California town. An insult to author,
publisher and reader.

760.   Carey, Mary Elizabeth. Alice O'Connor's
         Surrender. Boston: Angel Guardian Press,
         1897.

761.   Carmichael, Montgomery. Christopher and
         Cressida. New York: Macmillan, 1924.

A chivalric romance reflecting the divine
in human affairs.

762.   ———. The Life of John William Walshe.
         London: Burns & Oates, 1902.

A fictional portrait of a saintly layman,
including much Franciscan lore.

763.   ———. Solitaries of Sambuca. London:
         Burns & Oates, 1914.

A wealthy English Catholic finds happiness
and peace in an abandoned Italian hermitage.

764.   Carr, Philippa. The Miracle at St. Brunos.
         New York: Putnam, 1972.

A baby is found by monks in an abbey on
Christmas Day in the year 1522. Regarding it
as a miracle, the friars raise him. His
story is enmeshed with intrigue in the days
when Henry VIII looted the kindgom's monasteries.

765. Carrick, James. With O'Leary in the Grave.
      London: Heinemann, 1971.

      A Catholic member of the British army
      returns home to Londonderry at the time of
      the 1969 rioting.

766. Carroll, Consolata. I Hear In My Heart. New
      York: Farrar, Straus, 1949.

      The eldest daughter of an Irish Catholic
      family in Upstate New York becomes a nun.

767. ————. Pray Love, Remember. New York:
      Farrar, Straus, 1947.

      The joys of growing up in an Irish Catholic
      family.

768. Carroll, James. Madonna Red. Boston:
      Little, Brown, 1976.

      IRA sympathizers plan to assassinate the
      British ambassador in St. Matthew's Cathedral
      in Washington. Cardinals, priests and an
      order of contemplative nuns figure promi-
      nently in this superb thriller.

769. ————. Prince of Peace. Boston: Little,
      Brown, 1984.

      A powerful study of a charismatic, radical
      priest who fights the FBI, the Vietnam war,
      and a corrupt cardinal. The priest also
      loves his best friend's wife, an ex-nun. He
      leaves the church to marry her.

770. Carroll, Malachy Gerard. The Stranger.
      Milwaukee: Bruce, 1952.

      A defrocked priest appears in a remote
      Irish village and excites the curiousity of
      the people.

771. ————. Time Cannot Dim. Chicago: Regnery,
      1955.

      Life and times of St. Thomas Aquinas.

772.   Carroll, Patrick J. <u>Many Shall Come</u>. Notre
       Dame, IN: Ave Maria Press, 1937.

       A hard-driving Chicago businessman abandons
       his faith in a mad pursuit for wealth and
       social position. He and his family are won
       back to Catholicism.

773.   Carter, Charles Franmklin. <u>Rafael</u>. Los
       Angeles: Grafton, 1923.

       The California mission days.

774.   Caruso, Joseph. <u>The Priest</u>. New York:
       Macmillan, 1956.

       In an Italian slum in Boston a priest tries
       to save an innocent man condemned to death
       without violating the secrecy of the
       confessional. Mystery critic Anthony Boucher
       criticized the book for relying on miracles
       and for carelessness in matters of Catholic
       ritual and doctrine.

775.   Casey, Jack. <u>Lily of the Mohawks</u>. New York:
       Bantam, 1984.

       The life and good works of Kateri
       Tekakwitha, a 17th century native American
       girl.

776.   Casey, Robert. <u>The Jesus Man</u>. New York:
       Evans, 1979.

       A Boston priest gets involved in a murder.

777.   Cather, Willa. <u>Death Comes for the
       Archbishop</u>. New York: Knopf, 1927.

       A masterful study of the 19th century
       archbishop of Santa Fe.

778.   ————. <u>Shadows on the Rock</u>. New York:
       Knopf, 1931.

       A richly textured view of life in Catholic
       Quebec.

779.   Catalan, Henry. <u>Soeur Angele and the
       Bellringer's Niece</u>. New York: Sheed &
       Ward, 1957.

Soeur Angele is an intelligent, observant French nun who solves several murders. In this story she discovers who killed a bellringer whose niece may have seen visions of the Virgin Mary.

780. ————. *Soeur Angele and the Embarrassed Ladies.* New York: Sheed & Ward, 1955.

Soeur Angele discovers which of three lovers murdered a bargain-basement Don Juan.

781. ————. *Soeur Angele and the Ghosts of Chambord.* New York: Sheed & Ward, 1956.

Soeur Angele cuts through layers of evil to find a killer among a group of traveling players.

782. Catherwood, Mary Hartwell. *The Lady of Fort St. John.* Boston: Houghton, Mifflin, 1906.

St. Isaac Jogues.

783. Catto, Max. *The Devil at Four O'Clock.* New York: Morrow, 1959.

An Irish priest tries to rescue the inhabitants of a leper colony when a volcano erupts nearby.

784. ————. *I Have Friends in Heaven.* Boston: Little, Brown, 1966.

An orphan leads a caravan of elderly nuns with a statue of the Virgin and Child across war-torn Italy.

785. Caulfield, Malachy. *The Black City.* New York: Dutton, 1953.

A grim story of Belfast.

786. Cavanaugh, Arthur. *The Faithful.* New York: Morrow, 1986.

A Catholic boarding school is presided over by a nun and priest who fall in love but remain true to their vows.

787.   Cayzac, Joseph. <u>Mission Boy</u>. New York:
       Benziger, 1927.

       A tragic tale of missionaries in Nairobi.

788.   Cesbron, Gilbert. <u>Saints in Hell</u>. New York:
       Doubleday, 1954.

       A French priest works among the poorest of
       the poor.

789.   Chandler, David. <u>Father O'Brien and His
       Girls</u>. New York: Appleton, 1963.

       A Las Vegas priest and four nuns confront
       the world of gambling and prostitution. He
       breaks all the church's rules to reach out to
       the estranged and disillusioned.

790.   Charles, Robert J. <u>Broken Vows</u>. New York:
       Dembner, 1981.

       An ex-priest, now married, moves toward
       adultery with his best friend's wife, who is
       an ex-nun herself. Their profound betrayal
       of God, their church and each other sets in
       motion a tragic chain of events.

791.   Charques, Dorothy. <u>The Nunnery</u>. New York:
       Coward-McCann, 1960.

       In 16th century England a teenage girl
       tries to decide whether to become a nun. The
       prioress needs her estate to survive.

792.   Chavez, Fray Angelico. <u>The Lady from Toledo</u>.
       Fresno: Academy Guild, 1960.

       A statue of Our Lady inspires Spanish
       colonists to reconquer New Mexico in 1692.

793.   Chesterton, G.K. <u>The Ball and the Cross</u>.
       New York: Lane, 1909.

       A Scottish Catholic takes issue with an
       atheist editor and decides to resolve his
       dispute with a duel.

794. Chetwood, Thomas B. <u>Black and White</u>. New
      York: Wagner, 1928.

      A sister encourages her materialistic
      brother to think of spiritual and charitable
      things.

795. Christman, Elizabeth. <u>Ruined for Life</u>. New
      York: Paulist, 1987.

      A group of dedicated young Catholics spends
      a year helping the poor in the inner city.

796. Clark, Felicia. <u>The Cripple of Nuremberg</u>.
      New York: Eaton, 1900.

      Protestants and Catholics war against each
      other in 16th century Germany.

797. Clarke, A.M. <u>Fabiola's Sisters</u>. New York:
      Benziger, 1898.

      Christian martyrs in 3rd century Carthage.

798. Clarke, Mrs. DeWitt. <u>Lizzie Maitland</u>. New
      York: Dunigan, 1857.

      A propaganda novel proving the superiority
      of Catholicism.

799. Clarke, Isabel. <u>Altar of Sacrifice</u>. New
      York: Longmans, 1932.

      A poor English lady inherits an estate but
      is forbidden by the will ever to become a
      Catholic. She discovers that Catholicism is
      more valuable to her than any fortune.

800. ———. <u>Carina</u>. New York: Benziger, 1931.

      Catholicism's attraction and character-
      building qualities win over even the most
      bigoted.

801. ———. <u>A Case of Conscience</u>. New York:
      Benziger, 1927.

      Through her efforts to keep her half-
      sister's lover a loyal Catholic, the heroine
      discovers her love for him.

802. ————. Children of Eve. New York:
      Benziger, 1918.

      Religious differences cause an estrangement
      between a young couple until the birth of
      their first child.

803. ————. Cloudy Summits. New York:
      Longmans, 1939.

      Love and conversion.

804. ————. Degree Nisi. New York: Longmans,
      1933.

      An anti-divorce novel.

805. ————. Deep Heart. New York: Benziger,
      1919.

      A love triangle culminating in conversion.

806. ————. The Elstones. New York: Benziger,
      1919.

      A wealthy man is received into the church
      on his deathbed. His wife is bitter but each
      of the three children investigates the church
      and converts. One son becomes a priest.

807. ————. Eunice. New York: Benziger, 1919.

      The gradual unfolding of a woman into
      spiritual perfection and the joyful
      acceptance of Catholicism.

808. ————. Fine Play. New York: Benziger,
      1914.

      A Catholic woman discovers that her husband
      has been divorced, so she must leave him.

809. ————. It Happened in Rome. New York:
      Benziger, 1920.

      An adventure set in Rome during a Holy
      Year.

810. ————. An Italian Adventure. New York:
      Longmans, 1931.

"Charming, clean and Catholic," said
Catholic World.

811.   ———. Lady Trent's Daughter. New York:
        Benziger, 1920.

A man loves both a mother and her daughter.
His Catholic principles prevent his marrying
the daughter, but she becomes Catholic in the
end.

812.   ———. Lamp of Destiny. New York:
        Benziger, 1916.

The cloister is a refuge for the lovelorn.

813.   ———. Light on the Lagoon. New York:
        Benziger, 1921.

Catholic music and art attract aesthetes to
the church.

814.   ———. The Potter's House. New York:
        Hutchinson, 1931.

A divorced English woman is rejected by an
Italian Catholic lover. After much rebellion
and searching she enters the church.

815.   ———. Prisoner's Years. New York:
        Benziger, 1912.

A love story in which both bride and groom
are converted.

816.   ———. The Rest House. New York:
        Benziger, 1917.

A pampered young English woman becomes a
Catholic despite opposition from family and
friends.

817.   ———. Sweet Citadel. New York: Benziger,
        1913.

A Catholic wife preserves her faith and
eventually wins her husband to it.

818.   ————. Strangers of Rome. New York:
        Longmans, 1928.

        A melodramatic romance.

819.   ————. Subject to Authority. New York:
        Longmans, 1946.

        A Catholic family converts the son of a
        neighbor.

820.   ————. Tressider's Sister. New York:
        Benziger, 1921.

        A tragedy permeated with Catholic
        teaching. The London Times said Miss Clarke
        "has allowed religious enthusiasm to divert
        artistic integrity."

821.   ————. Ursula Finch. New York: Benziger,
        1920.

        An English woman goes to Rome as a
        governess and becomes a Catholic. Her
        English lover follows and also converts.

822.   ————. Villa by the Sea. New York:
        Benziger, 1925.

        A selfish woman tries to prevent her
        adopted son from practicing Catholicism.

823.   ————. Viola Hudson. New York: Benziger,
        1923.

        An attack on mixed marriage.

824.   ————. Welcome. New York: Longmans, 1943.

        In Jamaica two devout Catholic brothers
        fall in love with the same non-Catholic girl.

825.   ————. Whose Name Is Legion. New York:
        Benziger, 1919.

        Catholicism versus spiritualism. Catholic
        World in May 1921 commented, "Miss Clarke's
        novels are irreproachably moral and always
        strongly, splendidly and compellingly
        Catholic."

826. Clarkson, Tom. <u>Love Is My Vocation</u>. New
York: Farrar, Straus, 1953.

Imaginative life of St. Therese.

827. Cleary, John. <u>Peter's Pence</u>. New York:
Morrow, 1974.

The IRA plans to steal Vatican art
treasures and hold them for ransom, but the
plot goes haywire and they end up kidnapping
the Pope.

828. Clements, E.H. <u>The Other Island</u>. London:
Hodder, 1956.

A mystery set among monks on the Welsh
coast.

829. Clifford, Francis. <u>The Blind Side</u>. New
York: Coward-McCann, 1971.

A priest in war-torn Biafra tries to get
food and medicine to his people.   Back home
in England he gets entangled in political
intrigue.

830. ————. <u>The Trembling Earth</u>. London:
Hamish Hamilton, 1955.

831. Coccioli, Carlo. <u>Heaven and Hell</u>. New York:
Prentice-Hall, 1952.

The last sixteen years of an Italian
priest's life told in extracts from letters,
journals and reports.

832. ————. <u>The Little Valley of God</u>. New York:
Simon & Schuster, 1957.

Saints and sinners in Italy.

833. ————. <u>The White Stone</u>. New York: Simon &
Schuster, 1960.

A priest loses his faith during the war but
may have performed a miracle.   A writer who
had known him searches for the priest from
Mexico to Italy. <u>Library Journal</u> called it
"a spiritual detective story of high literary
caliber."

834. Cohen, Arthur Allen. The Carpenter Years.
      London: Hart-Davis, 1967.

835. Connolly, Francis X. Give Beauty Back. New
      York: Dutton, 1950.

      An artist returns to Catholicism and his
      work takes on new depth and meaning. One of
      his close friends converts. The title is
      from Gerard Manley Hopkins.

836. Connolly, Miles. The Bump on Brannigan's
      Head. New York: Macmillan, 1950.

      An ordinary man tries to apply the
      teachings of Christ to everyday life and
      finds to his amazement that they work. In
      this fantasy-satire the hero struggles
      towards sainthood despite bad temper and
      ulcers.

837. _____. Dan England and the Noonday Devil.
      Milwaukee: Bruce, 1951.

      An ex-reporter refuses to see evil in any
      man. He ennobles the lives of others.

838. _____. Mr. Blue. New York: Macmillan,
      1928.

      A fantasy satire on modern values. The
      hero lives in a large packing box and
      preaches love and kindness. The New York
      Times called him "a human paradox, a sort of
      modern St. Francis."

839. Conroy, Joseph. A Mill Town Pastor. New
      York: Benziger, 1921.

      A valiant and witty priest shapes the
      spiritual destiny of a small Ohio town.

840. Conway, Katherine Eleanor. Lalor's Maples.
      Boston: Pilot, 1901.

      A New England Irish Catholic family
      advances socially and politically.

841. Cook, Kenneth. Stormalong. London: Joseph,
      1963.

"I've been guilty of murder, adultery and despair," the hero tells a priest in confession as this story opens.

842. Cooke, Emma. <u>Eve's Apple</u>. Belfast: Blackstaff, 1985.

What does a 42-year-old Irish Catholic housewife do when she discovers herself pregnant as the result of a secret fling? Set in Ireland at the time of the 1983 abortion referendum.

843. Cooke, Frances. <u>Unbidden Guest</u>. New York: Benziger, 1909.

Love, religion and finance.

844. Cookson, Catherine. <u>A Grand Man</u>. New York: Morrow, 1975.

A child prays incessantly to allow her family to leave city slums for an idyllic country cottage.

845. Cooper, Elizabeth Ann. <u>No Little Thing</u>. New York: Doubleday, 1960.

A Catholic priest has an affair and marries a beautiful singer. He settles in an artist's colony in the Southwest, but his soul is not at peace. When a critically injured girl calls for a priest, he decides he must return. <u>Booklist</u> called it "a well-written and compassionate story of a would be saint." The title comes from <u>The Imitation of Christ</u> by Thomas a Kempis.

846. Corcoran, Charles T. <u>Blackrobe</u>. Milwaukee: Bruce, 1937.

The courage of Father Marquette.

847. Cormier, Robert. <u>A Little Raw on Monday Mornings</u>. New York: Sheed & Ward, 1963.

A widowed mother of three becomes pregnant and feels guilty.

848.   Corrington, John William.   The Upper Hand.
        New York: Putnam, 1967.

        A mentally unstable priest tries to make
        sense out of his life by driving a truck into
        St. Louis Cathedral in New Orleans.

849.   Cornwell, John.   Spoiled Priest.   London:
        Longmans, 1969.

        An English priest leaves the priesthood to
        identify himself with a "fallible sinful
        uncertain and blind world." His example
        encourages several other priests to leave.
        The author uses the liturgical year as the
        time frame for the story.

850.   Corvo, Baron.   Hadrian VII.   New York:
        Knopf, 1925.

        An enchanting fantasy about a worldly
        Englishman who becomes Pope. He is a
        stubborn eccentric who smokes cigarettes,
        scorns privilege and ceremony, and plans to
        sell Vatican treasures to help ease the
        world's misery. He is assassinated by a
        Protestant fanatic from Northern Ireland.
        Originally published in England in 1904.

851.   Costantin, M.M.   God and the Others.   Boston:
        Houghton, Mifflin, 1972.

        A young Irish girl grows up painfully
        amidst a strict Catholic school environment.
        She heads for Barnard College as the story
        ends, where she loses her faith.

852.   Coyne, John.   The Shroud.   New York:
        Berkley, 1983.

        Unspeakable horror follows a priest during
        the Christmas season.

853.   Coyne, Joseph E.   House of Exile.   Milwaukee:
        Bruce, 1964.

        A monastery in a Massachusetts town becomes
        a place of refuge for an order of missionary
        priests escaping Communist rule. A spy is in
        their midst.

854. ————. The Threshing Floor. New York:
      Putnam, 1956.

      A dull and tiresome story of a young man's
      journey from boyhood to priesthood.

855. Crawford, F. Marion. Adam Johnstone's Son.
      New York: Macmillan, 1896.

      Divorce and a violated vow of celibacy are
      the plot mainsprings.

856. ————. Casa Braccio. New York: Macmillan,
      1894.

      A nun renounces her vows and escapes from a
      convent to join her lover. Supposedly based
      on a true incident in Brazil, this was placed
      on the Index of Forbidden Books, despite the
      author's avowed Catholicism.

857. ————. Corleone. New York: Macmillan,
      1904.

      A man slays his brother in church, goes to
      confession immediately afterwards and then
      blames the murder on the priest. The villain
      relies on the seal of confessional to protect
      himself.

858. ————. Marzio's Crucifix. New York:
      Macmillan, 1887.

      A skeptical man hates his brother who is a
      priest.

859. ————. Rose of Yesterday. New York:
      Macmillan, 1897.

      Anti-divorce novel.

860. ————. Taquisara. New York: Macmillan,
      1896.

      This adventure tale's plot devices include
      the seal of confession, the validity of the
      saramental rite, and the power of a deacon's
      orders.

861.   ———. Via Crucis: A Romance of the Second
        Crusade. New York: Macmillan, 1899.

        The days of St. Bernard.

862.   ———. The White Sister. New York:
        Macmillan, 1909.

        A girl becomes a nun after she thinks her
        lover is dead. He returns and wants to marry
        her.

863.   Crone, Anne. Bridie Steen. New York:
        Scribner, 1948.

        A tragic and moving story of Catholic-
        Protestant conflict in Ireland.

864.   Cronin, A.J. Desmonde. Boston: Little,
        Brown, 1975.

        A young, talented seminarian loses his
        vocation and his chastity in Ireland. His
        marriage ends in divorce. Returning to his
        talent for singing, he turns his life around
        and redeems his failures by volunteering for
        missionary service in India.

865.   ———. The Green Years. Boston: Little,
        Brown, 1944.

        A Catholic orphan grows up painfully in a
        prejudiced town in Scotland. He becomes a
        doctor.

866.   ———. The Keys of the Kingdom. Boston:
        Little, Brown, 1941.

        A saintly, Scottish missionary priest wins
        admiration and respect in China.

867.   ———. A Pocketful of Rye. Boston:
        Little, Brown, 1969.

        A story of a young doctor in Switzerland.
        Sequel to Sixpence.

868.   ———. Shannon's Way. Boston: Little,
        Brown, 1948.

A continuation of The Green Years.

869.   ————. A Song of Sixpence. Boston:
        Little, Brown, 1964.

        A young Catholic doctor works in a small
        town in Protestant Scotland.

870.   Crowninshield, Mary. The Archbishop and the
        Lady. New York: McClure, 1900.

        A romance set in the French countryside.

871.   Cuddon, J.A. Acts of Darkness. New York:
        McKay, 1964.

        A confused novel about a young scientist's
        uncle, a priest, who is accused of rape by
        the unbalanced daughter of a local farmer.

872.   ————. A Multitude of Sins. New York:
        Sheed & Ward, 1963.

        A young monk-to-be leaves a monastery to
        do settlement work in a London slum. Despite
        losing his vocation, he helps an apostate
        priest return to the church. The novel
        reveals a good knowledge of moral theology,
        dogma and canon law.

873.   ————. The Six Wounds. New York: McKay,
        1965.

        A Brazilian priest receives the stigmata
        and pilgrims flock to see him. A villaneous
        man tries to make a financial killing out of
        it.

874.   Cullinan, Elizabeth. A Change of Scene. New
        York: Norton, 1982.

        A young American woman spends a year in
        Dublin, encountering, among other things, a
        very different kind of Catholicism.

875.   ————. House of Gold. Boston: Houghton,
        Mifflin, 1970.

        An Irish Catholic family reminisces at the
        deathbed of their devout mother, who has made
        the church her inspiration.

876. Cullinan, Thomas. <u>The Eighth Sacrament</u>. New
      York: Putnam, 1977.

      An attractive young Mother Superior is
      terrified when two of her nuns are murdered.
      While cooperating with the police she begins
      to fall in love with a detective. A sus-
      penseful novel with a surprise ending.

877. Cunliffe-Owen, Sidney. <u>The Ladies of</u>
      <u>Soissons</u>. Westminster, MD: Newman, 1960.

      A witty and warm-spirited story of a
      community of English nuns who try to preserve
      the faith in the days of James II.

878. Cunningham, Francis A. <u>The Awakening</u>. St.
      Louis: Herder, 1901.

      Two sisters are converted from atheism.

879. Cunningham, Michael. <u>The Bishop Finds a Way</u>.
      New York: Farrar, Straus, 1955.

      A stern bishop follows a much loved one as
      head of a Seattle diocese in the 1930s. He
      has a difficult time until he conquers
      himself.

880. Cunninghame, Lady Fairlie. <u>The Little Saint</u>
      <u>of God</u>. London: Hurst, 1901.

      Devout Catholics struggle against the Red
      Terror in Brittany.

881. Curran, Doyle. <u>The Parish and the Hill</u>.
      Boston: Houghton, Mifflin, 1948.

      An Irish-American girlhood in a New England
      mill town.

882. Currier, Charles Warren. <u>Dimitrios and</u>
      <u>Irene</u>. Baltimore: Gallery, 1894.

      The Muslim conquest of Constantinople seals
      the fate of Christians.

883. ————. <u>Rose of Alhambra</u>. New York: P.J.
      Kenedy, 1897.

884. Currier, Isabel. The Young and the Immortal.
     New York: Knopf, 1941.

     The heroine is expelled from a Canadian
     convent school and becomes a thoroughly evil
     person. A Pauline Privilege marriage to a
     psychiatrist helps her. Another strong
     character becomes a nun but must conquer
     herself. Harry Sylvester called this a
     "brave and honest book, free of the fearful
     mawkishness which has marked Catholic
     imaginative writing in this country."

885. Curtayne, Alice. House of Cards. Milwaukee:
     Bruce, 1939.

     An Irish woman must choose between marriage
     and a career.

886. Curtis, Felicia. In the Lean Years. St.
     Louis: Herder, 1913.

     A vivid story of the persecution of
     Catholics under George II.

887. ————. A More Excellent Way. St. Louis:
     Herder, 1916.

     A young woman converts to Catholicism
     despite prejudice and social disapproval.

888. ————. Under the Rose. St. Louis: Herder,
     1935.

     The persecutions under Elizabeth.

889. Cutler, Roland. The Seventh Sacrament. New
     York: Dell, 1984.

     A crazed monk stalks and murders nuns who
     have broken their vows. Sordid and gruesome.

890. Curtsinger, Josephine. Seldom Without Love.
     New York: Macmillan, 1965.

     An often zany story of a small-town Texas
     housewife who is determined to raise money to
     build a Catholic church in her town during
     the harsh Depression days. Whether prodding

the ladies society or tangling with the
bishop, she "lurches from crisis to crisis
with the spiritual aplomb of one seemingly
gifted with providential immunity."

891.   Daggett, Mary. The Higher Court. Boston:
         Badger, 1911.

         A California priest abandons his vocation
         for marriage and a secular career.

892.   Daley, Robert. A Priest and a Girl. New
         York: World, 1969.

         A young priest falls passionately and
         hopelessly in love with an experienced Air
         France stewardess. The Washington Post said
         this novel "will disturb and anger many
         Catholics...but it is honest, accurate and
         fair. It breaks no new ground in fiction,
         but for many of its readers the sympathetic
         portrayal of a Catholic priest's lust as a
         noble, rather than shameful, thing will be
         remarkable enough."

893.   Damon, Norwood. The Chronicles of Mount
         Benedict. Boston: privately printed,
         1837.

         A hilarious satire on the anti-Catholic
         novel. Replete with lustful priests,
         terrorized nuns and sinister Popish plots.

894.   Daniel, Mary Samuel. Choice. St. Louis:
         Herder, 1914.

         A gripping conversion story.

895.   Daniels, Ernest Darwin. Because of His
         Faith. New York: Humphries, 1937.

         An Austrian nobleman fights for the Church
         and the Pope during the Middle Ages.

896.   Daudet, Ernest. The Apostate. New York:
         Appleton, 1889.

         A priest renounces his vocation for a
         dissolute life but is tormented by his

defection. He returns to a monastery on
Easter Sunday and is banished to a Trappist
community where he atones for the rest of his
days.

897.   ———. Unfrocked. New York: Tousey, 1885.

898.   Dauncey, Rolanda. The Far Dwelling. London:
       Macmillan, 1955.

899.   Davis, Dorothy Salisbury. A Gentle Murderer.
       New York: Scribner, 1951.

A superb story of a man who confesses
murder to a priest. The priest must track
down the murderer to prevent further
violence. It turns out that the murderer
wants to become a priest but was ruled
psychologically unfit.

900.   ———. God Speed the Night. New York:
       Scribner, 1968.

A French novice gives up the cloister to
become a heroic fighter in the French
underground. To save a Jewish friend she
allows herself to be violated by an anti-
Semitic (and "very religious") police chief.

901.   ———. Men of No Property. New York:
       Scribner, 1956.

Irish Catholics battle the Know Nothings in
New York City in the 1850s.

902.   ———. Where the Dark Streets Go. New
       York: Scribner, 1962.

The unhappy pastor of a slum parish in New
York becomes a detective when a mysterious
murder occurs in his neighborhood.

903.   Davis-Gardner, Angela. Felice. New York:
       Random House, 1982.

Life in a convent school in Nova Scotia in
the 1920s. A sensitive girl grows spiritually and emotionally.

904.   Deasy, Mary. The Celebration. New York:
        Random House, 1963.

        The disintegration of a once-proud
        Midwestern family in the 1930s culminates at
        the 25th anniversary of the ordination of
        their son.

905.   DeFelitta, Frank. Golgotha Falls. New York:
        Simon & Schuster, 1984.

        A strange force has driven two priests
        insane in a small church in Massachsuetts.
        Exorcism and the second coming figure in the
        plot of this fantasy thriller.

906.   Dehon, Theodora. Heroic Dust. New York:
        Macmillan, 1940.

        Devoutly Catholic Normans rise up to
        protect family and faith during the French
        Revolution.

907.   Delafield, E.M. Turn Back the Leaves. New
        York: Harper, 1930.

        An English Catholic family keeps the faith
        despite obstacles, sorrows and deprivations.
        The New York Times called it "a faithful and
        convincing picture of Catholic life."

908.   Del Castillo, Michel. The Seminarian. New
        York: Holt, 1970.

        A Spanish seminarian questions his faith
        and falls in love with a fellow student.

909.   Deledda, Grazia. The Mother. New York:
        Macmillan, 1923.

        A Sardinian priest falls in love with a
        young woman.

910.   De Mille, Nelson. Cathedral. New York:
        Delacorte, 1981.

        IRA supporters terrorize St. Patrick's
        Cathedral in an effort to draw attention to
        their cause.

911. DeNavery, Raoul. <u>The Monk's Pardon</u>. New
York: Benziger, 1883.

A sculptor monk becomes a hero in 17th
century Spain.

912. Denham, Michael. <u>The Massingers: Or the
Evils of Mixed Marriages</u>. London: Burns &
Oates, 1862.

913. Dennehy, Henry. <u>The Flower of Asia</u>. London:
Burns & Oates, 1901.

The conversion of a Hindu girl.

914. DePolnay, Peter. <u>No Empty Hands</u>.
Indianapolis: Bobbs, Merrill, 1962.

A wealthy Catholic businessman has long
been separated from his wife and is adored by
his mistress. He wants to marry his lover
but religious reasons prevent it. When his
wife dies and he is free, he unexpectedly
enters a Benedictine monastery.

915. ————. <u>The Price You Pay</u>. London: Allen,
1973.

A Catholic couple is destroyed by the
husband's adultery. He is willing to twist
his faith to achieve his ends, but pays a
heavy price.

916. Dering, Edward H. <u>The Ban of Maplethorpe</u>.
London: Art and Book Company, 1894.

917. ————. <u>Florence Danby</u>. London:
Richardson, 1868.

918. ————. <u>Sherborne</u>. London: Art and Book
Company, 1875.

An Anglican clergyman's son is converted
but cannot take his place in society because
of social prejudices. A friend of his wants
to become a member of parliament, and
postpones his conversion. All three of
Dering's novels have much to say about the
disabilities of English Catholics in public
life. All his heroes are reluctant converts.

919. Derleth, August. <u>Evening In Spring</u>. New
      York: Scribner, 1941.

      A Catholic teenager's love for a Protestant
      girl produces antagonism in both families.

920. DeSario, Joseph P.   <u>Limbo</u>. New York:
      Doubleday, 1987.

      A Los Angeles priest becomes a suspect in a
      rape-murder case after it is discovered that
      he is mentally ill.

921. Descalzo, Martin. <u>God's Frontier</u>. New York:
      Knopf, 1959.

      A railway man in a Spanish village
      "resurrects" a dead woman but is stoned to
      death when he refuses to pray for rain during
      a drought. He encounters the devil disguised
      as an office worker. <u>Commonweal</u> thought the
      hero was "unquestionably the complete Christ
      figure in contemporary fiction."

922. Deaver, Joseph. <u>A Certain Widow</u>. Milwaukee:
      Bruce, 1951.

      An Irish Catholic mother in Boston tries to
      mold her sons in the image of their crusading
      father.

923. ————. <u>No Lasting Home</u>. Milwaukee: Bruce,
      1947.

      An Irish family faces life's vicissitudes
      with wit, grace and fortitude. An older
      brother sacrifices so that his talented
      younger brother can attend a Catholic college
      in Boston.

924. ————. <u>Three Priests</u>. New York:
      Doubleday, 1958.

      One priest is a maverick liberal who fights
      political corruption, while another is editor
      of a church newspaper. The third is a shrewd
      politician who rises to the top in the church
      hierarchy.

925. Devine, Edward James. The Training of Silas.
      New York: Benziger, 1907.

      A small town pastor establishes a Catholic
      library, and two of his book loving parish-
      ioners fall in love.

926. DeWohl, Louis. Citadel of God. Philadelphia:
      Lippincott, 1959.

      DeWohl was a Catholic historical novelist
      par excellence. He specialized in biographi-
      cal novels of the saints. This one deals
      with St. Benedict.

927. ————. The Golden Thread. Philadelphia:
      Lippincott, 1952.

      St. Ignatius Loyola.

928. ————. The Joyful Beggar. Philadelphia:
      Lippincott, 1958.

      St. Francis of Assisi.

929. ————. The Last Crusader. Philadelphia:
      Lippincott, 1956.

      Don Juan of Austria.

930. ————. Lay Siege of Heaven. Philadelphia:
      Lippincott, 1961.

      St. Catherine of Siena.

931. ————. The Quiet Light. Philadelphia:
      Lippincott, 1956.

      St. Thomas Aquinas.

932. ————. The Restless Flame. Philadelphia:
      Lippincott, 1951.

      St. Augustine.

933. ————. Set All Afire. Philadelphia:
      Lippincott, 1953.

      St. Francis Xavier.

934. Dickens, Charles. <u>Barnaby Rudge</u>. London:
      Chapman & Hall, 1849.

      A vivid portrait of the anti-Catholic
      Gordon Riots of 1780.

935. Dickson, Elizabeth Barbour. <u>A Maiden's
      Heritage</u>. Long Beach: Dickson, 1929.

      Five girls prepare for life in a convent
      mission school.

936. DiDonato, Pietro. <u>Christ In Concrete</u>.
      Indianapolis: Bobbs, Merrill, 1939.

      A realistic portrait of Italian-American
      life.

937. ————. <u>The Penitent</u>. New York: Hawthorn,
      1962.

      A tale of murder, redemption and forgive-
      ness based on the life of St. Maria Goretti.

938. ————. <u>Three Circles of Light</u>. New York:
      Messner, 1960.

      A scurrilous portrait of a Jesuit priest
      which <u>Commonweal</u> called a "cliché ridden
      overdone piece of hokum."

939. Diminno, Nicholas. <u>The Gentle Martyrdom of
      Brother Bertram</u>. New York: Crown, 1962.

      A humorous tale of a monk's attempt to find
      a market for the monastery's surplus cheese.

940. Dinnis, Enid. <u>The Anchorhold</u>. St. Louis:
      Herder, 1923.

      A beautiful lady of noble birth sells all
      she has and becomes an Anchorite nun. Only
      in rejecting the world can she find God and
      possess heaven.

941. ————. <u>Bess of Cobb's Hall</u>. Milwaukee:
      Bruce, 1940.

      A Benedictine nun, noted for holiness, is
      executed at Tyburn in 1534.

942. ————. <u>Mr. Coleman, Gent</u>. St. Louis:
Herder, 1930.

A story of self-sacrifice, love and
martyrdom during the Popish Plot.

943. ————. <u>The Road to Somewhere</u>. St. Louis:
Herder, 1928.

A mystical narrative of divine and human
love.

944. ————. <u>The Shepherd of Weepingwold</u>.
London: Sands, 1929.

The spiritual beauty and quaint charm of
medieval England.

945. Dobraczynski, Jan. <u>To Drain the Sea</u>.
London: Heinemann, 1964.

946. Dockman, Elizabeth. <u>The Lady and the Sun</u>.
Westminster, MD: Newman, 1954.

The miracle of Fatima.

947. Doner, Mary Frances. <u>O Distant Star</u>. New
York: Doubleday, 1944.

An Irish girl falls for a wealthy Boston
aristocrat but gives him up and marries an
Irish miner.

948. Donohue, James F. <u>Spitballs and Holy Water</u>.
New York: Avon, 1977.

A hilarious novel about a black nun who
tries to raise a million dollars for the
church by convincing Babe Ruth's invincible
Yankees to play a black team from Chicago.

949. Donovan, Cornelius Francis. <u>His Father's
Way</u>. Chicago: Meier, 1926.

A young journalist puts up a brave fight
for his principles and triumphs.

950. ————. <u>The Left Hander</u>. Chicago: Meier,
1925.

"An entertaining, instructive and novel piece of Catholic fiction" - <u>Commonweal</u>.

951. Donovan, Josephine. <u>Black Soil</u>. Boston: Stratford, 1930.

Irish and German Catholic pioneers in Iowa endure many hardships.

952. Dooley, Roger Burke. <u>Days Beyond Recall</u>. Milwaukee: Bruce, 1949.

953. ————. <u>Gone Tomorrow</u>. Milwaukee: Bruce, 1961.

954. ————. <u>The House of Shanahan</u>. New York: Doubleday, 1952.

The above three novels constitute a trilogy about Irish Catholic middle-class life in Buffalo during the early days of this century.

955. ————. <u>Less Than the Angels</u>. Milwaukee: Bruce, 1946.

A probing view of Catholic life in Milwaukee, where hypocrisy masqueraded in the trappings of piety. A Catholic brewery heiress, convinced of her saintliness, pushes her reluctant doctor-husband into a campaign for mayor. She does so to get even with upper-class Protestants who had rejected her. When her husband dies suddenly, she is forced to reexamine her values.

956. Dorsey, Anna Hanson. <u>Coaina, the Rose of the Algonquins</u>. New York: O'Shea, 1867.

The Catholic faith penetrates the lives of an Indian tribe living near Montreal, and the heroine dies rather than abandon her faith.

957. ————. <u>Conscience</u>. New York: Dunigan, 1856.

Two orphaned cousins have their ups and downs, but only Catholicism holds their lives together.

958. ———. The Flemmings. New York: O'Shea,
      1869.

      An Irish peddler settles on a farm in New
      Hampshire. As the first Catholics in the
      area they experience social ostracism and
      job discrimination.

959. ———. The Oriental Pearl. Baltimore:
      Murphy, 1848.

      Three German Catholic immigrants settle in
      Baltimore and rejoice in the religious and
      economic freedoms found here. They do not
      prosper materially but help to spread the
      faith.

960. ———. The Sister of Charity. New York:
      Dunigan, 1847.

      A shipwreck off the North Carolina coast
      brings a dedicated nun to a beautiful home
      occupied by a gentleman and his two
      daughters. She succeeds in converting the
      household, and even converts a neighboring
      Episcopalian clergyman and a judge.

961. ———. The Student of Blenheim Forest.
      Baltimore: Murphy, 1846.

      A wealthy young Virginian is convinced of
      the truth of Catholicism but his Episcopalian
      father tries bribery and threats to prevent
      it. The young man gives up everything for
      his newfound faith but soon dies. There is a
      tearful deathbed reconciliation scene.

962. Dostal, W. A. The Hand of God. New York:
      Benziger, 1934.

      A lapsed Catholic returns to the faith in a
      Czech community in Iowa.

963. Doty, William L. Button, Button. Huntington,
      IN: Our Sunday Visitor, 1979.

      An elderly cigar-loving monsignor in a
      small New York town investigates two gruesome
      murders.

964.   ———.   Fire In the Rain.   Milwaukee:
        Bruce, 1951.

        A priest tries to recapture the idealism of
        his early years.

965.   ———.   The Mark.   Milwaukee: Bruce, 1953.

        A young priest finds it difficult to adjust
        to the demands of teaching in a Catholic boys
        high school.

966.   ———.   The Rise of Father Roland.
        Milwaukee: Bruce, 1961.

        A newly ordained priest tries to cope with
        varied and unpredictable problems befalling
        him.

967.   Douglas, Lady Gertrude.   Linked Lives.
        London: Art and Book Company, 1876.

        A melodramatic conversion tale.

968.   Douglas-Irvine, Helen.   Fray Mario.   New
        York: Longmans, 1939.

        A little book of rare charm about a
        Franciscan monk in Peru who becomes a
        wandering minstrel.

969.   Drake, Henry Burgess.   The Woman and the
        Priest.   London: Davies, 1955.

        A man breaks from the church and decides to
        find his own way to God in a strongly
        Catholic village in France.   His decision
        leads to many trials and tribulations.   The
        author is critical of the church, which he
        calls "a force elemental, fateful and
        malign."

970.   Drummond, Hamilton.   For the Religion.   New
        York: Harper, 1898.

971.   ———.   A Man Of His Age.   New York:
        Harper, 1899.

        Two novels about Catholic-Huguenot conflict
        in France and Florida.

972. DuBois, Theodora. The Listener. New York:
      Doubleday, 1953.

      A novice enters a convent after her lovers
      death but is unsuited for this life. She is
      drawn into a murder mystery.

973. Dubus, Andre. Voices from the Moon.
      Boston: Godine, 1984.

      A deeply religious adolescent is distressed
      when his divorced father decides to marry his
      older brothers ex-wife. He tells a compas-
      sionate wise priest, "It will be very hard to
      be a Catholic in our house." The priest
      convinces him that love is neither simple nor
      smooth.

974. Dubus, Elizabeth Nell. To Love and To Dream.
      New York: Putnam, 1986.

      A beautiful Cajun Catholic woman, in love
      with a Jewish doctor about to be shipped to
      the Pacific during World War II, discovers
      she must choose between the dictates of her
      religious upbringing and the demands of her
      heart.

975. Ducharme, Jacques. The Delusson Family. New
      York: Funk, 1939.

      An upwardly-mobile French Canadian family
      in Massachusetts is overjoyed when their son
      becomes a priest.

976. Dudley, Owen Francis. The Coming of the
      Monster. New York: Longmans, 1936.

      Another adventure for the "Masterful Monk"
      who fights communism and paganism. Alfred
      Kazin said that the "Masterful Monk" tales by
      Dudley "have a narrow range and their appeal
      seems limited to Catholic readers."

977. ————. The Last Crescendo. New York:
      Longmans, 1954.

      A talented egocentric pianist, a non-
      practicing Catholic, is in love with a devout

girl. He loses his ability to play in a
cruel act of violence, but forgives his
assailant.

978.   ⸺. The Masterful Monk. New York:
        Longmans, 1929.

        His second appearance.

979.   ⸺. Michael. New York: Longmans, 1948.

        The monk helps an introverted young man
        rediscover purpose in life after the horrors
        of the World War.

980.   ⸺. The Pageant of Life. New York:
        Longmans, 1932.

        A young Englishman's disturbed life
        prevents his conversion.

981.   ⸺. The Shadow on the Earth. New York:
        Longmans, 1927.

        A young man crippled for life renounces
        religion, but is converted by the compas-
        sionate and pivotal influence of the
        "Masterful Monk."

982.   ⸺. The Tremaynes and the Masterful
        Monk. New York: Longmans, 1940.

        A depraved man is regenerated.

983.   Duggan, Alfred. Count Bohemond. New York:
        Pantheon, 1965.

        The First Crusade.

984.   ⸺. The Cunning of the Dove. New York:
        Pantheon, 1960.

        St. Edward the Confessor.

985.   ⸺. My Life for My Sheep. New York:
        Coward-McCann, 1955.

        St. Thomas Becket.

986. DuMaurier, Angela. The Road to Leenane.
      London: Davies, 1963.

         A woman is torn between her growing love
      for a married man and her devotion to
      Catholicism. They cannot marry. Years later
      when he is free to marry her, she has become
      a nun. They meet briefly when he sends his
      only daughter to the convent school where she
      teaches. They still love each other, but she
      has given her life wholly to God.

987. Duguid, Julian. Father Coldstream. New
      York: Appleton, 1938.

         An absorbing and dramatic story of the
      Jesuits in 18th century Paraguay.

988. Duncan, David. The Trumpet of God. New
      York: Doubleday, 1956.

         The Children's Crusade.

989. Dunne, John Gregory. True Confessions. New
      York: Dutton, 1977.

         A brilliant tale of two brothers in
      California. One is a monsignor rising
      rapidly in the church hierarchy; the other a
      detective whose investigation of a horrible
      murder leads to a prominent Catholic layman.
      The priest finds his soul only when he loses
      his status and is banished to a small town.

990. Dunphy, Jack. Nightmovers. New York:
      Morrow, 1968.

         A childless middle-aged widow finds it hard
      to cope with loneliness until a young cousin
      arrives from Ireland. Her only friend in her
      changing Brooklyn neighborhood has been an
      old and misunderstood priest.

991. Dunnett, Dorothy. The Game of Kings. New
      York: Putnam, 1961.

         Catholic-Protestant conflict in the
      Scotland of Mary Stuart.

992.   Dupre, Catherine. The Child of Julian Flynn.
       London: Collins, 1972.

       The sad story of an Irish priest's love
       affair.

993.   Earls, Michael. Melchior of Boston. New
       York: Benziger, 1911.

       A Boston businessman plays one of the Magi
       in a Christmas play. This awakens religious
       interest and he tries to bring Christian
       ethics to the marketplace.

994.   ————. The Wedding Bells of Glendalough.
       Huntington, IN: Our Sunday Visitor, 1913.

       Two young men are called to the priesthood
       at a Jesuit college in Boston.

995.   Eastwick, Mrs. Egerton. Beyond These Voices.
       New York: Benziger, 1901.

       A skeptical woman refuses to accept the
       Catholic way of life and commits suicide.

996.   ————. The Trial of Margaret Brereton. New
       York: Benziger, 1892.

       An attack on mixed marriage.

997.   Eastwood, Catherine. The Estranged Face.
       New York: Roy, 1957.

       An English missionary nun in Uganda is
       dispensed from her vows. Still unable to
       find personal peace, she eventually returns
       to Africa.

998.   Eastwood, Helen. Beloved Intruder. London:
       Eldon, 1949.

       Portrait of a self-sacrificing Catholic
       heroine.

999.   Eaton, Evelyn and Edward Roberts Moore. Heart
       in Pilgrimage. New York: Harper, 1948.

       Life and trials of Mother Seton.

1000.   Ebejer, Francis. A Wreath for the
        Innocents. London: Macgibbon, 1958.

1001.   Ebers, George. Barbara Blomberg. New York:
        Appleton, 1897.

        A historical romance of the reign of
        Charles V, which Catholic World said
        "inexcusably misrepresented Catholic
        purity."

1002.   Eca de Queiroz, Jose. The Relic. New York:
        Knopf, 1925.

        A scoundrel convinces an old lady to leave
        her fortune to him. He pretends to be pious
        but is really licentious. He takes a
        pilgrimage to Jerusalem and steals a relic,
        but he is found out and discredited.

1003.   ———. The Sin of Father Amaro. New York:
        St. Martin's, 1963.

        An orphan becomes a priest without any
        real calling and hides behind the cassock.
        He has a love affair and fathers a child. A
        bitterly anticlerical novel originally
        published in Portugal in 1874.

1004.   Eckstein, Ernst. A Monk of the Aventine.
        Boston: Roberts, 1894.

        A monk is imprisoned in 10th century Rome.

1005.   Eco, Umberto. The Name of the Rose. New
        York: Harcourt, 1983.

        An amazing bestseller about seven bizarre
        murders in a Franciscan abbey in 14th
        century Italy.

1006.   Edgar, A.H. John Bull and the Papists.
        London: Richardson, 1846.

        Conversion of an Anglican rector.

1007.   Edgar, Mary C. Father Drummond and His
        Orphans. Philadelphia: McGrath, 1854.

An Irish priest devotes his life and
energies to the care of the poor and
starving during the darkest days of Irish
travail.

1008.   Edwards, Edward J.   The Chosen.   New York:
           Longmans, 1949.

Five young men enter a seminary but only
one endures through ordination.

1009.   ————.   Dark Enemy.   New York: Longmans,
           1954.

A non-Catholic doctor in a Catholic
hospital is determined to save his wife.
She is pregnant and suffering from a heart
condition, but refuses to have an abortion.

1010.   ————.   These Two Hands.   Milwaukee:
           Bruce, 1942.

A missionary priest refuses a sick call to
a dying leper.   He is removed from his
teaching assignment and sent to a lonely
place, where he overcomes cowardice and ends
life as a hero.

1011.   ————.   This Night Called Day.   Milwaukee:
           Bruce, 1945.

After a man's wife dies, he thinks he
loves her sister.   A priest helps him make
the right decision.

1012.   ————.   Thy People, My People.   Milwaukee:
           Bruce, 1941.

A young American missionary in the
Philippines is well loved and labors
unselfishly.

1013.   ————.   White Fire.   Milwaukee: Bruce,
           1943.

American nuns works among Filipino lepers.

1014.   Egan, Maurice Francis.   The Disappearance of
           John Longworthy.   Notre Dame, IN: Ave
           Maria Press, 1890.

A wealthy young socialite steps back from the pressures of life, converts to Catholicism, and becomes a truly happy man.

1015. ———. Marriage of Reason. Baltimore: Murphy, 1893.

A "good and wholesome" portrait of American Catholic life.

1016. ———. The Success of Patrick Desmond. Notre Dame, IN: Ave Maria Press, 1893.

A materialistic man ruins his relationship with a lovely girl, driving her to a convent.

1017. ———. The Vocation of Edward Conway. Notre Dame, IN: Ave Maria Press, 1896.

A bright and ambitious young man, on the threshhold of a great business career, decides to become a priest.

1018. Eichler, Lillian. Stillborn. New York: Appleton, 1929.

A possessive mother dominates her son to overcompensate for her husband's desertion. She wants him to become a priest, but love causes him to change his ideas about life and religion.

1019. Eifel, Aloysius J. A Brother's Sacrifice. Techny, IL: Society of the Divine Word, 1909.

A priest tries to prove the innocence of a parishioner accused of murder.

1020. Eisinger, Jo. The Walls Came Tumbling Down. New York: Coward-McCann, 1943.

A newspaper gossip columnist tries to prove that his parish priest did not commit suicide.

1021. Eliot, Ethel Cook. Angel's Mirth. New York: Sheed & Ward, 1936.

Suicide and divorce in her family lead a young girl to conversion.

1022. ————. Her Soul To Keep. New York: Macmillan, 1935.

In a college town a middle-aged Catholic widow learns that her adopted daughter is pregnant by a married professor. Faith and courage triumph. "An impressive story of a woman's trust and faith." (Saturday Review)

1023. ————. Roses for Mexico. New York: Macmillan, 1946.

The Virgin Mary appears to Juan Diego at Guadelupe.

1024. Elsna, Hebe. The Abbot's House. London: Collins, 1969.

1025. ————. The Convert. London: Hale, 1952.

1026. ————. Gail Talbot. London: Hale, 1953.

The church heals sinners and brings peace to troubled marriages.

1027. ————. The Season's Greetings. London: Hale, 1954.

A Christmas story of Catholic family life.

1028. Endo, Shusaku. The Samurai. New York: Harper, 1982.

In 17th century Japan a samurai adopts the Christian faith for political reasons and journeys to the Vatican. His faith deepens and he dies for it. Endo has been called the Japanese Graham Greene.

1029. ————. Silence. New York: Harper, 1976.

An extraordinary and harrowing account of the martyrdom of Japanese Catholics in the 17th century. The main character is a Portuguese priest whose faith was not strong enough to withstand persecution.

1030. ———. Volcano. New York: Taplinger,
       1980.

       A defrocked French priest and a Japanese
       friend are obsessed by a volcano.

1031. ———. Wonderful Fool. New York: Harper,
       1983.

       A Christ-like French visitor to Japan
       befriends the poor and despised. He is
       considered a fool by his affluent friends.

1032. Englebert, Omer. The Wisdom of Father
       Pecquet. New York: McKay, 1951.

       Charming vignettes of a rural French
       pastor.

1033. Enriquez, Emigdio. The Devil Flower. New
       York: Hill & Wang, 1959.

       A Filipino schoolteacher indulges in a
       sensual attraction to an older married man,
       who once seduced a nun.

1034. Espinas, Jose Maria. By Nature Equal. New
       York: Pantheon, 1961.

       "Moving unpretentious story that has a
       firm spiritual undergirding." (America) Set
       in Spain.

1035. Estang, Luc. The Better Sons. New York:
       Pantheon, 1964.

       A man leaves his wife and lives with his
       mistress, but eventually comes to see what
       his selfishness has done to his family.

1036. Evans, Fallon. Pistols and Pedagogues. New
       York: Sheed & Ward, 1963.

       An English professor tries to combat a
       drug ring at a small Catholic college in the
       mid-West. A comedy mystery.

1037. ———. The Trouble With Turlow. New York:
       Doubleday, 1961.

The humorous exploits of a young English
professor at a small Catholic women's
college.

1038.   Evans, John. <u>Halo For Satan</u>. Indianapolis:
        Bobbs, Merrill, 1948.

The bishop of Chicago wants to obtain the
rarest religious relic in the world - a
manuscript allegedly written by Jesus.
Assorted mobsters also want it, if it
exists.

1039.   Faber, Christine. <u>Ambition's Contest</u>. New
        York: P.J. Kenedy, 1891.

A young man struggles to subdue his
intellectual ambitions before becoming a
Catholic and then a priest.

1040.   ————. <u>Burden of Honor</u>. New York: P.J.
        Kenedy, 1915.

The heroism of a noble Catholic girl.

1041.   Faber, Nancy W. <u>Strange Way Home</u>. Chicago:
        Regnery, 1963.

A young Jewish child is kidnapped by a
fanatical Catholic who takes him to a remote
Canadian town. The boy becomes a priest and
one day learns the true story of his family.

1042.   Fabricius, Johan Wigmore. <u>Son of Marietta</u>.
        Boston: Little, Brown, 1936.

The saga of an actress's daughter, whose
son was fathered by a bishop.

1043.   Faherty, William B. <u>A Wall for San
        Sebastian</u>. Fresno: Academy Guild, 1962.

A Franciscan missionary, once a soldier,
is torn between religious and military
methods when he tries to save his town.

1044.   Fairley, Michael. <u>With Friends Like That</u>.
        Port Washington, NY: Ashley, 1987.

A love story between a Catholic man and a
Protestant woman who meet accidentally when
they seek shelter from a Belfast bomb.

1045.   Farnum, Mabel. Carrack Sailed Away. Boston:
        Propagation of the Faith Press, 1938.

        The missionary journeys of Francis Xavier.

1046.   ———. The Town Landing. New York: P.J.
        Kenedy, 1923.

        A man is converted through the examples of
        a friend and a lover.

1047.   ———. The Wounded Face. Boston: Angel
        Guardian Press, 1912.

        Two well informed and zealous Catholic men
        engage in good works.

1048.   Farrell, James T. Father and Son. New
        York: Vanguard, 1940.

1049.   ———. Judgement Day. New York:
        Vanguard, 1935.

1050.   ———. My Days of Anger. New York:
        Vanguard, 1943.

1051.   ———. The Silence of History. New York:
        Doubleday, 1963.

1052.   ———. A World I Never Made. New York:
        Vanguard, 1936.

1053.   ———. Young Lonigan. New York: Vanguard,
        1932.

1054.   ———. The Young Manhood of Studs Lonigan.
        New York: Vanguard, 1934.

        All of Farrell's novels concentrate on
        Irish Catholic life in Chicago, emphasizing
        the estrangement of the young and intellec-
        tually talented from their Catholic
        upbringing. Items 1049, 1053 and 1054
        constitute the Studs Lonigan trilogy. Items
        1048, 1050 and 1052 are the Danny O'Neill

trilogy. Item 1051 is the portrait of Eddie
Ryan, a brilliant student at the University
of Chicago who rejects both his faith and
the world he lives in.

1055.   Farrell, Michael. Thy Tears Might Cease.
        New York: Knopf, 1964.

        A devoutly Catholic adolescent is plunged
        into the Irish rebellion. While he repu-
        diates Catholicism he remains culturally
        Catholic.

1056.   Fecher, Constance. King's Legacy. London:
        Hale, 1967.

1057.   Fedden, Marguerite. Dark Extremity.
        London: Burleigh, 1953.

        A devoted girl marries a nearly blind war
        hero. At the shrine of St. Anne de Beaupre,
        his sight is restored.

1058.   ————. Myrtle Among Thorns. London:
        Burleigh, 1948.

        Mixed marriage and divorce.

1059.   Feiner, Ruth. A Miracle for Caroline. New
        York: Coward-McCann, 1950.

        A British housewife, disappointed by life,
        petitions Our Lady to allow her to live it
        over again. She finds her real life
        infinitely better.

1060.   Fetler, Andrew. The Travellers. London:
        Golancz, 1966.

1061.   Fielding, Gabriel. Eight Days. New York:
        Morrow, 1959.

        A Catholic convert finds his faith tested
        and challenged in the sinister, amoral
        environment of Northern Africa. Chad Walsh
        called this "a powerful and haunting
        dramatization of the workings of conscience
        and an impressive exploration of a man's
        hidden life."

1062.   Firbank, Ronald. Concerning the Eccentrici-
        ties of Cardinal Pirelli. London:
        Richards, 1926.

        A Spanish cardinal is so strange that the
        Pope receives complaints. "With priests
        like Pirelli the church is in peril."

1063.   Fish, Horace F.X. The Saint's Theatre. New
        York: Huebsch, 1924.

        A pious Spanish girl performs miracles of
        healing but discovers that human love is the
        highest of all vocations.

1064.   Fisher, Anne B. Cathedral In the Sun. New
        York: Carlyle House, 1940.

        The Spanish missions in California.

1065.   Fitzgerald, Barbara. We Are Besieged. New
        York: Putnam, 1946.

        A Protestant family decides to stay in
        Catholic Ireland in the 1920s even though
        they feel "we may remain, as aliens
        besieged, in a land that has lost its
        welcome."

1066.   Fitzgerald, F. Scott. This Side of
        Paradise. New York: Scribner, 1920.

        The only Fitzgerald novel with Catholic
        elements, this first novel by the celebrated
        chronicler of the Lost Generation is
        notable for a strong portrait of a priest.
        Father Darcy may be based on a family
        friend, Father Sigourney Fay, to whom it is
        dedicated.

1067.   Fitzmaurice, Eugene. The Indulgence. New
        York: Freundlich, 1985.

        A fabulously wealthy Catholic family is
        involved in the destiny of the United
        States, from the Revolutionary War to 1900.
        The Vatican is seen as a background player,
        manipulating sources of great wealth.

1068.   Fitzsimons, Simon. How George Edwards
        Scrapped Religion. Boston: Stratford,
        1923.

        A young university professor loses his
        faith but regains it before his life ends.

1069.   Flaherty, Joe. Fogarty and Co. New York:
        Coward-McCann, 1973.

        A Brooklyn Irishman laments his fate after
        he deserts his wife and hankers after other
        women.   He sees himself a victim of his
        strict religious upbringing.

1070.   Fleischer, Leonore. Agnes of God. New
        York: New American Library, 1985.

        A nun is arrested for murdering a child,
        the origin of which she is totally unaware.
        She is judged sane and must stand trial, at
        which a lapsed Catholic psychiatrist and a
        strong-willed Mother Superior clash.   A
        novel based on a screenplay.

1071.   Fleming, Thomas J. All Good Men. New York:
        Doubleday, 1961.

        Fortunes of an Irish Catholic political
        family.

1072.   ————. The God of Love. New York:
        Doubleday, 1963.

        A priest, a big-city Catholic politician,
        and a neurotic girl are driven to self-
        destruction.

1073.   ————. The Good Shepherd. New York:
        Doubleday, 1974.

        A new American cardinal finds bitter
        personal and public conflicts threatening to
        destroy his priesthood.   When the Vatican
        opposes some of his decisions, he is pushed
        toward further torment and doubt.

1074.   ————. Romans, Countrymen, Lovers. New
        York: Morrow, 1969.

A Catholic intellectual loses his faith
and his marriage. He recovers his self
respect and confidence outside of his faith.

1075. Fleury, Barbara Frances. Faith, the Root.
New York: Dutton, 1942.

Christian Century called this character
study of a French Catholic priest in a small
Michigan town "a parable for preachers."

1076. Flood, Charles Bracelen. A Distant Drum.
Boston: Houghton, Mifflin, 1957.

A Harvard-educated Catholic lawyer is
rejected by his girlfriend partly for
religious reasons.

1077. ———. Love Is a Bridge. Boston:
Houghton, Mifflin, 1953.

A man divorces his wife and marries again
but the second marriage is a disaster. He
returns to his first - and in Catholic
doctrine - his only wife.

1078. ———. Tell Me, Stranger. Boston:
Houghton, Mifflin, 1959.

A Catholic photographer falls in love with
his boss, an attractive divorcee. He saves
her life and has an affair with her but is
bothered by his conscience. She ends the
affair in order to help him save his soul.

1079. Flynn, Brian. Running Nun. London: Long,
1952.

1080. ———. The Saints Are Sinister. London:
Long, 1960.

1081. Flynn, Daniel. Destiny; or the Priest's
Blessing. Baltimore: Kelly, 1871.

1082. Fogazzaro, Antonio. The Saint. New York:
Putnam, 1906.

An agnostic divorcee is deserted by her
lover, who is converted and becomes a

priest. He becomes a living saint but is a
scandal to the leaders of the church,
including the Pope. On his deathbed he
converts his former mistress. William
Roscoe Thayer wrote "The Saint is the story
of a man with a passion for doing good; in
the most direct and human way, who found the
church in which he believed, the church
which existed ostensibly to do good
according to the direct and human ways of
Jesus Christ, thwarting him at every step."
The Saint is still drawing attention. See
Peter Hebblethwaite, "A Novelist for the
Synod," The Tablet, 241 (5 September 1987):
939-940.

1083.   Fombona, Miriam Blanco. No True Life.
        London: Lincolns-Prager, 1955.

1084.   Fonseca, Rodolfo L. Tower of Ivory. New
        York: Messner, 1954.

        An exploration of the psychological effect
        on fifteen missionary nuns in China who are
        raped during anti-religious violence.

1085.   Forbes, Helen E. His Eminence. New York:
        Nash, 1904.

        An Italian cardinal awaits the Napoleonic
        invasion.

1086.   Forrest, David. After Me, the Deluge.
        London: Hodder, 1972.

        A priest in a tiny French village hears
        the voice of God warning that a second flood
        is coming. No one believes him.

1087.   Forrest, H.D. Father Justin. St. Louis:
        Herder, 1921.

1088.   Forton, Jean. The Better Part of Valour.
        London: Cape, 1963.

1089.   Fowler, Helen Marjorie. The Refugee. New
        York: Macmillan, 1961.

        A bereaved husband, a lukewarm Catholic
        convert, undergoes considerable anguish when
        his wife and children are murdered.

1090. Fowlie, Wallace. Sleep of the Pigeon.
       London: Harvill, 1951.

1091. Fractious, Father. Sister Teresita and the
       Spirit. San Francisco: Ignatious Press,
       1986.

       A light-hearted caricature of radical
       nuns.

1092. Frankau, Pamela. The Road Through the
       Woods. New York: Doubleday, 1960.

       A young man searches for his spiritual and
       psychological identity.

1093. Fraser, Antonia. Quiet as a Nun. New York:
       Viking, 1977.

       A glamorous television reporter returns to
       her convent school to investigate a bizarre
       story: A nun was found dead of starvation
       in a spooky tower.

1094. Frederic, Harold. The Damnation of Theron
       Ware. New York: Stone & Kimball, 1896.

       A Catholic priest and nun are certain of
       their faith but a young Methodist minister
       is tormented by doubt.

1095. Fremantle, Anne. By Grace of Love. New
       York: Macmillan, 1957.

       An English Protestant peer has a tempes-
       tuous affair at Oxford with a Catholic girl
       from an old and prominent family. When she
       refuses to marry him, he goes to Spain and
       fights in the civil war. When they meet
       again some years later, he has become a
       priest.

1096. Friedman, Ben. The Anguish of Father
       Rafti. New York: Two Continents, 1977.

       A powerful indictment of Catholic–Jewish
       relationships, set in the future.

1097. Fuentes, Carlos. The Good Conscience. New
       York: Obolensky, 1961.

The young heir to a fortune is torn
between the practicality of his father's
world and the idealism of his Catholic
education.

1098.   Fuller, Jack. <u>Mass</u>. New York: Morrow,
        1986.

        A spy novel using the Mass allegorically.

1099.   Fullerton, Lady Georgiana. <u>Constance
        Sherwood</u>. London: Moxon, 1865.

        Catholics in Elizabethan England.

1100.   ————. <u>Grantley Manor</u>. London: Moxon,
        1847.

        The damages of religious prejudice.

1101.   ————. <u>Ladybird</u>. London: Moxon, 1852.

        A Catholic widow refuses to marry her
        lover because she feels guilty about taking
        him from his calling. He becomes a
        missionary to China.

1102.   ————. <u>Mrs. Gerald's Niece</u>. London:
        Bentley, 1869.

        A High Church clergyman and his wife are
        converted.

1103.   Fumento, Rocco. <u>The Tree of Dark Reflection</u>.
        New York: Knopf, 1962.

        An exhaustive probing of the psychic and
        social causes of a family's descent into
        self-destruction. The hero is an Italian
        Catholic in love with a Jewish woman. She
        converts to Catholicism while he turns
        towards atheism.

1104.   Gallagher, Louis Joseph. <u>Episode on Beacon
        Hill</u>. New York: Benziger, 1950.

        An absorbing study of Catholic-Protestant
        relationships.

1105. Gallagher, Thomas Michael. The Monogamist.
       New York: Random House, 1955.

       An Irish Catholic businessman in Manhattan
       falls in love with a young pianist. But he
       cannot sacrifice his happy twenty-five year
       marriage, and becomes reconciled to his wife
       at Christmas time.

1106. Gallahue, John. The Jesuit. New York:
       Stein & Day, 1973.

       Three Jesuits undertake a secret mission
       to Moscow in 1931 at the behest of Pope Pius
       XI. "A spy story in ecclesiastical mufti."
       (New York Times)

1107. Gallico, Paul. The Small Miracle. New
       York: Doubleday, 1952.

       An Italian orphan and his sick donkey try
       to visit the crypt of St. Francis but it
       takes the Pope's intervention to grant the
       request.

1108. Gallie, Menna. You're Welcome to Ulster.
       New York: Harper, 1970.

       An English widow visits Catholic friends
       in Belfast and encounters militant Orangemen
       on the twelfth of July.

1109. Galvez, Manuel. Holy Wednesday. New York:
       Appleton, 1934.

       An Argentinian priest listens to sins in
       the confessional. While exhorting and
       comforting people, he is struggling against
       the same desires.

1110. Gambino, Richard. Bread and Roses. New
       York: Seaview, 1981.

       A grand saga of Italian-American life.
       One of the sons becomes a powerful priest
       with great influence at the Vatican.

1111. Garford, James. Camphor. London: Faber,
       1960.

An irreverent man thinks he has a late
vocation, but is possessed by sensual
interests.

1112.   ———. Seventeen Come Sunday. London:
         Faber, 1961.

This is a growing-up Catholic novel, with
the hero rebelling against his religion.
His priest tells him, "You've had a wonderful Catholic upbringing you don't appreciate
now, but you will when you meet others who
lack it."

1113.   Garvin, Viola. Child of Light. New York:
         Longmans, 1937.

This story of a spiritual development of
two friends - one a Protestant convert to
Catholicism, the other a born but lukewarm
Catholic - "glows with an ardent spiritual
fervor." (Manchester Guardian)

1114.   Gash, Joe. Priestly Murders. New York:
         Holt, 1984.

In a Chicago church a priest is shot dead
during Mass. Two police officers - both
lovers and lapsed Catholics - move rapidly
to solve the case which has embarrassed the
city.

1115.   Gaughan, Jessie A. The Story of Sir Charles
         Vereker. New York: P.J. Kenedy, 1927.

Cromwell's invasion of Ireland.

1116.   Gay, Laverne. Wine of Satan. New York:
         Scribner, 1949.

Pope Gregory and the Crusades.

1117.   Geddes, Paul. A State of Corruption. New
         York: Holt, 1985.

The Vatican creates a special group to
rout out evil during the famous bank
scandal.

1118. Gerard, Dorothea. <u>Orthodox</u>. New York:
Longmans, 1888.

An Austrian army officer loves a beautiful
Jewish girl but renounces her and enters a
monastery.

1119. ———. <u>The Unworthy Pact</u>. New York:
Benziger, 1913.

A young English man's faith is tested when
his uncle's will is discovered.

1120. Gerner, George B. <u>Crossroads</u>. Fresno:
Academy Library Guild, 1955.

1121. Gibbs, Henry. <u>A Long Probation</u>. New York:
Benziger, 1897.

An orphan grows up a good Catholic.

1122. Gibert, Julia Marion. <u>Outward and Visible
Signs</u>. New York: Viking, 1987.

A zany, eccentric group of Californians try
to make sense out of life. The author uses
the seven sacraments as a literary frame-
work.

1123. Gibson, Elizabeth. <u>The Water is Wide</u>.
Grand Rapids: Zondervan, 1984.

A young woman whose father is a staunch
and bigoted evangelical minister encounters
both Catholics and liberal Protestants while
attending college in Northern Ireland. Her
favorite professor is a priest who is killed
in a bomb explosion. She falls in love with
a man who aspires to the priesthood.

1124. Gide, Andre. <u>The Vatican Cellars</u>. London:
Penguin, 1959.

A swashbuckler, featuring Masons, Jesuits,
shady aristocrats and a plot to kidnap the
Pope.

1125. Gilbert, Rosa Mulholland. <u>Father Tim</u>.
London: Sands, 1910.

A young Irish priest fights alcohol abuse and poverty in the slums of Dublin.

1126. ————. O'Loughin of Clare. New York: P.J. Kenedy, 1916.

Anti-Catholic discrimination in eighteenth century Ireland.

1127. Gilford, Charles B. Quest for Innocence. New York: Putnam, 1961.

An avowed atheist visits a mid-western Catholic family of a comrade killed in Korea. He probes into the background of his friend - an ex-seminarian - and discovers unexpected truths.

1128. Gill, B.M. Nursery Crimes. New York: Scribner, 1987.

An insane child in a convent school continues her murderous ways in a chilling novel reminiscent of The Bad Seed.

1129. Gill, Brendan. The Trouble of One House. New York: Doubleday, 1950.

Complex inter-relationships in an Irish-Catholic family.

1130. Gillespie, Jane. A Man on a Pillar. London: Davies, 1956.

1131. Gilman, Dorothy. A Nun in the Closet. New York: Doubleday, 1975.

Two nuns from a poverty-stricken order go to check out a bequest of property. They get involved in some hilarious but often scary adventures.

1132. Gilmore, Florence. Dr. Dumont. St. Louis: Herder, 1911.

A man's faith helps him bear many trials.

1133. ————. The Parting of the Ways. St. Louis: Herder, 1914.

Two boyhood pals, parted for years, are reunited in the church.

1134.   Giovannetti, Alberto. Requiem for a Spy. New York: Doubleday, 1983.

The KGB places an agent in the Vatican diplomatic corps, but he returns to the Catholic faith of his childhood.

1135.   Gironella, Jose Maria. The Cypresses Believe in God. New York: Knopf, 1955.

A teenager willingly offers himself to God in reparation for the sins of the world and becomes a Catholic martyr during the Spanish Civil War.

1136.   Gittelson, Celia. Saving Grace. New York: Knopf, 1981.

A light-hearted, compassionate story of a Pope who leaves the Vatican for a few days to see life in the real world.

1137.   Glasco, Gordon. The Days of Eternity. New York: Doubleday, 1983.

One day in a Los Angeles church Anna, an American lawyer, sees a priest from out of her past. Nearly thirty years before they had been lovers in an Italian village when he was a lieutenant in the Nazi army. Her love for him still simmered.

1138.   Glaser, Dorothy. Brother Anselmo. New York: Brewer, 1930.

A Dominican monk in Avignon contemplates leaving his order to discover the joys of the world.

1139.   Gobineau, Arthur de. The Lucky Prisoner. New York: Doubleday, 1926.

A romance with a background of the Catholic-Huguenot conflict.

1140.   Godden, Rumer. Five for Sorrow, Ten for Joy. New York: Viking, 1979.

A French prostitute becomes a nun in this remarkable and inspiring novel.

1141. ————. In This House of Brede. New York: Viking, 1969.

A successful career woman renounces the world and enters a cloistered order of Benedictine nuns.

1142. Goldenberg, Isaac. Play by Play. New York: Persea, 1985.

A Catholic soccer player discovers that he has a Jewish father who wants to convert him to Judaism.

1143. Goldthorpe, John. The Summer of Desire. New York: Coward-McCann, 1960.

In an English village a middle-aged civil servant and novelist-convert, becomes infatuated with the young niece of the parish priest. "Vivid and compelling." (Catholic World)

1144. Gollin, James. Eliza's Galiardo. New York: St. Martin's, 1983.

The priest who heads an obscure religious order tries to sell a rare musical manuscript, but someone steals it.

1145. Goncourt, Edmond. Sister Philomene. London: Rutledge, 1890.

A French girl in a convent school becomes a nun but is terribly unfulfilled until she becomes a nursing sister in a hospital. She seems to have found her vocation until a young surgeon falls in love with her.

1146. Gordon, Caroline. The Malefactors. New York: Harcourt, 1956.

A middle-aged poet, living off a wealthy wife, undergoes a mid-life crisis by taking a mistress. He then returns to his wife who is working in a Catholic mission. He con-

verts to the Catholic faith after rejecting
it repeatedly. Brainard Chaney said this is
"a dramatic presentation of the freedom of
God's grace."

1147.   ———. The Strange Children. New York:
        Harcourt, 1951.

A young girl tries to make sense out of
the complex entanglements between her
parents and a group of friends who visit the
family's Tennessee farm. One visitor is a
millionaire and a convert who plans to give
away his money to the church. His wife does
not share his faith or enthusiasm and runs
off with another man. The convert is the
symbol of stability and order and his
Catholic faith provides the way of deliver-
ance from what Psalm 144 calls "the world of
the strange children."

1148.   Gordon, Mary. The Company of Women. New
        York: Random House, 1980.

A compelling and charismatic priest and
five intensely religious women come together
in this moving and brilliant novel.

1149.   ———. Final Payments. New York: Random
        House, 1978.

After her suffocatingly religious father's
death, a young woman searches for love in
unlikely places. A highly praised novel
about the obligation of loving the unlove-
able.

1150.   Gorman, Herbert. The Cry of Dolores. New
        York: Rinehart, 1947.

Father Hidalgo and the Mexican uprising of
1810.

1151.   Goudge, Elizabeth. Gentian Hill. New York:
        Coward-McCann, 1949.

A world-weary priest, an orphan girl and a
sailor figure prominently in this legend of
St. Michael's chapel.

1152. Goulet, Robert. <u>The Violent Season</u>. New
       York: Braziller, 1961.

       Sex versus religion in a lumberjack town
       in Quebec.

1153. Graeme, Bruce. <u>The Penance of Brother
       Alaric</u>. London: Hutchinson, 1930.

1154. Graham, James. <u>The Khufra Run</u>. New York:
       Doubleday, 1973.

       A nun tries to recover a religious relic.

1155. ———. <u>The Wrath of God</u>. London:
       Macmillan, 1971.

       The Mexican revolution of 1922 affects the
       church harshly.

1156. Granger, Bill. <u>Schism</u>. New York: Crown,
       1981.

       A Vatican diplomat and one-time missionary
       to Cambodia reappears twenty years after his
       presumed death. The CIA, the KGB and a
       beautiful reporter all want to know his
       secrets involving a Vatican treaty with
       Russia.

1157. Grant, Dorothy Freemont. <u>Devil's Food</u>. New
       York: Longmans, 1949.

       A young Catholic female student rebels
       against her upbringing, goes to a secular
       college and is seduced by a professor.

1158. ———. <u>Margaret Brent, Adventurer</u>. New
       York: Longmans, 1944.

       The heroism of early Catholic Maryland.

1159. ———. <u>Night of Decision</u>. New York:
       Longmans, 1946.

       Catholics fight persecution in late
       seventeenth century New York.

1160. Grass, Gunter. <u>Cat and Mouse</u>. New York:
       Harcourt, 1963.

A sickly teenager in wartime Germany idolizes the Virgin Mary.

1161. Gray, John. <u>Park</u>. New York: Carcanet, 1986.

Black Latin-speaking Catholics dominate the world of the future in this fantasy novel originally published in 1932.

1162. Gray, Mary Agatha. <u>Like Unto a Merchant</u>. New York: Benziger, 1915.

Earnest souls seek religious truth.

1163. ————. <u>The Tempest of the Heart</u>. New York: Benziger, 1912.

A young monk leaves his monastery for a successful musical career but eventually returns.

1164. ————. <u>The Towers of St. Nicholas</u>. New York: P.J. Kenedy, 1913.

Catholics struggle to endure in Elizabethan days.

1165. ————. <u>The Turn of the Tide</u>. New York: Benziger, 1910.

Humble Catholic fishermen live quiet lives on the east coast of England.

1166. Grayson, Richard. <u>The Death of Abbe Didier</u>. New York: St. Martin's, 1981.

A priest of a fashionable society church is stabbed to death in his own confessional.

1167. Greeley, Andrew M. <u>Angels of September</u>. New York: Warner, 1986.

A beautiful art gallery owner struggles to come to terms with her family, her new love and old-fashioned Catholicism.

1168. ————. <u>Ascent Into Hell</u>. New York: Warner, 1983.

A priest who defects finds life on the
outside not all that great. Neither wealth,
nor marriage, nor adultery brings him
happiness.

1169.   ———. The Cardinal Sins. New York:
         Warner, 1981.

Two Chicago brothers become priests and
struggle with love/sex problems. One
becomes a Cardinal.

1170.   ———. God Game. New York: Warner, 1986.

A science fiction novel with a priest
hero. "A trashy sword-and-sorcery yarn full
of caricatures who fight all day only to
settle their differences in bed."
(Publishers Weekly)

1171.   ———. Happy Are the Clean in Heart. New
         York: Warner, 1986.

Father Ryan solves a case of murder.

1172.   ———. Happy Are the Meek. New York:
         Warner, 1985.

The first of a projected series of mystery
novels based on the Beatitudes and featuring
Father Blackie Ryan, rector of Holy Name
Cathedral in Chicago. This fantastic tale
has everything: a locked room murder, devil
worship, and messages from beyond the grave.

1173.   ———. Happy Are Those Who Search for
         Justice. New York: Mysterious Press,
         1987.

Father Ryan solves a complicated murder.

1174.   ———. Lord of the Dance. New York:
         Warner, 1984.

The granddaughter of a prominent Irish
American family digs into the family's past
and discovers the unexpected. One character
is a priest-television personality.

1175.   ———. Patience of a Saint. New York:
         Warner, 1987.

         A hard-drinking Chicago newspaperman
         rediscovers faith in God and love for his
         wife.

1176.   ———. Rite of Spring. New York: Warner,
         1987.

         A lawyer's love affair with an elusive and
         mysterious Irish woman turns into a suspense
         tale when she disappears.

1177.   ———. Thy Brother's Wife. New York:
         Warner, 1982.

         Two brothers seek fame and fortune in
         different ways. One wants to be President,
         the other a Cardinal. The priest has always
         loved his brother's wife.

1178.   ———. Virgin and Martyr. New York:
         Warner, 1985.

         An energetic Irish American woman moves
         from the convent to Central American
         revolution and martyrdom.

1179.   Green, Julian. Each In His Darkness. New
         York: Pantheon, 1962.

         A young Catholic man, supposedly devout,
         is obsessed with sex and becomes dissolute.
         Examining his conscience, he becomes a
         better Catholic. The New York Times said
         "one of the most gifted religious novels to
         have been written in France since Bernanos,
         this visionary novel is haunted by religious
         anguish and a fear of damnation."

1180.   ———. If I Were You. New York: Harper,
         1949.

         The devil induces a frustrated French
         clerk to change personalities with people he
         envies. But Satan is powerless against
         God's grace.

1181. Greenberg, Joanne. <u>The King's Persons</u>.
       London: Gollancz, <u>1963</u>.

1182. Greene, Graham. <u>Brighton Rock</u>. New York:
       Viking, 1936.

       A brilliant suspense tale about a sadistic
       murderer, his girl and "the appalling
       strangeness of the mercy of God."

1183. ————. <u>A Burnt Out Case</u>. New York:
       Viking, <u>1961</u>.

       Priests, nuns and an atheist doctor care
       for an African lepers colony. "The conflict
       between faith and doubt is moving because
       Greene knows so well the difficulties of
       faith and feels so deeply the agonies of
       doubt." (<u>Saturday Review</u>)

1184. ————. <u>The End of the Affair</u>. New York:
       Viking, <u>1951</u>.

       Even an adulterous love affair may reflect
       the mysterious workings of God's grace.

1185. ————. <u>The Heart of the Matter</u>. New York:
       Viking, <u>1948</u>.

       A classic exposition of the sin of
       despair.

1186. ————. <u>Monsignor Quixote</u>. New York:
       Simon & Schuster, <u>1982</u>.

       The comic adventures of a small town
       Spanish priest and his friend, the town's
       unrepentant Communist mayor.

1187. ————. <u>The Power and the Glory</u>. New York:
       Viking, <u>1946</u>.

       An alcoholic and sexually-scarred priest
       continues to minister to his flock during
       the anti-clerical persecutions in Mexico.
       Captured by the secret police, he finds the
       courage to become a martyr.

1188. Greer, Ben. <u>Slammer</u>. New York: Atheneum,
       1975.

Two priests try to prevent a riot in a
South Carolina prison.

1189. Grey, Francis William. The Cure of St.
Philippe. London: Digby, 1899.

One of Canada's great novels, this is
about politics and religion in the 1890s.

1190. Griffin, C.F. Instead of Ashes. London:
Barrie & Rockliff, 1962.

1191. Griffin, John Howard. The Devil Rides
Outside. Ft. Worth: Smiths, 1952.

A young man goes to a monastery in France
to do research on Gregorian manuscripts but
his carnal desires war against his
spirituality.

1192. Grogger, Paula. The Door in the Grimming.
New York: Putnam, 1936.

Austrian Catholic peasants resist
Napoleon's invasion.

1193. Groseclose, Elgin Earl. The Carmelite. New
York: Macmillan, 1955.

The Pope sends a Spanish missionary to
Persia in the 17th century.

1194. Gross, William B. The Conquest of
California. Boston: Stratford, 1930.

Father Serra and the missions.

1195. Groves, Freda Mary. My Lady Rosia. New
York: Benziger, 1914.

Stirring historical romance of the 17th
century, with an appearance of St. Catherine
of Siena.

1196. Guareschi, Giovanni. Comrade Don Camillo.
New York: Farrar, Straus, 1964.

1197. ———. Don Camillo and His Flock. New
York: Farrar, Straus, 1952.

1198. ———. Don Camillo's Dilemma. New York:
       Farrar, Straus, 1957.

1199. ———. Don Camillo Meets the Flower
       Children. New York: Farrar, Straus,
       1970.

1200. ———. Don Camillo Takes the Devil by the
       Tail. New York: Farrar, Straus, 1957.

1201. ———. The Little World of Don Camillo.
       New York: Farrar, Straus, 1951.

       A series of delightful tales of an imper-
       turbable and resourceful Italian priest and
       his on-going fight with the hot-tempered
       Communist mayor of his village.

1202. Guevremont, Germaine. The Outlander. New
       York: McGraw-Hill, 1950.

       A mysterious stranger visits a French
       Canadian community and changes everyone's
       life.

1203. Guinan, Joseph. The Soggarth Aroon.
       Dublin: Talbot, 1944.

       Experiences of an Irish country curate.

1204. Guiney, Louise Imogen. Monsieur Henri. New
       York: Harper, 1892.

       The faithful Catholic peasants of the
       Vendee region of France fight to preserve
       their faith and values.

1205. Gwynn, Stephen. John Maxwell's Marriage.
       New York: Macmillan, 1903.

       Catholic-Protestant antagonisms in public
       and private life in 18th century Ireland.

1206. Hackett, Francis. The Green Lion. New
       York: Doubleday, 1936.

       Catholic education in Ireland receives
       severe criticism in this account of a young
       man who attended Jesuit schools.

1207.   Haffner, Katherine. <u>Play in the Sand</u>. New
         York: Pageant, 1953.

         A light-hearted view of Catholic-Protestant
         marriage.

1208.   Hagerue, G. de Bugny. <u>Romance of a Jesuit</u>.
         New York: Benziger, 1912.

         A young man enters a Jesuit novitiate as a
         spy for the French government. He is
         gradually converted to real faith, confesses
         his duplicity and becomes a novice.

1209.   Haien, Jeannette. <u>The All of It</u>. Boston:
         Godine, 1986.

         A touching tale of rural Ireland. A
         kindly world-weary priest comes to a small
         town and becomes privy to some startling
         information about a local couple.

1210.   Halegua, Lillian. <u>The Priest</u>. London:
         Owen, 1963.

         A depressing novel about a priest's
         descent into insanity.

1211.   Halevi, Zev Ben Shimon. <u>The Anointed</u>.
         Boston: Routledge & Kegan Paul, 1987.

         In Spain a Jewish convert to Christianity
         reverts to his ancestral faith despite the
         Inquisition.

1212.   Halevy, Ludovic. <u>The Abbe Constantin</u>.
         Chicago: Rand, McNally, 1882.

         A genial French abbot assists the love
         affairs of a rich American girl in a
         charming, loveable bestseller.

1213.   Hallack, Cecily. <u>The Happiness of Father
         Happe</u>. New York: P.J. Kenedy, 1938.

         An idiosyncratic priest-scholar serves a
         Franciscan monastery on the south coast of
         England and gets involved in outrageous
         exploits.

1214. ———. A Mirror for Toby. New York:
       Macmillan, 1933.

       A singer and artist loses his voice and is
       threatened with blindness. He flees to a
       monastery but a wise monk urges him to
       return to the world and become a husband and
       father. The New York Times said the novel's
       "interwoven themes are the eternal mysticism
       of life and the mysticism of Catholicism."

1215. ———. The Swordblade of Michael. London:
       Sands, 1929.

       The happy adventures of a young English
       Benedictine.

1216. Hallahan, William H. The Monk. New York:
       Morrow, 1983.

       An eerie horror story.

1217. Halley, Laurence. Abiding City. New York:
       Viking, 1986.

       A diplomat risks his life to prevent the
       assassination of the Pope at Canterbury
       Cathedral.

1218. Hamill, Desmond. Bitter Orange. New York:
       Morrow, 1980.

       A Catholic family in a Belfast ghetto
       becomes enmeshed in hatred and violence.

1219. Hamill, Pete. A Killing for Christ. New
       York: World, 1968.

       A plot to assassinate the Pope on Holy
       Thursday. The hero is an ex-priest with a
       prostitute girlfriend.

1220. Hanley, Gerald. Without Love. New York:
       Harper, 1957.

       An Irish Catholic paid killer begins to
       search his conscience. His sister searches
       for him and a prostitute loves him, but he
       is killed.

1221. Hanley, James. <u>Drift</u>. London: Partridge,
       1930.

       A Catholic man, in love with a Protestant
       woman, rebels against his strict religious
       upbringing. "God was so far away that even
       if he spoke to you you couldn't hear Him."

1222. ————. <u>The Furys</u>. New York: Macmillan,
       1935.

       A Catholic mother concentrates all her
       energies on convincing her son to become a
       priest.

1223. Hanlin, Tom. <u>The Miracle at Cardenrigg</u>.
       New York: Random House, 1949.

       Irish Catholic families overcome a
       disaster in a Scottish mining town.

1224. Hard, Margaret. <u>This is Kate</u>. New York:
       Holt, 1944.

       An English Protestant girl attends a
       convent school in Canada but is unable to
       appreciate Catholic customs and values.

1225. Harding, Michael P. <u>Priest</u>. Wolfeboro, NH:
       Blackstaff Press, 1986.

       The anguish of disillusioned priests in
       today's Ireland.

1226. Hardy, Ronald. <u>The Place of Jackals</u>. New
       York: Doubleday, 1955.

       A French chaplain in Indochina finds
       hostility and contempt until he recognizes
       his own failures. Riley Hughes wrote,
       "Hardy has caught the dark night of the
       spirit with insight, compassion and
       understanding."

1227. Harland, Henry. <u>The Cardinal's Snuff Box</u>.
       New York: Lane, 1900.

       A charming romance set in Italy featuring
       a delightful cardinal who assists in the
       conversion of an English Protestant in love
       with a Catholic girl.

1228. ————. The Lady Paramount. New York:
      Lane, 1902.

1229. ————. My Friend Prospero. New York:
      McClure, 1904.

      The above two novels extol the virtues of
      Italian Catholic life.

1230. Harper, Patrick. The Serpent's Circle. New
      York: St. Martin's, 1985.

      A cult plans to abduct the Pope on his
      visit to England.

1231. Harris, Mary Kathleen. Fear at my Heart.
      New York: Sheed & Ward, 1951.

      A child searches for religious truth but
      finds her parents uninterested.

1232. ————. The Niche Over the Door. New York:
      Sheed & Ward, 1948.

      Gloomy tale of an orphan girl.

1233. ————. A Safe Lodging. New York: Sheed &
      Ward, 1957.

      Anti-Catholic hysteria grips England in
      1780.

1234. Harris, Miriam. Tents of Wickedness.
      Boston: Houghton, Mifflin, 1907.

      Fashionable New York life is contrasted
      with a French convent school.

1235. Harrison, Edith. Clemencia's Crisis.
      Chicago: McClurg, 1915.

      An American naval officer falls in love
      with a Spanish lady who has promised to
      become a nun.

1236. Harrison, J. Kind Hearts and Coronets. New
      York: Benziger, 1904.

      A family is divided by religion. "Aunt
      Estelle would rather endow a home for

indigent canaries with her money than let it
go to the R.C. church."

1237.   Harsanyi, Zsolt. The Star Gazer. New York:
           Putnam, 1939.

        Galileo and his times.

1238.   Hartley, J.M. With Crooked Lines.
           Milwaukee: Bruce, 1948.

        A brain surgeon searches for religious
        truth and meaning. He makes friends with a
        Jesuit priest, falls in love with the
        priest's niece, and converts.

1239.   Hartley, L.P. My Fellow Devils. New York:
           British Book Centre, 1959.

        An agnostic woman marries a nominally
        Catholic movie star. Their marriage ends
        when she can no longer condone his moral
        defections. Nevertheless, she is gradually
        attracted by the faith he neglects and
        converts at the end.

1240.   Harley, Olga. Anne. Philadelphia:
           Lippincott, 1920.

        A pure and virtuous girl becomes Catholic.

1241.   Hassler, Jon. Grand Opening. New York:
           Morrow, 1987.

        A Catholic family opens a grocery store in
        a small Minnesota town and has to overcome
        religious prejudice to survive.

1242.   ―――――. A Green Journey. New York:
           Morrow, 1985.

        A devout Catholic schoolteacher joins her
        bishop's tour group to Ireland, where she
        has her last chance at love.

1243.   Hawthorne, Nathaniel. The Marble Faun.
           Boston: Ticknor & Fields, 1860.

        Two Americans studying art in Rome fall in
        love with a mysterious female artist, a

handsome nobleman, and an evil monk. The
nobleman murders the monk but gives himself
up. The artist embarks on a penitential
pilgrimage, and the American girl converts
to Catholicism.

1244.   Hayes, Charles Edward. The Four Winds. New
        York: Macmillan, 1942.

        Not even religion can save an Irish farm
        family from despair in rural Kansas during
        the Depression.

1245.   Hays, Hoffman Reynolds. Takers of the City.
        New York: Reynal, 1946.

        Father de las Casas fights the mistreat-
        ment of the Indians in Mexico.

1246.   Heagney, Harold J. Others Will Come. St.
        Nazianz, WI: Salvatorian Press, 1945.

1247.   ————. Victory. Ozone Park, NY: Catholic
        Literary Guild, 1941.

        A two-volume fictional biography of the
        founder of the Salvatorian Fathers.

1248.   Hegerty, Walter. The Price of Chips.
        London: Davis-Poynter, 1973.

        The lives of two Catholics in Northern
        Ireland from 1930 to 1970.

1249.   Heidish, Marcy. Miracles. New York: New
        American Library, 1984.

        Saint Elizabeth Seton.

1250.   Hemon, Louis. Maria Chapdelaine. New York:
        Macmillan, 1921.

        A heroic French Canadian woman's story.

1251.   Henderson, Isaac. The Prelate. Boston:
        Ticknor, 1886.

        A critical look at the intrigues of the
        Italian Church.

1252. Henderson, Jane. The Little Green Truck.
       London: Miles, 1948.

       A moving story of American Catholic life.

1253. Henderson, Nancy. Full of Grace. New York:
       Doubleday, 1983.

       A young girl working in a home for aged
       nuns encounters senility, suffering and
       mental imbalance. Her faith is destroyed
       when a nun tells her there is no God.

1254. Henry-Ruffin, Margaret Ellen. The Shield of
       Silence. New York: Benziger, 1914.

       A priest refuses to disclose what he knows
       about a murder.

1255. Henty, G.A. Orange and Green. New York:
       Scribner, 1888.

       Catholic-Protestant conflict in 1690
       Ireland.

1256. Herron, Edward. Life Returns to Die. New
       York: Benziger, 1934.

       "An intelligent example of Catholic
       fiction." (America)

1257. Herron, Shaun. The Whore Mother. London:
       Cabe, 1973.

       A young American Catholic joins the IRA
       out of a romantic attachment to an ideal.
       He becomes disillusioned and tries to
       escape.

1258. Heuser, Herman Joseph. The Archbishop's
       Pocketbook. New York: P.J. Kenedy, 1928.

       Humorous and idealistic novel of priestly
       life.

1259. ————. The Chaplain of St. Catherines.
       New York: Longmans, 1925.

       A priest deepens his spiritual life as
       chaplain to a convent of cloistered nuns.

1260.   ———. <u>Pastor Halloft</u>. New York:
         Longmans, 1919.

         An American parish priest has many
         grievances against the church establishment.

1261.   Hewlett, Francesca. <u>Told by Brother Giles</u>.
         London: Sands, 1928.

1262.   Heydon, J.K. <u>World D</u>. New York: Sheed &
         Ward, 1935.

         A fantasy novel about the creation of a
         new world.

1263.   Heywood, J.C. <u>How Will It End?</u> London:
         Burns & Oates, 1872.

         Conversion.

1264.   Hibbert, Eleanor. <u>Defenders of the Faith</u>.
         London: Hodder, 1956.

         The wrath of the Inquisition.

1265.   Hichens, Jacobine. <u>The Marriage of
         Elizabeth Whitacker</u>. New York: Duell,
         1953.

         An Anglican widow falls in love with a
         Catholic but cannot decide whether to marry
         him. "An ill natured and rather irritating
         attack on the Catholic church." (<u>Catholic
         World</u>)

1266.   ———. <u>Noughts and Crosses</u>. London:
         Putnam, 1952.

1267.   Hichens, Robert Smythe. <u>The Garden of
         Allah</u>. New York: Stokes, 1904.

         A woman longing for peace has a love
         affair with a renegade monk, but he returns
         to the monastery to save his soul.

1268.   Hickey, Emily. <u>Lois</u>. London: Burns &
         Oates, 1908.

         Conversion of a young woman author.

1269.   Hicks-Beach, Susan Emily. Cardinal of the
        Medici. New York: Macmillan, 1937.

        A Cardinal's life in Renaissance Italy.

1270.   Higgins, Jack. Confessional. New York:
        Stein & Day, 1985.

        A KGB assassin posing as a priest is
        assigned to kill the Pope.

1271.   ———. A Prayer for the Dying. New York:
        Holt, 1973.

        A man trying to renounce the IRA is
        trapped in an evil world of his own
        creation. He tangles with a priest who
        knows his darkest secrets. The tormented
        killer plays the church organ as a hobby,
        falls in love with a blind girl, but still
        goes to confession hoping to relieve his
        gilt-ridden soul.

1272.   Higgins, Margaret. Unholy Sanctuary. New
        York: Ace, 1971.

1273.   Hilburn, Samuel. The Spider Love. New
        York: Exposition, 1962.

        A young Catholic teacher is involved in
        numerous problems in a Catholic boarding
        school.

1274.   Hilkert, Robert C. The Hell Catholic. New
        York: Sheed & Ward, 1952.

        A young Catholic layman who serves God
        more from a fear of hell than from the
        motivation of love discovers the grace of
        God on a Holy Year pilgrimage.

1275.   Hill, Cecilia. Can These Things Be?
        London: Hutchinson, 1923.

        The mystery of Lourdes.

1276.   Hillman, Mary V. In the Jersey Hills. New
        York: P.J. Kenedy, 1927.

        Romance in a Catholic college.

1277.   Hinkemeyer, Michael T. Fourth Down Death.
        New York: St. Martin's, 1985.

        The Virgin Mary may be appearing to the
        sexually repressed wife of a fanatically
        religious college professor. The murder of
        a student adds to the perplexity.

1278.   Hinkson, Pamela. Golden Rose. New York:
        Knopf, 1944.

        A missionary nun tries to convince a
        married woman to stay with her husband even
        though she has fallen in love with another.

1279.   Hobbes, John Oliver. Robert Orange. New
        York: Macmillan, 1900.

1280.   ————. The School for Saints. New York:
        Macmillan, 1898.

        These two novels have been called the
        finest Catholic novels of the Victorian age
        and should be read together since they are
        continuous. Robert loves Bridget, unhappily
        married to a wretch. The husband's apparent
        death leaves them free to marry, but on
        their honeymoon they hear he is alive. They
        must part, since as Catholics they cannot
        divorce. Some years later when the husband
        in question finally dies and the two can
        marry, Bridget renounces Robert because he
        is on the verge of entering the priesthood.
        Margaret Maison argues that in these two
        novels the author, whose real name was Pearl
        Craigie, "has told a story of tremendous
        moral and spiritual force, a tale of tragic
        grief and frustration redeemed and ennobled
        by the Catholic faith."

1281.   Hoff, Rhoda. The Silver Answer. New York:
        Dodd, Mead, 1945.

        An American girl divorces her philandering
        husband and gives all her attention and love
        to a priest in a novel that is quietly
        written and touched with mysticism.

1282.   Hoffman, Mary Jane. Agnes Hilton. New
        York: O'Shea, 1864.

A woman from a fashionable family embraces Catholicism and faces their horror and dismay.

1283. Hogan, Pendleton. The Bishop of Havana. New York: Washburn, 1933.

A Bishop makes an annual visit to St. Augustine from Cuba. Before each voyage he asks Mother Marie to foretell his fate.

1284. Holder, Charles Frederick. The Adventures of Torqua. Boston: Little, Brown, 1902.

An Indian resists Spanish missionaries.

1285. Holland, John. There Is No Peace. London: Bles, 1970.

1286. ————. The Relic. London: Bles, 1971.

1287. Hollis, Christopher. With Love, Peter. New York: McMullen, 1948.

The joys of family life.

1288. Holme, Timothy. The Assisi Murders. London: Macmillan, 1985.

Murder strikes at pilgrims, and an irreligious policeman must find the solution in a series of 13th century letters.

1289. Holms, G. Randolph. The Hounds of the Vatican. New York: Vantage Press, 1986.

An absurd pastiche of Sherlock Holmes, who is called upon the save the world from a sinister band of Freemasons. The Masons try to upset the balance of power by destabilizing the religious situation and placing a pretender on the Papal throne.

1290. Holton, Leonard. A Corner of Paradise. New York: St. Martin's, 1977.

Father Bredder's last case, a tale of stolen jewelry and murder.

1291.   ————. Deliver Us From Wolves. New York:
              Dodd, Mead, 1963.

         On a trip to the shrine at Fatima in
         Portugal Bredder becomes enmeshed in a
         frightening tale of werewolves and jewel
         thieves. He combats superstition and shows
         compassion and understanding for an atheist
         schoolteacher.

1292.   ————. The Devil to Play. New York:
              Dodd, Mead, 1974.

         A second baseman is murdered during a game
         that Bredder is attending. Then a radical
         priest is shot.

1293.   ————. Flowers by Request. New York:
              Dodd, Mead, 1964.

         An ex-convict dies soon after turning down
         Bredder's request to sing in the church
         choir.

1294.   ————. The Mirror of Hell. New York:
              Dodd, Mead, 1972.

         A brilliant student is bludgeoned to death
         in the rose garden of a Baptist college
         where Bredder's friend Barbara is taking
         summer courses.

1295.   ————. Out of the Depths. New York:
              Dodd, Mead, 1966.

         While fishing from a pier, Bredder finds
         the body of a scuba diver.

1296.   ————. A Pact with Satan. New York:
              Dodd, Mead, 1960.

         A wealthy widow insists that her dead
         husband is trying to kill her.

1297.   ————. A Problem in Angels. New York:
              Dodd, Mead, 1970.

         A violinist in a string quartet drops dead
         during a concert attended by Bredder.

1298.   ———. The Saint Maker. New York: Dodd,
        Mead, 1959.

        The first case for Father Joseph Bredder,
        a kindly humble priest who is chaplain to
        the Convent of the Holy Angels in Los
        Angeles. He loves baseball, pipes, flowers
        and old books. He is a friend to Barbara, a
        convent school girl, whose father is a
        policeman. In case after case Bredder
        assists her father by following "spiritual
        fingerprints," clues which enable him to see
        into the human soul. In this brilliant case
        a person with a twisted religiosity is
        killing others before they can sin, thus
        creating saints.

1299.   ———. Secret of the Doubting Saint. New
        York: Dodd, Mead, 1961.

        A 400 karat diamond, supposedly given to
        St. Thomas in India, is said to be cursed
        and causes death to all of its owners.

1300.   ———. A Touch of Jonah. New York: Dodd,
        Mead, 1968.

        Death strikes suddenly during a boat race.

1301.   Hope, Graham. A Cardinal and his Conscience.
        New York: Smith & Elder, 1901.

        A French Cardinal is involved in the
        Huguenot wars.

1302.   ———. The Lady of Lyte. London:
        Methuen, 1905.

        The Popish Plot.

1303.   Horgan, Paul. One Red Rose for Christmas.
        New York: Longmans, 1952.

        A warm, sentimental tale of an orphanage,
        a rebellious girl and an elderly nun.

1304.   ———. The Saintmaker's Christmas Eve.
        New York: Farrar, Straus, 1955.

A Christmas Eve miracle in 1809 New
Mexico.

1305.   ———. Things As They Are. New York:
          Farrar, Straus, 1964.

An introspective look at growing up
Catholic.

1306.   Hornman, Wim. The Stones Cry Out.
          Philadelphia: Lippincott, 1972.

Camilio Torres, the revolutionary priest.

1307.   Hosea, John. The Compassionate People.
          London: Heinemann, 1952.

Nuns help to comfort prisoners in wartime
France.

1308.   Houghton, Bryan. Judith's Marriage.
          Evanston, IL: Credo House, 1987.

A new convert suffers from today's liberal
Catholics but she becomes an unassuming
saint.

1309.   ———. Mitre and Crook. New York: Roman
          Catholic Book Publishers, 1986.

A bishop discovers heresy in his parishes
and seminaries and proceeds to restore the
Old Faith. Both of these novels are bitter
attacks on post Vatican II Catholicism.

1310.   Hoult, Norah. Father Hone and the Tele-
          vision Set. London: Hutchinson, 1956.

1311.   Houselander, Caryll. The Dry Wood. New
          York: Sheed & Ward, 1948.

After an old priest in the London slums
dies, his parishioners seek a miracle so he
can be canonized. Their prayers for the
recovery of a little crippled boy are not
answered. "Written with striking beauty and
skill, with a subtle sensitive ability to
translate the emotions of religion in terms
of individual lives." (New York Times)

1312. Houston, Jane. The Faith and the Flame.
       New York: Sloane, 1958.

       A Catholic lady falls in love with a
       Protestant captain during the religious
       wars.

1313. How, Louis. The Penitentes of San Rafael.
       Indianapolis: Bobbs, Merrill, 1900.

       A suspenseful tale of a bizarre sect in
       New Mexico.

1314. Hoyt, Francis Deming. Catherine Sidney.
       New York: Longmans, 1912.

       "Soundly Catholic principles." (Catholic
       World)

1315. ————. The Coming Storm. New York: P.J.
       Kenedy, 1914.

       Catholics versus socialists.

1316. ————. The Modernist. Lakewood, NJ:
       Lakewood Press, 1915.

       A novel contrasting the ideals and values
       of Catholics and non-Catholics in the upper
       class.

1317. Hubbard, Margaret Ann. Murder at St.
       Dennis. Milwaukee: Bruce, 1952.

       Murder strikes a Catholic hospital.

1318. ————. Murder Takes the Veil. Milwaukee:
       Bruce, 1950.

       A convent school in the Louisiana Bayous
       becomes a place of terror when a murderer,
       dressed in a nun's habit, stalks the
       inhabitants.

1319. ————. Sister Simon's Murder Case.
       Milwaukee: Bruce, 1959.

       Sister Simon, a supervisor in a convent
       hospital, finds a body under a plum tree.
       She becomes the detective.

1320.   Hudson, Jay W. <u>Abbe Pierre</u>. New York:
        Appleton, 1922.

1321.   ————. <u>Abbe Pierre's People</u>. New York:
        Appleton, 1928.

        Lighthearted story of an old French
        priest, his villagers, and an American man.
        Rich in local color.

1322.   Hughes, Richard. <u>Unholy Communion</u>. New
        York: Doubleday, 1982.

        A fanatic, obsessed and haunted by fears
        of a wrathful God, commits several murders
        in a Vermont town.

1323.   Hughes, Riley. <u>The Hills Were Liars</u>.
        Milwaukee: Bruce, 1955.

        Only the church survives after an atomic
        explosion in this fantasy novel.

1324.   Hughs, Mary. <u>The Two Schools: A Moral Tale</u>.
        Baltimore: Lucas, 1835.

        An early Catholic novel promoting a kind
        of sheltered religious fervor.

1325.   Hulme, Kathryn. <u>The Nun's Story</u>. Boston:
        Little, Brown, 1956.

        A sympathetic treatment of a woman who
        cannot adjust to the arduous discipline of
        convent life. After 17 years she is
        released from her vows. A bestseller and a
        popular film.

1326.   Hunt, Joseph. <u>Satan's Daughter</u>. London:
        Hale, 1970.

1327.   Hunter, Herman Leslie. <u>The Miracles of the
        Red Altar Cloth</u>. New York: Exposition,
        1949.

1328.   Huntington, Jedediah Vincent. <u>Alban</u>. New
        York: Putnam, 1851.

        A bright young Yale graduate explores all
        the Christian churches before he concludes

that Catholicism is a civilizing, stabiliz-
ing force in society and therefore true.

1329.   ———. Blond and Brunette. New York:
         Appleton, 1858.

A rich Irish Catholic marries off his
daughters. Filled with mixed marriages,
conversions, and satire on American artistic
tastes.

1330.   ———. The Forest. New York: Redfield,
         1852.

A missionary priest guides a settlement of
Indians into a kind of pristine existence.

1331.   ———. Rosemary. New York: Sadlier, 1860.

A complex and mystical love story.

1332. Hure, Anne. The Two Nuns. New York: Sheed
      & Ward, 1964.

Hatred and meanness spoil the atmosphere
of a French convent. "Her nuns emerge as
complex human beings, tangible yet
mysterious, familiar yet inexplicable."
(Bestsellers)

1333. Hurley, Doran. Monsignor. New York:
      Longmans, 1936.

An Irish priest fights against pride and
hunger for power in a small New England
factory town.

1334.   ———. The Old Parish. New York:
         Longmans, 1938.

Irish Catholic life in a small Massachusetts town has a quality of folklore in it.

1335.   ———. Says Mrs. Crowley, Says She. New
         York: Longmans, 1941.

Similar to item 1334.

1336. Hurst, Fannie. Appassionata. New York:
      Knopf, 1926.

A sensuous girl, frustrated in love,
sublimates her strong sexual desires by
moving toward religious mysticism and
becoming a novice. Catholic reviewers were
unfavorable to this Jewish author's book.

1337. Huxley, Aldous. The Devils of Loudun. New
York: Harper, 1951.

Religious hysteria and sexual mania erupt
in a French convent, causing a priest to be
burned alive.

1338. ————. Grey Eminence. New York: Harper,
1940.

The strange career of a contemplative
priest with intense spiritual longings who
puts them aside to serve Cardinal Richelieu.

1339. Huysmans, Joris Karl. The Cathedral. New
York: Dutton, 1922.

A profligate French nobleman comes to
believe in God, becomes a Catholic at
Chartres Cathedral, and joins the
Benedictines.

1340. ————. En Route. New York: Dutton, 1920.

Conversion and spiritual development of a
French novelist.

1341. ————. The Oblate. New York: Dutton,
1924.

A Benedictine struggles against French
anticlericalism.

1342. Innes-Brown, Mrs. Honour Without Renown.
London: Burns & Oates, 1907.

1343. ————. Three Daughters of the United
Kingdom. New York: Benziger, 1903.

1344. Irons, Genevieve. The Damsel Who Dared.
London: Sands, 1909.

A novel of conversion.

1345. ———. In the Service of the King. St.
Louis: Herder, 1913.

Four English Catholic girls try to serve
Christ through noble and heroic work.

1346. ———. Mystery of the Priest's Parlour.
St. Louis: Herder, 1911.

A pastor is forced to become a detective
when he finds a dead man in his parlour.

1347. Jackson, Helen Hunt. Ramona. Boston:
Roberts, 1884.

The romance of the California missions.

1348. Janey, Russell. The Miracle of the Bells.
New York: Prentice-Hall, 1946.

A Hollywood actress asks to be buried in a
poor Pennsylvania town with all the church
bells ringing. Sentimental trash but a
bestseller.

1349. Jessey, Cornelia. Consuela Bright. New
York: Sheed & Ward, 1962.

A Jewish woman defends her faith
throughout the novel but abruptly becomes a
Catholic and then a nun at the end.
(Published in England under the title The
Plough and the Harrow.)

1350. Johnson, Anna. Father John. New York:
American Tract Society, 1907.

In 1831 a girl searches for her father and
discovers by accident that he is a priest.

1351. Johnson, Grace and Harold. The Broken
Rosary. Milwaukee: Bruce, 1959.

1352. ———. Roman Collar Detective. Milwaukee:
Bruce, 1953.

A parish priest unexpectedly becomes a
sleuth when murder strikes a small Ohio
town.

1353.   Johnston, Sue Mildred. Star Inn. Notre
        Dame, IN: Ave Maria Press, 1953.

        A man who hunts down priests for the crown
        in Elizabethan days converts to the church
        he has persecuted.

1354.   Johnston, William. The Priest's Wife. New
        York: Lancer, 1971.

        A lighthearted satire on celibacy centered
        around a rock and roll singer who falls in
        love with a priest in modern day Rome.

1355.   Johnstone, William W. Jack-in-the-Box. New
        York: Zebra, 1986.

        A silly horror story about an angelic
        child, her possession by a demon in a box,
        and a priest.

1356.   Jokai, Maurus. Peter the Priest. New York:
        Fenno, 1897.

        A beggar monk becomes a missionary during
        the Reformation and is pursued by a woman
        who adores him.

1357.   Jordan, Elizabeth Carver. Faith Desmond's
        Last Stand. Chicago: Extension, 1924.

        A miraculous story of love and courage.

1358.   Jordan, Mary V. Now and Forever.
        Milwaukee: Bruce, 1945.

        Just before she takes her final vows to
        become a nun, a girl leaves and marries an
        atheist doctor. She succeeds in converting
        him just before his death in World War II.

1359.   Joyce, James. A Portrait of the Artist as a
        Young Man. New York: Viking, 1916.

        The classic anticlerical condemnation of
        Catholic education in Ireland.

1360.   Joyce-Prendergast, K.M. This Is My Land.
        Dublin: Gill, 1944.

1361. ———. Vintage. Dublin: Gill, 1945.

A charming picture of Catholic Ireland.

1362. Judah, Charles Burnet. Christopher Humble. New York: Morrow, 1956.

The Popish Plot.

1363. Just, Bela. The Gallows and the Cross. London: Gollancz, 1956.

A Budapest prison chaplain is in prison for helping a condemned man escape.

1364. Kavanagh, James. Celibates. San Francisco: Harper, 1985.

A sleazy story of two priests who struggle with celibacy. One falls in love with a woman but remains chaste even after being removed from the priesthood. The other becomes a veritable whoremonger who eventually marries a paramour, hides her existence for a few years, and is then defrocked.

1365. Kaye, D. Michael. To Live Alone. New York: Stokes, 1933.

A girl leaves a convent school to become a promising playwright in Hollywood.

1366. Kaye-Smith, Sheila. Superstition Corner. New York: Harper, 1934.

A young woman remains loyal to the Catholic faith even after her father and a local priest have defected. The story takes place in England shortly after the defeat of the Spanish Armada.

1367. ———. The View from the Parsonage. New York: Harper, 1954.

An Anglican pastor becomes an atheist and raises his daughters without religion. After an unhappy marriage, one daughter becomes a Catholic and a nun.

1368.   Kazantzakis, Nikos.   St. Francis.   New York:
        Simon & Schuster, 1962.

        Unsentimental view of the Poverello.

1369.   Keable, Robert.   Ann Decides.   New York:
        Putnam, 1927.

        A Catholic missionary loses his faith,
        leaves the church and falls in love with a
        divorcee.   He lives with her but is
        preoccupied with spiritual concerns.   After
        his death his lover comes to appreciate his
        anguish.   Published in England under the
        title Lighten Our Darkness.

1370.   Keenan, Edward P.   The Burden Light.   New
        York: P.J. Kenedy, 1938.

        A typical week in the life of a parish,
        where three priests try to help their
        parishioners.   One of the priests discovers
        he is dying.

1371.   Kelley, Francis Clement.   Pack Rat.
        Milwaukee: Bruce, 1942.

        A satire on World War II politics from a
        religious perspective.

1372.   Kelley, William.   Gemini.   New York:
        Doubleday, 1959.

        A young man from the New York slums enters
        the seminary to atone for his sexual sins
        and lustful urges.   But he is consumed by
        passion and rejects the Catholic faith
        altogether.

1373.   ————.   The God Hunters.   New York: Simon
        & Schuster, 1964.

        A seminarian returns to his wacky family
        for a holiday.   His mother is religious, his
        sister is a nun, his twin brother is insane,
        his father is divorced and remarried, and
        his stepsister tries to seduce him.
        Bestsellers called this controversial novel
        "one of the most significant efforts ever

achieved in the tradition of frank,
realistic and probing Catholic fiction."
But the New York Times called it "a phony
gambit."

1374. Kelly, Mary. A Cold Coming. New York:
       Walker, 1968.

       An Edinburgh nunnery is used for some
       shady schemes.

1375. Keneally, Thomas. The Place at Whitton.
       New York: Walker, 1965.

       A mad priest descends into a maelstrom of
       violence in an Australian seminary in this
       powerful and frightening story of the nature
       of evil.

1376. ———. Three Cheers for the Paraclete.
       New York: Viking, 1969.

       Conflict erupts between a young liberal
       intellectual priest and his hidebound Irish
       superiors in an Australian seminary.

1377. Kennedy, Eugene. Father's Day. New York:
       Doubleday, 1981.

       A well-told tale of a Notre Dame
       president.

1378. Kennedy, John P. Rob of the Bowl.
       Philadelphia: Lea & Blanchard, 1838.

       Catholic-Protestant conflict in late 17th
       century Maryland. Still in print.

1379. Kent, Michael. The Mass of Brother Michel.
       Milwaukee: Bruce, 1942.

       A crippled man takes refuge in a monastery
       and develops an overpowering desire to
       celebrate Mass.

1380. Keon, Grace. Broken Paths. Chicago:
       Extension, 1923.

       A defense of the indissolubility of
       marriage.

1381.   ————. High Road. New York: P.J. Kenedy,
         1930.

         Divorce threatens a family.

1382.   ————. Stars In My Heaven. Ozone Park,
         NY: Catholic Literary Guild, 1941.

         A saintly Catholic woman finds happiness
         in duty, patience and sorrow. She is
         divorced by her worthless husband but she
         cannot marry again. In a convenient ending
         he and his new wife are killed in a train
         wreck, enabling the heroine to marry.

1383.   ————. When Love Is Strong. St. Louis:
         Herder, 1907.

         Antidivorce.

1384.   Kern, Alfred. L'Amour Profane. New York:
         Pantheon, 1961.

         A French priest loses his vocation but
         must stay in the priesthood to earn a
         living. He becomes chaplain to a convent
         run by a domineering Mother Superior.

1385.   Kernan, Thomas. Now With the Morning Star.
         New York: Scribner, 1944.

         The Nazis dissolve an ancient monastery in
         the Black Forest and force all the monks
         into a strange and hostile world.

1386.   Kerr, Lady Amabel. The Whole Difference.
         St. Louis: Herder, 1903.

         The evils of mixed marriage.

1387.   Kersey, Clare. The Fiery Cross. London:
         Hale, 1970.

         The Jacobite wars.

1388.   Kieffer, Alfonso. The Padre of the Plains.
         Atlanta: Brown, 1936.

         A missionary's adventures.

1389. Kiely, Benedict. <u>Call for a Miracle</u>. New
York: Dutton, 1951.

1390. ————. <u>There Was an Ancient House</u>.
London: Metheun, 1955.

Two novices find life difficult in an
Irish seminary.

1391. Kienzle, William X. <u>Assault With Intent</u>.
Kansas City: Andrews, McMeel, 1982.

A zany satire on ultra-conservative
Traditionalists who plan to execute liberal
seminary professors but are too stupid to
succeed.

1392. ————. <u>Deadline for a Critic</u>. Kansas
City: Andrews, McMeel, 1987.

Using the new Catholic funeral liturgy as
the setting for each chapter, Kienzle weaves
a compelling tale of the murder of a corrupt
nominally Catholic fine arts critic.

1393. ————. <u>Deathbed</u>. Kansas City: Andrews,
McMeel, 1986.

Strange happenings in a Catholic hospital.

1394. ————. <u>Death Wears a Red Hat</u>. Kansas
City: Andrews, McMeel, 1980.

An unknown assailant is depositing the
decapitated heads of criminals who have
escaped justice on the headless shoulders of
the statues of saints.

1395. ————. <u>Kill and Tell</u>. Kansas City:
Andrews, McMeel, 1984.

An auto executive is murdered and many
people stand to profit from his demise.

1396. ————. <u>Mind Over Murder</u>. Kansas City:
Andrews, McMeel, 1981.

A monsignor is missing and many people had
good reason to do away with him.

1397.   ———. The Rosary Murders. Kansas City:
         Andrews, McMeel, 1979.

         The first appearance of Father Robert
         Koesler, Detroit priest and newspaper editor
         who assists police in solving crimes.   In
         his debut he searches for a psychopath who
         is murdering priests and nuns and draping
         their bodies with rosaries.

1398.   ———. Shadow of Death. Kansas City:
         Andrews, McMeel, 1983.

         Cardinals are being murdered all over the
         world in an apparent plot to destroy the
         Papacy.

1399.   ———. Sudden Death. Kansas City:
         Andrews, McMeel, 1985.

         A shocker about the murder of a pro
         football star. Koesler joins the "God
         Squad," a Bible study group for football
         players, and uses religious motivation and
         color blindness to trap the murderer.

1400.   Kilpatrick, Mary G. The Test. Philadel-
         phia: Kilner, 1907.

         A graduate of a convent school plans to
         marry outside her faith, but her boyfriend
         returns to Catholicism even though it means
         being disinherited.

1401.   King, Pauline. Snares of the Enemy. New
         York: Scribner, 1986.

         A superior mystery about murder in a
         monastic boys school in England.

1402.   King, Verna. Mrs. Foley, God Bless Her.
         Indianapolis: Bobbs, Merrill, 1951.

         An uproarious romp about a Catholic
         convert who interferes in every aspect of
         church life.

1403.   Kinsley, Peter. Pimpernel 60. New York:
         Dutton, 1968.

A Jesuit priest who helps dissidents
defect from Communist countries heads for
Albania - the most anti-religious country on
earth.

1404. Klarmann, Andrew. <u>Lark's Creek</u>. New York:
Pustet, 1927.

Conversion story.

1405. Kline, Nancy E. <u>The Faithful</u>. New York:
Morrow, 1968.

A spirited teenager visits a French
convent, where she is encouraged to exercise
caution and prudence to moderate her life
style.

1406. Koch, C.J. <u>The Doubleman</u>. New York:
McGraw-Hill, 1986.

An allegorical tale about a youth who
rejects his religion for a successful
musical career.

1407. Koch, Claude. <u>Light in Silence</u>. New York:
Dodd, Mead, 1958.

Extraordinary goings-on at a Catholic
college run by an order of teaching
brothers.

1408. Kocher, Paul H. <u>Alabado</u>. Chicago:
Franciscan Herald, 1978.

California mission days.

1409. Kossak, Zofja. <u>Angels in the Dust</u>. New
York: Roy, 1947.

1410. ———. <u>Blessed Are the Meek</u>. New York:
Roy, 1944.

Both of these are about the Crusades.

1411. Kovacs, Imre. <u>The Ninety and Nine</u>. New
York: Funk, 1955.

A Hungarian Jesuit fights communism.

1412. Krueger, Carl. St. Patrick's Battalion.
       New York: Dutton, 1960.

       Irish Catholic immigrants defect from the
       U.S. Army during the Mexican War.

1413. Kuehnelt-Leddihn, Erik von. Black Banners.
       Caldwell, ID: Caxton, 1954.

       A German aristocrat and his American wife
       witness the destruction of their way of life
       in a Europe gone mad. His Catholic faith
       offers security and she converts.

1414. ————. Moscow 1979. New York: Sheed &
       Ward, 1940.

       A fantasy novel in which all of Europe is
       controlled by Russia, while American is a
       Catholic country ruled by a Filipino Pope
       living in San Francisco. An American goes
       to Russia as a secret Catholic missionary
       but he is discovered and executed.

1415. Kuhl, Arthur. Royal Road. New York: Sheed
       & Ward, 1941.

       In Kentucky a black Catholic is unjustly
       imprisoned for a murder he did not commit.
       He is executed but dies forgiving his
       persecutors.

1416. Lagerkvist, Per. Pilgrim at Sea. New York:
       Random House, 1964.

       A strange allegory about a defrocked
       priest on a pirate ship.

1417. Lake, Elizabeth. The First Rebellion.
       London: Cresset, 1952.

1418. Lambert, Derek. The Saint Peter's Plot.
       New York: Bantam, 1979.

       With Nazi Germany about to collapse,
       Hitler plans to kidnap Pope Pius XII.

1419. Lane, Jane. Rabbits in the Hay. West-
       minster, MD: Newman, 1958.

The Babington Plot of 1585.

1420.   ———. Thunder on St. Paul's Day.
         Westminster, MD: Newman, 1954.

London has gone mad during the hysteria of
the Popish Plot.

1421. Lange, Monique. A Little Girl Under a
       Mosquito Net. New York: Viking, 1973.

A Jewish girl growing up in wartorn Paris
and Saigon searches for God and nearly
becomes a Catholic.   When confronted with
the reality of the martyrdom of her people,
she chooses to remain Jewish.

1422. Langgaesser, Elisabeth.   The Quest.   New
       York: Knopf, 1953.

Seven pilgrims go to a monastery to seek
atonement after the fall of Berlin.

1423. Lansdowne, Jane.   The Shadow of Eversleigh.
       New York: Benziger, 1908.

Faithful Catholics struggle to survive in
17th century England.

1424. Lappin, Peter.   The Land of Cain.   New York:
       Doubleday, 1958.

Catholics and Protestants kill one another
in the streets of Belfast in the 1920s.

1425. Lardner, Ring, Jr.   The Ecstasy of Owen
       Muir.   New York: Cameron & Kuhn, 1955.

An ironic tale of a young American who
converts to Catholicism so that he can marry
his secretary.   He becomes a devout Catholic
while she remains a lukewarm one.   They
finally part and he goes to a monastery.
Very critical of the church.

1426. Lash, Jennifer.   The Prism.   New York:
       Doubleday, 1963.

A brilliant monk, lacking in humility and
the ability to love, is transformed when he
discovers people in need.

1427. Lathen, Emma. <u>Ashes to Ashes</u>. New York:
       Simon & Schuster, 1971.

       An irate parents group is fighting to save
       their parochial school in Queens, New York.
       Its leader is murdered.

1428. Lauder, Stuart. <u>Disorderly House</u>. London:
       Longmans, 1966.

       A bishop is concerned that all is not well
       at an enclosed order of nuns. He asks a
       sensible Catholic friend to enter the
       convent as a lay worker to investigate, and
       she discovers a terrifying scene.

1429. Lauritzen, Jonreed. <u>The Cross and the
       Sword</u>. New York: Doubleday, 1965.

       Father Serra and the California missions.

1430. Laverty, Maura. <u>Liffey Lane</u>. New York:
       Longmans, 1947.

       The simple faith of the Irish poor, as
       seen through a small girl's vision.

1431. Lawrence, Josephine. <u>Let Us Consider One
       Another</u>. New York: Appleton, 1945.

       Religious prejudice threatens to destroy a
       young couple's happiness.

1432. Lawson, F.X. <u>Sidney Carrington's Contumacy</u>.
       St. Louis: Herder, 1909.

       Conversion of a high-principled girl.

1433. Laxalt, Robert. <u>A Man in the Wheat Field</u>.
       New York: Harper, 1964.

       An allegorical novel about the nature of
       evil set in an Italian community in the
       southwest. A local priest has had a
       recurring dream about a man dressed in
       black. When a stranger comes to town, the
       local people shun him.

1434. Leary, Francis. <u>This Dark Monarchy</u>.
       London: Evans, 1950.

1435. Leckie, Robert. Ordained. New York:
       Doubleday, 1969.

       An army chaplain becomes a high church
       official.

1436. Lecky, Walter. Gremore. New York:
       Sadlier, 1886.

1437. ————. Mister Billy Buttons. New York:
       Benziger, 1896.

1438. ————. Pere Monniere's Ward. New York:
       Benziger, 1898.

       Three tales of Franco-American life in
       rural upstate New York.

1439. Lee, Minnie Mary. The Brown House at
       Duffield. New York: P.J. Kenedy, 1886.

       Conversions at a convent school.

1440. LeFort, Gertrud von. The Pope from the
       Ghetto. New York: Sheed & Ward, 1934.

       By a combination of extraordinary
       circumstances, a Jewish Christian becomes
       Pope in 12th century Rome.

1441. ————. The Song at the Scaffold. New
       York: Sheed & Ward, 1933.

       A group of Carmelite nuns faces death with
       serenity and courage when they are martyred
       by an atheist government in Paris in 1794.

1442. ————. The Veil of Veronica. New York:
       Sheed & Ward, 1932.

       A young poet serves as a sort of Everyman,
       representing secular modern man's attempt to
       escape from the values of Catholic tradi-
       tion.

1443. Leger, Jack-Alain. Monsignore. New York:
       Dell, 1982.

       An unflattering portrait of the Vatican.

1444. Lemelin, Roger. In Quest of Splendour.
       Toronto: McClelland, 1955.

       A French Canadian leaves the seminary but
       retains his spiritual values.

1445. Leonard, Elmore. Touch. New York: Arbor
       House, 1987.

       A former brother in a religious order, now
       caring for alcoholics in a Detroit hospice,
       is able to heal others. He also exhibits
       the stigmata. Promoters and right-wing
       extremists both try to exploit the reclusive
       gentle man who, in the meantime, has fallen
       in love with an attractive woman.

1446. Leslie, Peter. The Extremists. London:
       New English Library, 1970.

       Protestants and Catholics clash in
       Belfast.

1447. Lewis, Ada Cook. The Longest Night. New
       York: Rinehart, 1958.

       The massacre of St. Bartholomew's Eve.

1448. Lewis, C.S. Pilgrim's Regress. New York:
       Sheed & Ward, 1935.

       An allegorical tale of a modern pilgrim's
       journey to Catholicism.

1449. Lewis, Maynah. The Future Is Forever.
       London: Hurst, 1967.

1450. Lewis, Robert. Michel, Michel. New York:
       Simon & Schuster, 1967.

       A young boy is torn between Jewish
       relatives in Israel and his Catholic foster
       parents who baptized him during the
       Holocaust. "An honest and researched
       exposure of traditional and modern anti-
       Semitism in the church." (America)

1451. L'Heureux, John. The Clang Birds. New
       York: Macmillan, 1972.

A savage satire on radical priests and nuns of the early seventies. Protest and promiscuity replace poverty, chastity and obedience.

1452. ———. <u>Tight White Collar</u>. New York: Doubleday, 1972.

A newly ordained Jesuit dislikes his family but goes home to preside at a wake and evaluate his feelings. He is selfish and uncharitable and cannot give himself to Christ because he cannot see himself in others.

1453. Lieberman, Rosalie. <u>The Man Who Captivated New York</u>. New York: Doubleday, 1960.

Further adventures of Brother Angelo.

1454. ———. <u>The Man Who Sold Christmas</u>. New York: Longmans, 1951.

Brother Angelo, a lowly friar, believes he is told by God to bring the meaning of Christmas to people through selfless acts of kindness. Conveys a spiritual message gently.

1455. ———. <u>Sister Innocent and the Wayward Miracle</u>. Westminster, MD: Newman, 1965.

A hilarious fantasy about a zealous nun who sprouts wings and takes to the air. Her Mother Superior tries desperately to ground her and calls on the bishop for help.

1456. Lindop, Audrey Erskine. <u>The Judas Figures</u>. New York: Appleton, 1956.

Father Keogh and his fellow priests fight superstition and terror in a small Mexican town during Holy Week.

1457. ———. <u>The Singer, Not the Song</u>. New York: Appleton, 1953.

Father Keogh fights an evil bandit.

1458. Lindsay, Jack. <u>Fires in Smithfield</u>. Bath,
       England: Chivers, 1972.

       Religious persecution under Queen Mary.

1459. Lingard, Joan. <u>The Lord On Our Side</u>.
       London: Hodder, 1970.

       Protestants and Catholics in Belfast both
       believe their cause is blessed by God.

1460. ———. <u>Sisters by Rite</u>. New York: St.
       Martin's, 1984.

       Three girls, two Protestants and one
       Catholic, grow up together on the same
       Belfast street and become friends for life.
       Religious hatreds alter their relationships
       somewhat. One of the Protestants becomes a
       Catholic years later for reasons never
       explained.

1461. Linney, Romulus. <u>Heathen Valley</u>. New York:
       Atheneum, 1962.

       A strange tale about an Episcopalian
       missionary bishop in North Carolina who
       converts to Catholicism in 1859.

1462. Lister, Stephen. <u>Delorme in Deep Water</u>.
       London: Davies, 1958.

       The genial Father Delorme becomes an
       amateur detective when he tries to unravel
       some crimes in his beloved French village.

1463. ———. <u>Peace Comes to Sainte Monique</u>.
       London: Davies, 1947.

       Father Delorme is the leading citizen of a
       French fishing village that lives on sun-
       shine and sardines.

1464. Litsey, Edwin Carlile. <u>Grist</u>. Philadel-
       phia: Dorrance, 1826,

       A young man falls in love with a friend's
       wife and flees to a Trappist monastery to
       repress his passion.

1465. ──────. Stones for Bread. Caldwell, ID:
           Caxton, 1940.

           Two old paupers die in misery in a
           Kentucky town, scorned by all but a
           compassionate priest.

1466. Litta, The Duke. The Soul of a Priest. New
           York: Doubleday, 1908.

           An Italian priest struggles against doubts
           and legalism, but leaves the priesthood at
           the end.

1467. Livingston, Armstrong. The Monk of
           Hambleton. London: Henkle, 1928.

1468. Llewellyn, Richard. Sweet Morn of Judas
           Day. New York: Doubleday, 1964.

           A Brazilian Catholic family struggles
           against spiritism and Satanism. (Judas Day
           is a time of prayer for the souls of
           betrayers and evildoers.)

1469. Lodge, David. The British Museum is Falling
           Down. New York: Holt, 1967.

           A delicious satire on birth control. The
           novel chronicles one day in the life of an
           impoverished British graduate student who
           fears that his wife may be pregnant for the
           fourth time. (Published in paperback as
           Vatican Roulette.)

1470. ──────. The Picturegoers. London:
           Macgibbon & Kee, 1960.

           A lapsed Catholic intellectual falls in
           love with a girl who chose not to become a
           nun. An intelligent look at spiritual
           discontent seen through the modern obsession
           with the cinema.

1471. ──────. Souls and Bodies. New York:
           Morrow, 1982.

           A social comedy about middle-class,
           university-educated British Catholics whose

marital and sexual lives have changed
dramatically since the 1950s. Many of their
hopes for renewal and renovation in the
church have been dashed. (Published in
England under the title How Far Can You Go.)

1472. Longueville, Thomas de. A Romance of the
       Recusants. London: Kegan Paul, 1888.

       Some English folk remain loyal Catholics
       despite severe disabilities.

1473. Lord, Daniel A. Murder in the Sacristy.
       St. Louis: Queens Work, 1941.

       A melodramatic mystery tale crowded with
       Communists, Nazis, and a priest who wants to
       convert Russia.

1474. Lothar, Ernst. Beneath Another Sun. New
       York: Doubleday, 1943.

       A family of Austrian Catholic carvers of
       wooden statues fights for faith and freedom
       in Nazi-occupied Czechoslovakia.

1475. Lucas, Anne M. The Pendulum. New York:
       Buechler, 1936.

       An artistic and convincing conversion
       tale.

1476. Lugt, Arie van der. The Crazy Doctor. New
       York: Random House, 1954.

       A kind Dutch priest tries in vain to
       convert an agnostic doctor who has left his
       wife and abandoned God. After the priest's
       death, the doctor realizes the truth of the
       priest's constant refrain, "God is love. He
       won't leave you alone."

1477. Lynam, Shevawn. The Spirit and the Clay.
       Boston: Little, Brown, 1954.

       A saintly priest leads some of his
       disillusioned flock back to the faith during
       the harrowing days of the Spanish Civil War.

1478. Lynch, Liam. <u>Tenebrae</u>. Dublin: Wolfhound Press, 1985.

An Irish priest, losing his faith and contemptuous of his parishioners, encounters supernatural grace when he ministers to a dying woman.

1479. MacArthur, Adella R. <u>That Romanist</u>. Boston: Arena, 1896.

The courtship of a Protestant and Catholic faces serious problems from the mean-spirited mother of the groom. At the end the couple renounces both religions for a kind of liberal universalism.

1480. MacCabe, William Bernard. <u>Adelaide, Queen of Italy</u>. Boston: Marlier, 1856.

Medieval religious devotion.

1481. MacFarlane, Peter Clark. <u>Hell to Answer</u>. Boston: Little, Brown, 1916.

A man performing good deeds in a small mission church is harmed by a spiteful actress who raises suspicions about him.

1482. MacGillivray, Anne. <u>Isle of Youth</u>. London: Hale, 1957.

1483. Macken, Walter. <u>Seek the Fair Land</u>. New York: Macmillan, 1959.

In the days of Oliver Cromwell a priest dies for his faith and a merchant flees religious persecution.

1484. Mackenzie, Compton. <u>Heavenly Ladder</u>. New York: Doran, 1924.

An Anglo-Catholic priest is persecuted by the Protestant faction of the Church of England and becomes a private in the First World War. As a layman he goes to Italy where he finds peace in the Church of Rome.

1485. Mackinder, Dorothy. <u>A Forest of Feathers</u>. London: Macdonald, 1950.

A French woman tries to find spiritual
peace and self respect.

1486.   ———. The Miracle at Lemaire.   London:
          Macdonald, 1952.

A French pastor resists those who try to
exploit a false miracle, and in so doing
brings about a change of heart in his
people.

1487.   ———. The Silver Fountains.   New York:
          McMullen, 1947.

A French curate defends a woman's reputa-
tion from slander and gossip, but his
integrity and outspokenness cause him to
lose his parish.

1488.   ———. The Violent Take It By Storm.   New
          York: Sheed & Ward, 1939.

A Spanish actress meets by accident an old
friend who has become a worldly monsignor.
She urges him to recover his lost humility,
and then enters a convent herself.

1489.   ———. The Wandering Osprey.   Milwaukee:
          Bruce, 1948.

An unconventional Christian writer falls
in love with the daughter of a respectable
conventional family. The family prevents
the marriage, and the writer becomes rich
and famous. The unhappy girl plans to
become a nun. "In the core of their deepest
sorrow, they discern always the loving
purposes of God."

1490.   ———. The Wooden Statue.   London:
          Macdonald, 1951.

During a stay at a convent, an atheist
physician begins to search for spiritual and
emotional health.

1491.   MacLennan, Hugh.   Two Solitudes.   New York:
          Duell, 1945.

Catholics vs. Protestants in Canada.

1492. Macleod, Alison. <u>City of Light</u>. Boston:
Houghton, Mifflin, 1969.

Religious conflict in the Reformation.

1493. ———. <u>The Jesuit</u>. London: Hodder, 1972.

A Jesuit novice returns to England in
disguise during the days of Queen Elizabeth.
When he is jailed, he discovers a secret war
raging among his fellow Catholics. He is
soon convinced that his fellow Jesuits are
traitors, and he is expelled from the order.

1494. MacManus, Francis. <u>American Son</u>. New York:
Knopf, 1960.

Relationships between a fallen-away
priest, a convert and an Irish scholar.

1495. ———. <u>The Greatest of These</u>. Huntington,
IN: Our Sunday Visitor, 1976.

A compelling novel about a priest's
painful revolt against the church and his
dramatic return to it.

1496. Madden, Deirdre. <u>Hidden Symptoms</u>. Boston:
Little, Brown, 1987.

A grieving Catholic university student in
Belfast struggles to find a purpose in
living in this sad and deeply moving novel
of today's Northern Ireland.

1497. Maher, Mary. <u>Fidelity</u>. London: Burns &
Oates, 1898.

A plea for the Catholic education of
youth. The heroine suffers much but
achieves earthly and eternal happiness.

1498. Maher, Richard A. <u>The Heart of a Man</u>. New
York: Benziger, 1915.

A strike in a New York town pits Catholics
against socialists.

1499.   ————. Shepherd of the North. New York:
         Macmillan, 1916.

         A Catholic bishop converts several people.

1500.   Mahoney, Sister Irene. An Accidental Grace.
         New York: St. Martin's, 1982.

         Sister Ruth returns to a convent after a
         ten year absence. Seeking peace and
         certitude, she finds constant change and
         uncertainty. She is unsure whether she
         should have come back at all. An intelli-
         gent, perceptive and honest presentation of
         the joys and difficulties of a religious
         life that ends on a triumphant, affirmative
         note.

1501.   Mahyere, Eveline. I Will Not Serve. New
         York: Dutton, 1960.

         In a convent school a rebellious French
         girl falls in love with one of her teachers.

1502.   Maisel, Eric. The Blackbirds of Mulhouse.
         New York: Maya, 1984.

         A Catholic tour guide at Strasbourg
         Cathedral marries an American Jewish woman,
         but his family's prejudice and his own
         weakness doom the relationship.

1503.   Maitland, Sara. Virgin Territory. New
         York: Beauford, 1986.

         A morbid portrait of a nun who tries to
         recover from a breakdown after a fellow nun
         is raped in a South American village. She
         leaves the convent and drifts into feminism
         and lesbianism.

1504.   Mallet-Joris, Francoise. The Favorite. New
         York: Farrar, Straus, 1962.

         A girl endures the corruption of the
         French Court and becomes a nun at the
         suggestion of Cardinal Richelieu.

1505. Mallin, Tom. <u>Dodecahedron</u>. New York:
       Outerbridge and Lazard, 1972.

       An allegorical story about the murder of a
       girl expelled from a convent. "Misanthropy
       masquerading as morality." (<u>New York Times</u>)

1506. Mallock, William Hurrell. <u>The Old Order
       Changes</u>. London: Bentley, 1886.

1507. Mancini, Anthony. <u>The Miracle of Pelham Bay
       Park</u>. New York: Dutton, 1982.

       The Virgin Mary may have appeared to a
       little Italian girl in the Bronx, but no one
       believes her tale - the nuns who teach her,
       an unscrupulous journalist who exploits her,
       or the archbishop of New York who tries to
       squelch all public interest in the reported
       apparition.

1508. Mann, Anthony. <u>Tiara</u>. London: Bodley
       Head, 1973.

       A Vatican thriller.

1509. Mann, Thomas. <u>The Holy Sinner</u>. New York:
       Knopf, 1951.

       Imaginative and powerful story of a
       medieval Pope. "An <u>Oedipus</u> with a happy
       ending, thanks to God's mercy." (<u>Time</u>)

1510. Mannin, Ethel. <u>Bavarian Story</u>. New York:
       Appleton, 1950.

       A Bavarian schoolteacher holds fast to her
       Catholic faith and her love for a local
       music teacher despite her attraction to a
       materialistic American soldier.

1511. ————. <u>Late Have I Loved Thee</u>. New York:
       Putnam, 1948.

       A masterful portrait of a 20th century St.
       Augustine, a dissolute and talented author
       who becomes a priest. His conversion and
       his miraculous gift of healing are beauti-
       fully depicted.

1512.   Mannix, Mary Ellen. Chronicles of the
        Little Sisters. Notre Dame, IN: Ave
        Maria Press, 1899.

        Vignettes about an order of charitable
        nuns.

1513.   Manzoni, Alessandro. The Betrothed. Many
        editions, 1828.

        A kind of Catholic War and Peace.

1514.   Marchand, Margaret. Pilgrims on the Earth.
        New York: Crowell, 1940.

        Irish life in a steel town near
        Pittsburgh.

1515.   Marcotte, Gilles. The Burden of God. New
        York: Vanguard, 1964.

        A newly ordained priest in a French
        Canadian town tries to find a place for
        himself, and when he cannot, flees to a
        monastery. There he is reconciled with God
        and himself.

1516.   Marie, Josephine. Let No Man Put Asunder.
        New York: Benziger, 1898.

        A woman marries her lover's brother when
        she thinks that he has married another.
        Even when she discovers her mistake, she
        remains married.

1517.   Marsh, Anne. Father Darcy. London:
        Chapman & Hall, 1846.

        The Gunpowder Plot.

1518.   Marshall, Bruce. The Bishop. New York:
        Doubleday, 1970.

        A hard-nosed conservative bishop intends
        to enforce the Pope's decree on birth
        control despite widespread opposition.

1519.   ————. The Fair Bride. Boston: Houghton,
        Mifflin, 1963.

A priest loses his faith, leaves the priesthood, and falls in love with a dancehall entertainer. He works with the Communists in Spain as the Civil War erupts, but regains his faith and is arrested while celebrating Mass.

1520. ————. Father Hillary's Holiday. New
York: Doubleday, 1965.

Witty tale of an outspoken Franciscan friar's escapades in a Latin American police state.

1521. ————. Father Malachy's Miracle. Boston:
Houghton, Mifflin, 1947.

A hilarious satire on irreligion and skepticism, subtitled "A heavenly story with an earthly meaning."

1522. ————. Flutter in the Dovecote. London:
Hale, 1986.

An imaginative story about a conservative bishop who gets involved in international espionage.

1523. ————. Marx the First. London:
Constable, 1971.

A futuristic novel about a completely radical and unbelieving church where a Communist agent is elected to the throne of Peter.

1524. ————. Peter the Second. London:
Constable, 1974.

The Papacy is now all-powerful since its occupant is a Russian, and the Soviet government supports it. The Russian Pope has restored the Latin Mass, abolished clerical marriage, and resisted the permissive society. He is overthrown and executed when a radical female cardinal from Holland takes over.

1525. ————. Satan and Cardinal Campbell.
Boston: Houghton, Mifflin, 1959.

A Scottish priest has a running conflict
with his superiors. He seeks a miracle at
Lourdes for one of his converts, and
eventually becomes a cardinal, to the
suprise of many.

1526.   ————. To Every Man a Penny. Boston:
         Houghton, Mifflin, 1949.

A French priest tries to remain a faithful follower of God and a dispenser of grace
to all humanity despite the upheaval of war.

1527.   ————. Urban the Ninth. London:
         Constable, 1973.

A Russian Pope disappears on a trip to
Poland and is succeeded by a conservative
cardinal who wants to restore the church to
orthodoxy.

1528.   ————. The World, the Flesh and Father
         Smith. Boston: Houghton, Mifflin, 1945.

A wonderfully evocative tale of a priest's
long and useful life in the anti-Catholic
environment of Scotland.

1529.   Marshall, Marguerite. Nurse with Wings.
         Philadelphia: Macrae, 1952.

1530.   Marshall, May. Mulberry Leaf. London:
         Hutchinson, 1954.

1531.   Marshall, Robert K. Little Squire Jim. New
         York: Duell, 1949.

The impact of Catholicism on North
Carolina mountain folk.

1532.   Martin, Eliza G. Going Home. Philadelphia:
         Cummiskey, 1872.

Romance and conversion.

1533.   ————. Katherine. New York: Holt, 1886.

A New England woman moves from Methodism
to Unitarianism and agnosticism before

finding peace in Rome. A fair-minded
presentation which respects other traditions
but emphasizes Catholicism's ability to
provide a haven of stability and security.

1534.   ———. Whom God Hath Joined. New York:
         Holt, 1886.

         Two American Protestants are converted in
         Rome.

1535.   Martin, George Victor. The Bells of St.
         Mary's. New York: Grosset & Dunlap,
         1946.

         A novelization of the popular film about a
         priest and a nun in a run-down parish.

1536.   Martin, Malachi. Vatican. New York:
         Harper, 1986.

         Filled with weak characters, this purports
         to be a tale of an American priest who joins
         the Vatican in 1945 and becomes the confi-
         dant of five Popes.

1537.   Martin, M.C. The Other Miss Lisle.
         Huntington, IN: Our Sunday Visitor,
         1906.

         Catholic life in turn-of-the-century South
         Africa.

1538.   Martin, Valerie. A Recent Martyr. Boston:
         Houghton, Mifflin, 1987.

         A young novice has been asked to leave her
         convent and return to her family in New
         Orleans because her passion for God is too
         fervent. She becomes immersed in a decadent
         bankrupt city where a mysterious and fatal
         disease is spreading uncontrollably.

1539.   Martindale, C.C. Jock, Jack and the
         Corporal. London: Burns & Oates, 1922.

         A memorable novel about how the suffering
         of an English Catholic soldier in the World
         War leads to the regeneration of his
         comrades.

1540.   Martindale, Joseph.   Dry Mass.   London:
        Eyre & Spottiswoode, 1969.

        A pious university professor drives his
        girlfriend to suicide in this novel of
        despair which uses Catholic symbolism.

1541.   ————.   Found Wanting.   London: New
        Authors, 1967.

        A monk who cannot accept discipline and
        obedience leaves the order.

1542.   Martin du Gard, Roger.   Jean Barois.   New
        York: Viking, 1949.

        A professor's agnosticism causes his
        dismissal from a French Catholic college and
        separation from his devout wife.   Years
        later he spends time with his daughter whom
        he had not seen since her birth.   His
        child's love and his fear of death cause his
        return to religion.

1543.   Martucci, Dontato.   The Strange September of
        1950.   New York: Horizon, 1962.

        Stalin visits the Pope in this fantasy.

1544.   Masten, Richard L.   Saint Udo.   Boston:
        Houghton, Mifflin, 1930.

        A scholarly monk invents a new saint
        because he doesn't care for the two Udos in
        the calendar.   The phony saint begins to
        work real miracles.

1545.   Masterson, Whit.   Hunter of the Blood.   New
        York: Dodd, Mead, 1977.

        A legendary federal investigator becomes a
        Jesuit priest, but is called back into
        service to prevent an embittered ex-Jesuit
        from blowing up the Vatican.

1546.   Mathew, David.   The Mango on the Mango Tree.
        New York: Knopf, 1951.

        A philosophical novel about the mercy of
        God.

1547. Mathews, Francis X. The Concrete Judasbird.
       Boston: Houghton, Mifflin, 1968.

       An impressionistic portrait of a parochial
       school student.

1548. ———. The Frog in the Bottom of the Well.
       Boston: Houghton, Mifflin, 1971.

       A lonely 12-year-old boy finds solace in a
       statue of an angel in a local church. One
       day the statue speaks to him and sheds
       tears. The church is soon exploited as a
       shrine of alleged healings.

1549. Matthews, Ronald. Red Sky at Night.
       London: Hollis & Carter, 1951.

       Christianity conquers Communism.

1550. Mauck, Hilda. Wings of Hope. New York:
       Kendall, 1932.

       A young Catholic couple's first year of
       marriage is difficult as they try to live in
       accordance with the church's teachings.

1551. Maugham, W. Somerset. Catalina. New York:
       Doubleday, 1948.

       A crippled Spanish girl is healed through
       the intercession of the Virgin Mary.

1552. Mauriac, Francois. Flesh and Blood. New
       York: Farrar, Straus, 1955.

       A man leaves a seminary, discovering that
       he had no real vocation.

1553. ———. The Lamb. New York: Farrar,
       Straus, 1955.

       On a train a seminarian meets a corrupt
       young man who asks him to save his soul.
       The seminarian goes to an estate where he
       meets tremendous temptation and death.

1554. ———. Lines of Life. New York: Farrar,
       Straus, 1957.

A dissipated man, recovering from an
illness in a remote French village, awakens
spiritual thoughts in a bitter woman. She
realizes her emptiness is due to a lack of
awareness of God.

1555.   ————. The Loved and the Unloved. New
York: Pellegrini, 1952.

A novel showing humanity untouched by
grace.

1556.   ————. Maltaverne. New York: Farrar,
Straus, 1970.

A story of responsibility to God, to the
truth of things, to one's own freedom.

1557.   ————. The Mask of Innocence. New York:
Farrar, Straus, 1953.

A priest, himself caught in a web of
scandal, finds his life entwined with a man
whose evil is so profound that all around
him are destroyed.

1558.   ————. Therese. New York: Farrar,
Straus, 1947.

Therese, a sinful woman, is acquitted for
trying to poison her husband (though in fact
she was guilty). Mauriac sees her as shar-
ing in the guilt of mankind. The mysterious
currents that move within Therese and carry
her to her death exist in everyone.

1559.   ————. Viper's Tangle. New York: Sheed &
Ward, 1933.

A millionaire is wretchedly unhappy
because he lacks love. But God's love
pursues him to the end.

1560.   ————. Woman of the Pharisees. New York:
Farrar, Straus, 1951.

A self-righteous woman destroys the life
of a devoted priest. His example of
forgiveness triumphs at the end.

1561. ————. Young Man in Chains. New York:
       Farrar, Straus, 1965.

       An idle rich intellectual encounters true
       love and devoted religious faith and casts
       off the chains of materialism.

1562. Maxwell, Allan. The Priest's Secret.
       London: Amalgamated, 1936.

1563. May, Naomi. Troubles. London: Calder,
       1976.

       Catholic-Protestant strife in Ulster.

1564. Maynard, Theodore. The Divine Adventure.
       New York: Stokes, 1921.

       Two young men choose the monastic life but
       both are unsuited.

1565. McAuley, Eileen. The Call. London:
       Laurie, 1955.

1566. McCabe, Ellen Pauline. Rings of Love.
       Glasgow: Burns, 1952.

       A Catholic-Jewish love story.

1567. McCarthy, Justin. The God of Love. New
       York: Harper, 1909.

       The life of Dante.

1568. McClure, James. The Hanging of the Angels.
       New York: Random House, 1969.

       All hell breaks loose when a former priest
       is seduced by a prostitute. "In certain
       Catholic circles outrage may be the response
       to this novel." (Bestsellers)

1569. McCollum, Robert. And Then They Die. New
       York: St. Martin's, 1985.

       A Charismatic Catholic and the parish
       priest are murdered in a small Texas town.

1570. McCorry, Peter. Mount Benedict. Boston:
       Donahoe, 1871.

The burning of the Charlestown convent.

1571.   McCorry, Vincent P. <u>Monsignor Connolly of</u>
        <u>St. Gregory's Parish</u>. New York: Dodd,
        Mead, 1960.

        A serene and beloved pastor seems to make
        things turn out the way they should.

1572.   McCullough, Coleen. <u>The Thorn Birds</u>.   New
        York: Harper, 1977.

        An Australian priest loves a farmer's wife
        and fathers a child by her.   He becomes a
        cardinal and encounters his own son years
        later.

1573.   McCullough, Esther. <u>The Five Devils of</u>
        <u>Kilmainham</u>.   Freeport, ME: Taylor, 1955.

        Romantic suspense in Catholic Ireland.

1574.   McCullough, John H. <u>Galloway Heather</u>.
        London: Jackman, 1955.

1575.   McDermott, John. <u>Father Jonathan: or, The</u>
        <u>Scottish Converts</u>.   Philadelphia:
        McGrath, 1853.

        Catholic courage in hostile Scotland.

1576.   McGarry, Jean. <u>The Very Rich Hours</u>.   Balti-
        more: Johns Hopkins University Press, 1987.

        A parochial school graduate has an uneasy
        time at Harvard.

1577.   McGehee, Mrs. Junius. <u>Glen Mary: A Catholic</u>
        <u>Novel</u>.   Baltimore: Murphy, 1887.

1578.   McGerr, Patricia. <u>My Brothers, Remember</u>
        <u>Monica</u>.   New York: P.J. Kenedy, 1964.

        St. Monica prays for her son Augustine.

1579.   McGovern, Milton. <u>The Twilight Rendezvous</u>.
        New York: P.J. Kenedy, 1925.

        A beautiful English novice leaves the
        convent but returns to it after many
        adventures.

1580. McGrath, Canon. <u>Via Dolorosa</u>. St. Louis:
      Herder, 1904.

      Two young men decide against the priest-
      hood. One falls in love while the other
      turns to rationalism.

1581. McGrath, Fergal. <u>The Last Lap</u>. New York:
      Benziger, 1925.

      Catholic college life in Ireland.

1582. McGrath, Maura. <u>Out in the Sunset</u>. New
      York: Pageant, 1957.

      Irish Catholic pioneers in Kansas.

1583. McGratty, Arthur. <u>Face to the Sun</u>.
      Milwaukee: Bruce, 1942.

      Pro-Catholic view of the Spanish Civil
      War.

1584. McHale, Tom. <u>Farragan's Retreat</u>. New York:
      Viking, 1970.

      A grotesque caricature of conservative
      Irish Catholics in Philadelphia.

1585. ———. <u>Principato</u>. New York: Viking,
      1971.

      Another satire on Irish-American life.

1586. McInerny, Ralph. <u>The Basket Case</u>. New
      York: St. Martin's, 1987.

      Father Dowling solves a murder rooted in a
      long-buried crime.

1587. ———. <u>Bishop as Pawn</u>. New York:
      Vanguard, 1978.

      Missing bishops, ex-priests, and a
      vanished husband create a lively case for
      Dowling.

1588. ———. <u>Connolly's Life</u>. New York:
      Atheneum, 1983.

      When a dissident theologian is reported

killed in a plane crash, an old friend
decides to write the dead man's biography.
"A wickedly funny, poignantly bittersweet,
and profoundly serious tale of the Catholic
chaos of the last twenty years," said Andrew
Greeley.

1589.   ———.   Gate of Heaven. New York: Harper,
        1975.

Internal disputes threaten to destroy a
Catholic college in Ohio.

1590.   ———.   Getting A Way With Murder. New
        York: Vanguard, 1984.

Greed leads to murder in this Dowling
tale.

1591.   ———.   The Grass Widow. New York:
        Vanguard, 1983.

A young woman comes to Dowling, expressing
fear for her life. When she is found dead
the next day, supposedly a suicide, the
priest sees murder.

1592.   ———.   Her Death of Cold. New York:
        Vanguard, 1977.

The first appearance of Father Roger
Dowling, a middle-aged priest in a Chicago
suburban parish. A recovered alcoholic and
disillusioned veteran of the marriage
tribunal, Dowling is a compassionate man
whose insights into character enable him to
solve crimes.

1593.   ———.   Leave of Absence. New York:
        Atheneum, 1986.

A woman's husband and her best friend, a
nun, have an affair. The betrayed woman
wants to become a nun herself but cannot
because she is still married. A moving
novel about religious faith and its
obligations.

1594.   ———.   A Loss of Patients. New York:
        Vanguard, 1982.

Dowling tries to prove a dentist guilty of multiple murders.

1595. ———. Lying Three. New York: Vanguard, 1979.

A Dowling case involving terrorism, politics and baseball.

1596. ———. The Noonday Devil. New York: Atheneum, 1985.

The KGB places an agent in the American hierarchy. When the archbishop of New York dies, the battle for succession reveals the evil one.

1597. ———. The Priest. New York: Harper, 1973.

A young priest, back in Ohio from his studies in Rome, encounters confusion and intellectual sterility.

1598. ———. Rest in Pieces. New York: Vanguard, 1985.

A Dowling case involving radical priests, Latin American politics and drugs.

1599. ———. Romanesque. New York: Harper, 1978.

A youthful scholar wins a fellowship to do research at the Vatican Library, where he falls in with thieves, devious priests and a sensuous divorcee.

1600. ———. Second Vespers. New York: Vanguard, 1980.

A Dowling tale involving authors, scholars, book dealers and murder.

1601. ———. The Seventh Station. New York: Vanguard, 1977.

At a retreat house a businessman is found with an icepick in his chest at the seventh station of the cross.

1602.   ———. Thicker Than Water. New York:
              Vanguard, 1981.

         A Dowling case involving drugs and
         organized crime.

1603.   McLaverty, Michael. Call My Brother Back.
              Dublin: Figgis, 1939.

         Poverty and sectarian animosity plague a
         poor Catholic family in the Belfast of the
         1920s.

1604.   ———. In This Thy Day. New York:
              Macmillan, 1947.

         A priest tries to persuade a domineering
         widow to let her son marry the girl he
         loves.

1605.   ———. Truth In the Night. New York:
              Macmillan, 1951.

         Religious faith supplies the vitality and
         fortitude for a harsh life on a windswept
         Irish island.

1606.   McMahon, Thomas Patrick. The Issue of the
              Bishop's Blood. New York: Doubleday,
              1972.

         A mafia don's daughter receives the
         stigmata and performs genuine acts of
         healing. Rome sends a bishop to verify the
         authenticity of her sanctity but various
         evil people try to misappropriate her
         goodness.

1607.   McNamara, Lena. The Penance Was Death.
              Milwaukee: Bruce, 1964.

         A woman is murdered shortly after leaving
         the confessional.

1608.   McNeill, Orange. A Jesuit of Today. New
              York: Tait, 1895.

         A pampered rich Yale man renounces atheism
         and becomes a Catholic. He then gives up
         his girlfriend to study for the priesthood.

1609. McSherry, James. Pere Jean; or The Jesuit
       Missionary. Baltimore: Murphy, 1847.

1610. ———. Willitoft; or The Days of James the
       First. Baltimore: Murphy, 1851.

1611. Meade, Marion. Stealing Heaven. New York:
       Morrow, 1979.

       Ill-fated love affair of Heloise and
       Abelard.

1612. Meadows, Denis. Tudor Underground. New
       York: Devin-Adair, 1950.

       A stirring historical novel about the
       Jesuit attempt to bring back a vigorous
       Catholicism to England in the days when the
       Faith was outlawed.

1613. Meagher, Joseph William. Tippy Locklin.
       Boston: Little, Brown, 1960.

       Catholic family life in Brooklyn.

1614. Meeker, Mrs. Ogden. Fortune's Football.
       London: Burns & Oates, 1864.

       Catholics in Elizabethan England.

1615. Meany, Mary L. Grace Morton. Philadelphia:
       Cunningham, 1864.

       A novel about the painful circumstances of
       being a Catholic in Protestant America.
       Filled with conversions.

1616. Meersch, Maxence van der. The Dynamite
       Factory. London: Kimber, 1953.

       A man rebels against God because of Job-
       like miseries. Through monastic solitude he
       finds healing.

1617. ———. Fishers of Men. New York: Sheed &
       Ward, 1947.

       The Young Christian Workers in France.

1618. Meline, Mary. The Montarges Legacy.
       Philadelphia: Cunningham, 1869.

1619. ———. The Mobrays and the Harringtons.
       Baltimore: Baltimore Publishing Company,
       1884.

1620. Melville, James. The Wages of Zen. New
       York: Fawcett, 1985.

       An Irish priest is found murdered at a
       Buddhist temple in Japan.

1621. Memmi, Albert. Strangers. New York:
       Orion, 1960.

       A Jewish-Catholic marriage fails.

1622. Mergendahl, Charles Henry. The Bramble
       Bush. New York: Putnam, 1958.

       A doctor has an affair with the wife of a
       dying man. When she becomes pregnant, the
       doctor gives her husband an overdose of
       morphine. He is acquitted of mercy killing
       and marries his beloved but she dies in
       chldbirth. He is a lapsed Catholic who
       tries to pray again.

1623. Mewshaw, Michael. Earthly Bread. New York:
       Random House, 1976.

       A priest becomes embroiled in an attempt
       to deprogram a Pentecostal. A serio-comical
       morality tale.

1624. Meyer, Conrad F. The Saints. New York:
       Simon & Schuster, 1930.

       The murder of Thomas Becket.

1625. Mian, Mary Lawrence. Merry Miracle.
       Boston: Houghton, Mifflin, 1949.

       Satirical fantasy about some French
       villagers who invite a half dozen obscure
       saints to return from heaven for a visit.

1626. Michelfelder, William A. Be Not Angry. New
       York: Atheneum, 1960.

A desperately lonely priest has a brief affair with a spinster in his parish.

1627.   ————. A Seed Upon the Wind. Indiana-
          polis: Bobbs, Merrill, 1954.

In a Catholic hospital a doctor and a nurse reject the church. Both are forced to leave after they become lovers.

1628.   Miles, George Henry. The Governess.
          Baltimore: Hedian & Obrien, 1851.

A Catholic governess quietly converts numerous members of a Protestant household.

1629.   ————. Loretto. Baltimore: Hedian &
          Obrien, 1851.

A saintly girl wants to become a nun but her lapsed Catholic guardian refuses permission. Her good example leads many to convert.

1630.   ————. The Truce of God. Baltimore:
          Murphy, 1871.

The days of Pope Gregory VII.

1631.   Miller, Lucy Henry. Ash Wednesday.
          Richmond: Keenan, 1882.

1632.   Miller, Walter M., Jr. A Canticle for
          Leibowitz. Philadelphia: Lippincott,
          1960.

A futuristic novel about an order of monks who preserve the remains of a destroyed civilization.

1633.   Mitchell, Gladys. Convent on Styx. London:
          Joseph, 1975.

1634.   ————. St. Peter's Finger. New York: St.
          Martin's, 1987.

A student is murdered at an English convent school.

1635. Molloy, Frances. <u>No Mate for the Magpie</u>.
       New York: Persea, 1986.

       A feminist satire on clergy and convent
       life, set in troubled Northern Ireland.

1636. Molloy, Robert. <u>A Multitude of Sins</u>. New
       York: Doubleday, 1953.

       A charming and heartwarming tale of a
       Charleston widow who tries to reclaim a
       dying cousin to the Faith, so that the soon-
       to-be-deceased can go to heaven and be
       buried in consecrated ground, so as not to
       disgrace the family.

1637. ————. <u>Pound Foolish</u>. Philadelphia:
       Lippincott, 1950.

       A Charleston family has to contend with
       Yankee relatives and a Protestant-Catholic
       marriage.

1638. ————. <u>Pride's Way</u>. New York: Macmillan,
       1945.

       A splendid portrait of Catholic life in
       Charleston around 1910. The main character
       spends a great deal of time praying and
       attending Mass, but pride stands in the way
       of reconciliation with her sister. She is
       also given to visions of the Virgin Mary and
       the Holy Ghost.

1639. Monlaur-Reynes, Madame. <u>Dead Altars</u>.
       London: Burns & Oates, 1931.

       The devastating effects of war bring about
       many conversions.

1640. ————. <u>Sister Clare</u>. New York: McBride,
       1918.

       An elderly nun is driven from her convent
       by the German army.

1641. Monsarrat, Nicholas. <u>The Kappillan of
       Malta</u>. New York: Morrow, 1974.

An heroic priest goes into seclusion.

1642. Montano, Paulo. Godhead. London:
       Arlington, 1971.

1643. Montaurier, Jean. A Passage Through Fire.
       New York: Holt, 1965.

       An old priest, considered a failure, is
       transferred to a parish where a young priest
       decides to leave the priesthood at
       Christmas. The elderly man invites the
       disillusioned priest to remain with him to
       find his soul. They search together for
       integrity and grace. The younger priest is
       reborn and returns to his parish as the old
       man learns he is dying. "Both as literature
       and as a Christian document of our times, it
       is a giant among novels." (Library Journal)

1644. Monteilhet, Hubert. The Road to Hell. New
       York: Simon & Schuster, 1964.

       In a small French town an anonymous letter
       writer plays God by ferreting out the hidden
       sins of the town's most important people and
       punishing them. When the sinners unite
       against the inquisitor tragedy occurs. A
       witty satire on religion, especially
       confession.

1645. Montherlant, Henry de. The Boys. London:
       Weidenfeld, 1974.

1646. Moore, Brian. Black Robe. New York:
       Dutton, 1985.

       A Jesuit priest tries to convert Indians
       in Canada.

1647. ———. Catholics. New York: Holt, 1973.

       Sometime in the future the Vatican sends a
       representative to convince a group of monks
       who have kept the old faith to change with
       the times. They have preserved the Latin
       Mass and traditional Catholicism on an Irish
       island. Their leader is a monk who has
       secretly lost his faith.

1648.   ————. <u>Cold Heaven</u>. New York: Holt,
        1983.

        A dazzling and disturbing novel about an
        agnostic, 'adulterous wife who sees the Virgin
        Mary. It is an insightful and compassionate
        study of a tormented woman who does not want
        to believe what she has seen.

1649.   ————. <u>The Color of Blood</u>. New York:
        Dutton, 1987.

        A cardinal in an Eastern European country
        survives an assassination attempt and is
        placed under house arrest by security
        officers, allegedly for his own protection.
        He escapes in order to prevent a riot when
        the faithful protest Soviet oppression at a
        religious ceremony.

1650.   ————. <u>The Feast of Lupercal</u>. Boston:
        Little, Brown, 1957.

        A Catholic teacher develops a friendship
        with a Protestant girl, and his enemies try
        to ruin him. A critique of Catholic
        education in Ireland.

1651.   ————. <u>The Lonely Passion of Judith
        Hearne</u>. Boston: Little, Brown, 1955.

        A desperately lonely woman takes out her
        rage against God.

1652.   Moore, George. <u>Evelyn Innes</u>. New York:
        Appleton, 1898.

        A passionate Catholic actress and singer
        is torn between sexual love and religious
        faith.

1653.   ————. <u>Heloise and Abelard</u>. New York:
        Boni, 1925.

        A massive biographical novel.

1654.   ————. <u>The Lake</u>. London: Heinemann,
        1905.

In a small Irish town a priest banishes
the parish schoolteacher because she is
pregnant. He feels intense guilt and writes
to her in her English exile. A wistful,
melancholy and poetic novel.

1655. ———. Sister Teresa. Philadelphia:
Lippincott, 1901.

Evelyn (see item 1652) becomes a nun.
"Life is the will of God, and to enter into
the will of God we must forget ourselves."

1656. Moran, J.J. The Dun Ferry Risin'. London:
Digby, 1894.

A Methodist shopkeeper is terrified of
Popery.

1657. Morgan, Al. Minor Miracle. New York:
Dodd, Mead, 1961.

An eleven-year-old witnesses a weeping
picture of Jesus and brings unexpected
notoriety to a New York City parish.

1658. Mullins, Helene. Convent Girl. New York:
Harper, 1929.

Unfavorable look at a Catholic boarding
school for young ladies, where the nuns all
seem petty, mean-spirited and neurotic.

1659. Munro, Neil. Children of Tempest.
Edinburgh: Blackwood, 1903.

Life among British Catholic farmers.

1660. Murdoch, Iris. Henry and Cato. New York:
Viking, 1977.

A complex character study of a convert
priest and his boyhood friend Henry. While
Henry sees his life as less meaningful than
Cato's ministry to a rundown London mission,
Cato is becoming obsessed by Beautiful Joe,
a ghetto youth. Joe is the catalyst, setting off a whirl of extortion, kidnapping
and violent death.

1661.   ———. Nuns and Soldiers. New York:
         Viking, 1981.

         A former nun who has lost her faith
         encounters a vision of Christ in this
         complex study.

1661a.   ———. The Red and the Green. London:
         Chatto, 1965.

         A tragic tale of Catholic-Protestant
         conflict in Ireland during the Easter
         Rebellion. One character says, "Catholicism
         is the curse of this country." Another was
         horrified that so many of his relatives had
         become Catholic converts. A third character
         laments that in Ireland "religion was a
         matter of choosing between one appaling
         vulgarity and another."

1662.   Murnane, Gerald. A Lifetime on Clouds.
         Melbourne: Heinemann Australia, 1976.

         A young man in a Catholic secondary school
         is torn between sexual impulses and a desire
         to enter the priesthood.

1663.   Murphy, Edward Francis. Angel of the
         Delta. New York: Doubleday, 1958.

         A saintly woman helps the forgotten people
         in the Irish Channel district of New
         Orleans.

1664.   ———. Bride for New Orleans. New York:
         Doubleday, 1955.

         Priests and nuns minister to the "casket
         girls," who came to early New Orleans to
         find husbands.

1665.   ———. Mademoiselle Lavalliere. New York:
         Doubleday, 1948.

         A French actress leaves the glamorous
         world, embraces Catholicism and becomes a
         woman of sanctity and self-sacrifice.

1666.   ———. Pere Antoine. New York:
         Doubleday, 1947.

    In 18th century New Orleans a Spanish
priest is transformed from a mean-spirited
to a tolerant and kindly man who is beloved
by his parishioners.

1667. Murphy, Leo. The Golden Heritage. New
       York: P.J. Kenedy, 1929.

    A portrait of devout Catholics in Nova
Scotia.

1668. ———. Silver Glade. New York:
       Salvatorian, 1947.

1669. Murphy, Walter F. The Vicar of Christ. New
       York: Macmillan, 1979.

    A talented American becomes a diplomat, a
Supreme Court justice, a Trappist monk, and,
finally, Pope.

1670. Murray, David Leslie. The Bride Adorned.
       New York: Harcourt, 1929.

    A beautifully written story of love
between an English Protestant girl and an
Italian member of the Papal guards.

1671. Mussolini, Benito. The Cardinal's
       Mistress. New York: Boni, 1928.

    A melodramatic tale of intrigue and
corruption in the church, written by Italy's
atheist dictator.

1672. Mydans, Shelley. Thomas. New York:
       Doubleday, 1965.

    The martyrdom of Thomas Becket.

1673. Myers, Mary. A Candle to St. Anthony.
       London: Hutchinson, 1954.

1674. ———. The Thin Gold Ring. London:
       Hutchinson, 1950.

    A mixed marriage is held together by faith
and love.

1675.   Nagayo, Yoshiro. The Bronze Christ. New
        York: Taplinger, 1961.

            Catholics suffer persecution in 17th
        century Japan.

1676.   Nash, N. Richard. The Last Magic. New
        York: Atheneum, 1978.

            As the Pope lies dying, a bitter struggle
        for succession occurs. "A novel of
        compelling richness and power...dramatizes
        morally, intellectually and physically the
        great conservative-liberal issue that
        threatens to tear apart the R.C. church."
        (Publishers Weekly)

1677.   Neill, Esther W. Barbara's Marriage and the
        Bishop. New York: Macmillan, 1925.

            A bishop helps his niece survive an
        unhappy marriage.

1678.   ———. The Red Ascent. New York: P.J.
        Kenedy, 1914.

            A Southern convert becomes a seminarian
        under difficult conditions, but must return
        home to care for his family.

1679.   Neill, Robert. The Golden Days. London:
        Hutchinson, 1972.

            The Popish Plot.

1680.   ———. Traitor's Moon. New York:
        Doubleday, 1952.

            A gripping tale about anti-Catholicism in
        17th century England.

1681.   Newman, John Henry. Callista. London:
        Longmans, 1856.

            Conversion of a third century pagan woman.

1682.   ———. Loss and Gain. London: Longmans,
        1848.

            The classic conversion novel, leisurely,
        illuminating and intellectual. Despite

separation from loved ones and familiar
places, the hero finds peace and serenity,
"like the stillness which almost sensibly
affects the ears when a bell that has long
been tolling stops, or when a vessel, after
much tossing at sea, finds itself in
harbor."

1683. Newman, Robert H. <u>Fling Out the Banner</u>.
Philadelphia: Lippincott, 1941.

A boy clings to his Catholic faith in a
New England Protestant boarding school.

1684. Newton, William W. <u>The Priest and the Man</u>.
Boston: Cupples, 1883.

Abelard and Heloise.

1685. Nichols, Thomas Low. <u>Father Larkin's
Mission in Jonesville</u>. Baltimore: Kelly,
1860.

1686. Niebelschutz, Wolf von. <u>Children of
Darkness</u>. London: Allen & Unwin, 1963.

1687. Niggli, Josefina. <u>A Miracle for Mexico</u>.
Greenwich: New York Graphic Society,
1964.

The Virgin Mary appears to Juan Diego.

1688. Niwa, Fumio. <u>The Buddha Tree</u>. London:
Owen, 1966.

1689. Noble, Frances. <u>Not For This World Only</u>.
St. Louis: Herder, 1909.

An attack on secular education.

1690. ————. <u>The Temptation of Norah Leecroft</u>.
New York: Benziger, 1904.

A happy love story between a Catholic
governess and a Protestant Englishman.

1691. Nolan, Winefride. <u>Rich Inheritance</u>. New
York: Macmillan, 1952.

Catholic endurance in Elizabethan England.

1692. Norman, Mrs. George. <u>Brigit</u>. New York:
       Benziger, 1930.

       An orphan girl must choose between
       marriage and the convent.

1693. ———. <u>Hylton's Wife</u>. New York:
       Benziger, 1929.

       A Catholic wife struggles to preserve her
       marriage despite temptations.

1694. ———. <u>The King's Mountain</u>. London:
       Hurst, 1931.

1695. ———. <u>The Night of Spring</u>. London:
       Hurst, 1933.

1696. ———. <u>The Town on the Hill</u>. New York:
       Benziger, 1927.

       Love, marriage and divorce are treated
       from the Catholic point of view in a novel
       set amidst the serene beauty of the Italian
       countryside.

1697. Norman, James. <u>Father Juniper and the
       General</u>. New York: Morrow, 1956.

       A picturesque and satirical novel about a
       new priest in a Mexican town.

1698. Norris, Kathleen. <u>Little Ships</u>. New York:
       Doubleday, 1925.

       Family life in the 1920s. "The story's
       Catholic characters live their lives within
       the framework of Catholic institutions,
       beliefs, practices and traditions, and
       engage the world with a distinctive
       philosophy of life drawn from their
       religious faith." (Arnold Spann)

1699. ———. <u>Martie, the Unconquered</u>. New York:
       Doubleday, 1917.

       The Catholic heroine refuses to marry a
       divorced man and becomes a successful
       author.

1700.   ———.   Mother.   New York: Macmillan,
        1911.

        A condemnation of birth control and
        selfishness in marriage.

1701.   Norwood, Frank.   The Pope Must Die.   New
        York: Charter, 1985.

        A new Pope is stricken by a mysterious
        paralysis.   Summoned to his bedside, a young
        American neurologist can find no medical
        explanation.

1702.   Novak, Michael.   Naked I Leave.   New York:
        Macmillan, 1970.

        A former seminarian becomes a journalist
        covering the Vatican Council.   He has
        numerous sexual problems and encounters.

1703.   ———.   The Tiber Was Silver.   New York:
        Doubleday, 1961.

        A magnificent novel about a young American
        seminarian's life in Rome preceding his
        ordination.   The hero is also a talented
        painter torn between his desire to create
        and his consecration to God.

1704.   Nowinson, Marie L.   The Legacy of Gabriel
        Martel.   New York: Appleton, 1950.

        A devoutly Catholic lawyer tries to follow
        Christ's precepts in his daily and profes-
        sional life, but is disappointed by
        everyone, including his children.   He
        accepts his failures as the just and
        inscrutable will of God.

1705.   Obermeyer, Rosemary.   Golden Apples of the
        Sun.   New York: Dutton, 1944.

        A gypsy girl leaves a convent school and
        searches for happiness in the company of an
        elderly missionary priest and an atheist
        musician.

1706. O'Brien, Kate. <u>The Anteroom</u>. New York:
       Doubleday, 1934.

       For three days a priest prays by the
       bedside of a dying woman while her children
       try to sort out personal conflicts and
       crises.

1707. ————. <u>The Land of Spices</u>. New York:
       Doubleday, 1941.

       The Mother Superior of an Irish convent
       reviews the course of her life in a series
       of flashbacks.

1708. O'Connell, Charles C. <u>Light Over Fatima</u>.
       Cork: Mercier, 1947.

       The Virgin Mary appears at Fatima.

1709. O'Connell, Marvin R. <u>McElroy</u>. New York:
       Norton, 1980.

       A Catholic Congressman, an ex-seminarian,
       struggles to overcome his arrogance and to
       serve others.

1710. O'Connor, Edwin. <u>The Edge of Sadness</u>.
       Boston: Little, Brown, 1961.

       A priest, a recovered alcoholic, is so
       wounded that he tries to avoid his
       parishioners' personal problems. Winner of
       the Pulitzer Prize, 1962.

1711. ————. <u>The Last Hurrah</u>. Boston: Little,
       Brown, 1956.

       Catholicism and politics in Boston.

1712. O'Connor, Joseph. <u>The Norway Man</u>. New
       York: Macmillan, 1949.

       An Irish couple finds meaning in life by
       caring for a shipwrecked seaman.

1713. O'Connor, Mary Garland. <u>Thy Wedded Husband</u>.
       Boston: Houghton, Mifflin, 1958.

       A Catholic wife sees her husband falling
       in love with another woman.

1714. O'Connor, Patricia. <u>Mary Doherty</u>. London: Sands, 1939.

A mixed marriage in Belfast in the 1920s.

1715. O'Donovan, Gerald. <u>Vocations</u>. New York: Boni, 1922.

After a priest tries to seduce a sister in an Irish convent, she determines to break her vows. Realistic and critical handling of a controversial theme.

1716. Oemler, Marie C. <u>Slippy McGee</u>. New York: Appleton, 1917.

A priest in a small South Carolina town narrates a charming story about a crippled burglar.

1717. O'Faolain, Julia. <u>No Country for Young Men</u>. New York: Carroll & Graf, 1987.

A troubled nun relives her days in the Irish Civil War of the early 1920s.

1718. ————. <u>Women in the Wall</u>. New York: Viking, 1975.

In 6th century France a princess establishes a convent to provide sanctuary and peace for spiritual-minded women. She becomes increasingly fanatical.

1719. O'Faolain, Sean. <u>Come Back to Erin</u>. New York: Viking, 1940.

The rebellious son of a pious Irish family becomes a spiritual exile in America.

1720. O'Flaherty, Liam. <u>Skerrett</u>. New York: Macmillan, 1932.

A disgraced schoolmaster comes in conflict with an arrogant and avaricious parish priest.

1721. O'Grady, Patrick. <u>Dark Was the Wilderness</u>. Milwaukee: Bruce, 1945.

Jesuit missions in the 17th century.

1722.   O'Grady, Standish. The Flight of the Eagle.
        Dublin: Sealy, 1889.

        Oppression of Catholics in Ireland.

1723.   O'Leary, Con. The Lost Rosary. Boston:
        Donahoe, 1870.

        A saga of the "trials, temptations and
        triumphs" of Irish-Catholic immigrant girls
        in a hostile environment.

1724.   Oldenbourg, Zoe. The Awakened. New York:
        Pantheon, 1957.

        A mixed marriage saga.

1725.   ————. Cities of the Flesh. New York:
        Pantheon, 1963.

        In 12th century France a Catholic man weds
        a woman who supports the Albigensian heresy.

1726.   Older, Cora Miranda. Savages and Saints.
        New York: Dutton, 1936.

        A priest, having violated his vow of
        celibacy, is sent as penance to restore a
        ruined California mission. In rebuilding
        and ministering to his scattered flock he
        finds peace.

1727.   Oldmeadow, Ernest J. Antonio. New York:
        Century, 1909.

        A young monk tries to survive when
        monasteries are abolished in Portugal.

1728.   Oliver, John Rathbone. Article Thirty Two.
        New York: Macmillan, 1931.

        A psychological novel about celibacy and
        marriage.

1729.   ————. Greater Love. New York:
        Macmillan, 1936.

        The mother and brother of a man executed
        for murder try to make their lives an
        atonement for his sin.

1730.   ———. Rock and Sand. New York:
         Macmillan, 1930.

         A novel about the cultural clash between
         American Protestants and French Catholics in
         Quebec. The author, an Episcopal priest,
         was berated by Christian Century, which
         complained, "He fails to understand the
         vital, creative consecrated spirit which is
         a part of real Protestantism but when Oliver
         enters the door of the Catholic sanctuary,
         he writes with confidence and power."

1731.   Olmstead, Florence. Father Bernard's
         Parish. New York: Scribner, 1916.

         A kindly priest gets involved with the
         problems of his parishioners on Manhattan's
         Upper West Side.

1732.   Olsen, Paul. The Virgin of San Gil. New
         York: Holt, 1965.

         A statue of the Virgin is stolen from a
         church in a remote Mexican village. An
         innocent man is accused of the crime, and a
         young curate protests the injustice.

1733.   O'Malley, Michael. Miners Hill. New York:
         Harper, 1962.

         An Irish boy's emotional and spiritual
         problems before and after entering a
         seminary.

1734.   O'Marie, Sister Carol Anne. Advent of
         Dying. New York: Delacorte, 1986.

         Sister Mary Helen tries to discover who
         murdered her quiet secretary. The author
         uses the Advent liturgy effectively and
         brings the case to a resolution on Christmas
         Eve.

1735.   ———. A Novena for Murder. New York:
         St. Martin's, 1984.

         A spunky 75-year-old nun at a Catholic
         college in San Francisco investigates the
         murder of a faculty member.

1736.   O'Meara, Kathleen. <u>Mabel Stanhope</u>. Boston:
        Roberts, 1886.

        An absorbing study of French convent
        school life. The heroine wants to become a
        Catholic but her father, enraged, casts her
        off.

1737.   O'Meara, Walter. <u>The Devil's Cross</u>.
        London: Hodder, 1958.

        The Children's Crusade.

1738.   O'Neal, Charles. <u>The Three Wishes of Jamie</u>
        <u>McRuin</u>. New York: Messner, 1949.

        A dreamy young Irishman becomes a horse
        trader in Georgia, marries and hopes to have
        a son. A fascinating look at a small
        Catholic community in the deep South, who
        barely preserve their religious faith in a
        hostile environment.

1739.   Orczy, Baroness. <u>Fire in Stubble</u>. London:
        Methuen, 1912.

        The Popish Plot.

1740.   Ormond, Czenzi. <u>Laughter from Downstairs</u>.
        New York: Farrar, Straus, 1948.

        Bohemian family life in the Pacific
        Northwest.

1741.   Otis, Raymond. <u>Miguel of the Bright</u>
        <u>Mountain</u>. Albuquerque: University of New
        Mexico Press, 1977.

        Hispanic life in New Mexico between the
        World Wars.

1742.   Oxenhandler, Neal. <u>A Change of Gods</u>. New
        York: Harcourt, 1962.

        A Jewish man and a Catholic woman rush
        into marriage in Florence, but find reli-
        gious differences a problem. The Jewish
        husband converts, but the Catholic charac-
        ters seem corrupt and hypocritical.

1743. Palacio-Valves, Armando. <u>Jose</u>. New York:
        Barrons, 1961.

        Spiritual faith and moral courage enable
        fisherman in a Spanish village to overcome
        hardships.

1744. Papazoglou, Orania. <u>Sanctity</u>. New York:
        Crown, 1986.

        A chilling tale of murder and madness in a
        convent.

1745. Pape, Richard Bernard. <u>The House of the
        Misty Orchid</u>. London: Gibbs, 1963.

1746. Paradise, Jean. <u>Savage City</u>. New York:
        Crown, 1955.

        Catholics and blacks are victims of mob
        hysteria in New York in 1740.

1747. Paretsky, Sara. <u>Killing Orders</u>. New York:
        Morrow, 1985.

        A Dominican priory in Chicago in robbed of
        stock certificates. A tough female private
        eye confronts a secret Catholic society,
        the Vatican, and the Mafia to find the
        culprits.

1748. Parise, Goffredo. <u>Don Gastone and the
        Ladies</u>. New York: Knopf, 1955.

        A witty novel about a young and handsome
        priest who ministers in an Italian slum.
        Published in England as <u>The Priest Among the
        Pigeons</u>.

1749. Park, Ruth. <u>Serpent's Delight</u>. New York:
        Doubleday, 1962.

        A young girl in a middle-class Australian
        family claims to have seen the Blessed
        Virgin. The resulting publicity affects the
        lives of everyone. Published in England as
        <u>The Good Looking Women</u>.

1750. Parker, John. <u>Iron in the Valleys</u>. London:
        Ronald, 1959.

A devoted priest serves in an industrial area.

1751. Parr, Oliver. The White-Handed Saint. London: Washbourne, 1913.

A saintly English priest has a terrible accident the day after his ordination, which prevents him from celebrating Mass.

1752. Parsons, Gertrude. Thornberry Abbey. London: Burns & Oates, 1846.

Conversion of a Protestant clergyman and his fiancé.

1753. Pascal-Dasque, M.L. Lucinie. New York: P.J. Kenedy, 1959.

A young French nursing sister works miracles in Algeria.

1754. Patch, Howard R. The Cupid on the Stairs. New York: Sheed & Ward, 1942.

A satire on selfishness and illicit love.

1755. Patterson, Frances Taylor. The Long Shadow. New York: Sheed & Ward, 1956.

Saint Jean de Brebeuf.

1756. ————. White Wampum. New York: Longmans, 1934.

Indian converts in early Canada.

1757. Patterson, James. Virgin. New York: McGraw-Hill, 1980.

A metaphysical horror story that strains credulity.

1758. Patterson, Joseph Medill. Rebellion. Chicago: Reilly & Britton, 1911.

A Catholic wife tries everything to preserve a disintegrating marriage, but finally seeks a divorce despite church disapproval.

1759. Pauco, Joseph. <u>Unconquerable</u>. New York:
       Vantage, 1958.

       Struggle for religious freedom in
       Communist Slovakia.

1760. Paul, Phyllis. <u>Rox Hall Illuminated</u>.
       London: Heinemann, 1956.

       A scholarly widow sends her exuberant
       daughter to a convent school, where she is
       converted. Part of the plot revolves around
       an alleged apparition.

1761. Percy, Walker. <u>Love in the Ruins</u>. New
       York: Farrar, Straus, 1971.

       A remarkable satire on American Catholics
       subtitled "The Adventures of a Bad Catholic
       at a Time Near the End of the World."

1762. ———. <u>The Moviegoer</u>. New York: Knopf,
       1961.

       A gentle satire on a young man who avoids
       responsibility and lives in the fantasy of
       movie theatres. Highly praised.

1763. Perdue, Lewis. <u>The Linz Testament</u>. New
       York: Donald I. Fine, 1985.

       Terrorists, spies and the Vatican all vie
       to obtain a long lost relic, the shroud of
       Veronica.

1764. Perera, Victor. <u>The Conversion</u>. Boston:
       Little, Brown, 1970.

       An outrageously ribald series of
       adventures of a young American Jew in Spain
       who battles a mad priest for his soul.

1765. Perriam, Wendy. <u>The Stillness, The
       Dancing</u>. London: Joseph, 1986.

       A novel about loss of faith and subsequent
       revelation.

1766. Peters, Ellis. <u>Dead Man's Ransom</u>. New
       York: Morrow, 1985.

Cadfael investigates the death of a prisoner.

1767. ————. <u>The Devil's Novice</u>. New York:
        Morrow, 1984.

A young novice upsets the peace of a monastic community. Murder results.

1768. ————. <u>An Excellent Mystery</u>. New York:
        Morrow, 1986.

Refugees from civil strife cause trouble at Cadfael's abbey.

1769. ————. <u>The Hermit of Etyon Forest</u>.
        London: Headline, 1987.

The fourteenth case for Brother Cadfael.

1770. ————. <u>The Leper of Saint Giles</u>. New
        York: Morrow, 1982.

Cadfael proves that a young man hiding from his enemies in a leper sanctuary did not strangle his girlfriend's lover on the eve of the wedding.

1771. ————. <u>Monk's Hood</u>. New York: Morrow,
        1981.

Cadfael solves the murder by poisoning of his childhood sweetheart's husband.

1772. ————. <u>A Morbid Taste for Bones</u>. New
        York: Morrow, 1978.

The first appearance of Brother Cadfael, the 12th century Welsh monk who solves crimes from his English monastery. Sent to Wales to bring back the bones of St. Winifred, Cadfael gets involved with the murder of a local squire.

1773. ————. <u>One Corpse Too Many</u>. New York:
        Morrow, 1980.

Cadfael tries to discover why an extra body is found when he prepares to bury rebels executed in civil war.

1774. ————. The Pilgrim of Hate. New York:
          Morrow, 1986.

          Cadfael sees the connection between the
       murder of a knight in a distant town and
       pilgrims gathering at a sacred shrine.

1775. ————. The Raven in the Foregate. New
          York: Morrow, 1986.

          A cruel priest is murdered just before
       Christmas, and Cadfael must find the slayer.

1776. ————. The Rose Rent. New York: Morrow,
          1987.

          A young monk is found murdered near a rose
       bush at the same time a widow disappears.

1777. ————. Saint Peter's Fair. New York:
          Morrow, 1981.

          A merchant is slain on the eve of a
       festive summer fair.

1778. ————. The Sanctuary Sparrow. New York:
          Morrow, 1983.

          A young minstrel is given sanctuary by
       Cadfael when a mob threatens to hang him for
       a crime he did not commit.

1779. ————. The Virgin in the Ice. New York:
          Morrow, 1982.

          Cadfael discovers who killed a young girl
       and placed her body in the ice.

1780. Peyrefitte, Roger. The Keys of St. Peter.
          New York: Criterion, 1956.

          A satirical novel dealing with the educa-
       tion of a French seminarian who goes to Rome
       to serve a wealthy cardinal. The Chicago
       Tribune wrote scathingly, "Uninformed
       readers will derive considerable misinfor-
       mation about Catholic doctrine. Prejudiced
       readers will find alleged horrors to gloat
       over or elaborate distortions to be shocked
       at."

1781.   ————. The Knights of Malta. New York:
         Phillips, 1959.

         A cardinal tries to bring the Order of
         Malta under the Vatican's control.

1782.   ————. Special Friendships. New York:
         Vanguard, 1950.

         Penetrating study of adolescents in a
         French Catholic college.

1783.   Pezeril, Daniel. Rue Notre Dame. New York:
         Sheed & Ward, 1953.

         A moving portrait of the sanctity of a
         French priest.

1784.   Phelan, Francis. Four Ways of Computing
         Midnight. New York: Atheneum, 1985.

         A remarkable exploration of a man's
         vocation and seminary days, abruptly ending
         in his unexplained loss of faith.
         "Beautifully conceived and elegantly
         written." (Library Journal)

1785.   Phelan, Thomas P. Arthur Lee. New York:
         P.J. Kenedy, 1935.

         A sympathetic look at a "simple, indus-
         trious, holy, sincere and manly" priest.

1786.   Philbrick, W.R. Ice for the Eskimo. New
         York: Beaufort, 1987.

         Several Boston-area Catholic clergy are
         involved in homosexual scandals and murder.

1787.   Phillip, Quentin Morrow. We Who Died Last
         Night. St. Meinrad, IN: Grail, 1941.

         A man's Catholic faith helps him recover
         from poverty and despair during the
         Depression. When he meets a woman he loves,
         he cannot marry her because of church
         teachings on divorce.

1788.   Pinckney, Josephine. Three O'Clock Dinner.
         New York: Viking, 1945.

A charming comedy about family life in Charleston, including a miserably unhappy Protestant-Catholic marriage.

1789. Pintauro, Joseph. State of Grace. New York: Times, 1983.

A Jesuit missionary returns to Brooklyn, falls in love and considers leaving the priesthood.

1790. Piovene, Guido. Confession of a Novice. London: Kimber, 1950.

A novice in an Italian convent finds her vocation lacking. Despair turns to murder.

1791. Pise, Charles Constantine. Father Rowland. Baltimore: Lucas, 1829.

The hero is a genteel, Maryland-born Jesuit who presents the claims of Catholicism to a general and his family, who occupy an elegant mansion overlooking the Potomac.

1792. ————. The Indian Cottage, A Unitarian Story. Baltimore: Lucas, 1831.

Conversion of a Unitarian woman.

1793. ————. Zenosius; or, The Pilgrim Convert. New York: Dunigan, 1845.

An angel appears to a young man and guides him on the path of truth. He visits Rome, meets the Pope and is converted. His sister is also converted and becomes a nun.

1794. Plagemann, Bentz. The Heart of Silence. New York: Morrow, 1967.

In a wealthy Chicago family religion is to be expressed discreetly and fervor is discouraged. The devout younger son flees to Mexico where he finds God and vows to remain until the end of his days "praying for the salvation of the world." While there he is the recipient of the miracle of the stigmata.

1795.   ———. Into the Labyrinth. New York:
         Farrar, Straus, 1948.

         During Lent a very religious 18-year-old
         schoolboy is seduced by a married woman.

1796.   Plante, David. The Catholic. New York:
         Atheneum, 1986.

         A powerful meditation on the conflict
         between homosexual obsession and Catholic
         faith.

1797.   ———. The Family. New York: Farrar,
         Straus, 1978.

         Growing-up Catholic in a French family in
         Providence in the 1950s.

1798.   Player, Robert. Let's Talk of Graves, of
         Worms, and Epitaphs. London: Gollancz,
         1975.

         A bizarre fantasy about an English Protes-
         tant clergyman who converts to Catholicism
         and becomes Pope. Apparently he murdered
         his wife along the way.

1799.   Plummer, Catherine. All About Brother Bird.
         New York: Doubleday, 1966.

         A monk in a California monastery is
         plagued by clumsiness and stupidity. But he
         has the unique gift of levitation, a talent
         he resents because he has no control over
         it.

1800.   ———. The Rose on the Summit. New York:
         Putnam, 1951.

         Insightful and well-written story of a
         convent schoolgirl.

1801.   Polland, Madeline A. Sabrina. New York:
         Delacorte, 1979.

         An Irish girl is supposed to become a nun
         but she wants to get married.

1802. Potter, Jeremy. A Trail of Blood. London:
Constable, 1970.

A monk discovers in the abbey archives who
really killed the princes in the tower.

1803. Power, Crawford. The Encounter. New York:
Sloane, 1950.

A priest struggles against pride and has a
strange encounter with a carnival performer
and his girlfriend.

1804. ———. The Hungry Grass. New York: Dial,
1969.

A dying Irish priest feels that he has
failed his parishioners and his life has had
little meaning and few accomplishments.

1805. Power, Edith Mary. Her Father's Share. New
York: Benziger, 1916.

Portuguese Catholic life.

1806. ———. A Knight of God. St. Louis:
Herder, 1910.

Persecution of Catholics in Yorkshire.

1807. Powers, J.F. Morte D'Urban. New York:
Doubleday, 1962.

A basically good priest becomes an
operator and manipulator, loves the golf
course more than his parishioners, and gets
caught up in the pettiness of ecclesiastical
jealousies. "Powers uses corrosive irony to
expose the problems of religion and the
religious life in modern society." (New
York Herald Tribune)

1808. Powers, John R. Do Black Patent-Leather
Shoes Really Reflect Up? Chicago:
Regnery, 1975.

1809. ———. The Last Catholic in America. New
York: Saturday Review, 1973.

1810. ————. The Unoriginal Sinner and the Ice
       Cream God. Chicago: Contemporary, 1977.

       A wonderful trilogy about the joys and
       tribulations of growing up Catholic in
       Chicago. Sin, punishment and confession
       come in for a great deal of ribbing.

1811. Prantera, Amanda. Strange Loop. New York:
       Dutton, 1985.

       Philosophical novel set in a convent.

1812. Prescott, H.F.M. The Man on a Donkey. New
       York: Macmillan, 1952.

       Rich and graceful historical novel about
       the Pilgrimage of Grace, a rebellion of
       loyal Catholics against Henry VIII.

1813. Pressburger, Emeric. Killing a Mouse on
       Sunday. New York: Harcourt, 1961.

       A Spanish priest is an important character
       in this suspenseful tale about a Loyalist
       exile in Franco's Spain.

1814. Preston, Margaret Mary. As a White Candle.
       New York: Pageant, 1952.

       Three novices take secular courses at a
       university. An atheist professor ridicules
       their faith until he becomes a Catholic.

1815. Prose, Francine. Household Saints. New
       York: St. Martin's, 1981.

       A warm portrait of Italian-American life
       in New York's Little Italy in the 1950s when
       Catholicism was vibrant and pervasive.

1816. Purcell, Mary. The Pilgrim Came Late.
       Dublin: Clonmore, 1948.

       A man condemned for murder returns to God.

1817. Queffelec, Henri. Island Priest. New York:
       Dutton, 1952.

A sacristan poses as a priest to Breton fishermen.

1818. Quigley, Hugh. The Cross and the Shamrock. Boston: Donahoe, 1853.

An Irish orphan remains a devout Catholic despite hostility. He makes converts and eventually becomes a bishop.

1819. ———. Profit and Loss. New York: O'Kane, 1873.

Melodramatic tale of Irish immigrants in Wisconsin.

1820. ———. The Prophet of the Ruined Abbey. New York: Dunigan, 1855.

An Irish priest is sentenced to death for presiding over an interfaith marriage. As he attempts to escape to America, his ship is wrecked and he becomes a hermit on a remote island.

1821. Quill, Monica. And Then There Was Nun. New York: Vanguard, 1984.

A sleuthing nun investigates a woman's soccer team to find a murderer.

1822. ———. Let Us Prey. New York: Vanguard, 1982.

Four promiscuous women are strangled by a religious fanatic.

1823. ———. Not a Blessed Thing. New York: Vanguard, 1981.

Prolific author Ralph McInerny, using a pen name, began this series about Sister Mary Teresa, an aged former professor of medieval history. Sister M.T. and two young nuns, the only remainders of a religious order, live in an old Chicago house where they solve crimes. In this case they help a terrified socialite.

1824.   ————. Nun of the Above. New York:
            Vanguard, 1985.

         When a woman who wanted to become a nun
         (but became a tramp instead) is strangled,
         Sister M.T. has one of her toughest cases.
         The ending is surprising but religiously
         satisfying.

1825.   Quinn, Simon. The Devil in Kansas. New
            York: Dell, 1974.

         The first of a series of six cloak and
         dagger novels featuring "Francis Xavier
         Killy," an ex-CIA man who becomes a lay
         brother in the Militia Christi, the
         Vatican's counter-espionage service. This
         series takes the Vatican thriller to a nadir
         of absurdity. In this debut Killy,
         investigating a suspicious war college, is
         captured and brainwashed to kill the Pope.

1826.   ————. His Eminence, Death. New York:
            Dell, 1974.

         Killy is the bodyguard for an African
         cardinal whose boyhood friend, his country's
         dictator, is planning to kill him.

1827.   ————. Last Rites for the Vulture. New
            York: Dell, 1975.

         A Franciscan monk, a one-time associate of
         Al Capone, is murdered. Killy and a Vatican
         official are sent to investigate claims that
         the deceased is a saint.

1828.   ————. The Last Time I Saw Hell. New
            York: Dell, 1974.

         Killy struggles against an ex-priest who
         collaborated with the Nazis.

1829.   ————. The Midas Coffin. New York: Dell,
            1975.

         Killy must hijack a shipment of Soviet
         gold.

1830. ————. <u>Nuplex Red</u>. New York: Dell, 1974.

> Terrorists take over a nuclear power plant.

1831. Quinnell, A.J. <u>In the Name of the Father</u>. New York: New American Library, 1987.

> The Vatican and the Kremlin engage in secret plots to destroy each other.

1832. Rab, Gusztav. <u>Sabaria</u>. London: Sidgwick & Jackson, 1963.

> Catholics and Communists clash in Hungary.

1833. Radmore, Marian. <u>The Devil's Brew</u>. London: Hale, 1971.

1834. Randolph, Edmund. <u>Mostly Fools</u>. London: Low, 1886.

> Satire on English Catholic institutions.

1835. Raymond, Ernest. <u>The Visit of Brother Ives</u>. London: Cassell, 1974.

1836. Raymond, Father M. <u>The Family That Overtook Christ</u>. New York: P.J. Kenedy, 1942.

> St. Bernard of Clairvaux.

1837. Rayner, Elizabeth. <u>Not All Saints</u>. New York: Longmans, 1933.

> An innocent Catholic girl joins a newspaper and gets caught up in a worldly life style. Published in England as <u>The Net Is Cast</u>.

1838. Raynolds, Robert. <u>The Sinner of St. Ambrose</u>. Indianapolis: Bobbs, Merrill, 1952.

> Catholicism confronts paganism in 4th century Italy.

1839. Read, Piers Paul. <u>A Married Man</u>. Philadelphia: Lippincott, 1979.

A Catholic wife contemplates adultery
while her agnostic husband plans to kill
her. Filled with delicious irony and
insight.

1840. ———. Monk Dawson. Philadelphia:
         Lippincott, 1970.

A priest renounces his ministry and has
numerous love affairs and marriages. After
losing his faith he regains it.

1841. Reade, Charles. The Cloister and the
         Hearth. New York: Dutton, 1906.

A man, once a student for the priesthood,
falls in love. Thinking his beloved is
dead, he engages in riotous living, attempts
suicide and then enters a monastery. Later
he finds his lover alive and learns that he
has a son. But he remains a monk.

1842. Reed, Kit. At War As Children. New York:
         Farrar, Straus, 1964.

Three young friends grow up during World
War II. One of them has a religious crisis.
"One of the best conceived and most convin-
cingly executed Catholic novels." (America)

1843. ———. Catholic Girls. New York: Donald
         Fine, 1987.

Four Catholic college roommates meet at a
funeral twenty years after graduation. Most
have departed radically from acceptable
Catholic lifestyles, but all recognize that
actions have consequences.

1844. Reeves, John. Murder Before Matins. New
         York: Doubleday, 1984.

The prior of a Canadian abbey is pushed
from a high tower to his death shortly
before he was to be named abbot. The
Toronto police investigate.

1845. Regnier, Paule. The Abbey of Evolayne. New
         York: Harcourt, 1935.

A Paris doctor is "reconverted" to
Catholicism by a priest-friend. He wants to
become a priest and his wife accedes to his
request, though loving him desperately. He
becomes a priest, and his wife enters a
convent. But while he is happy, his wife is
not.

1846. Reid, Christian. <u>Armine</u>. New York:
Catholic Publication Society, 1884.

A Louisiana family moves to France, where
they fight for conservative Catholic causes.
The daughter Armine joins a convent and
triggers the conversion of several friends.

1847. ⸻. <u>Child of Mary</u>. Notre Dame, IN:
Ave Maria Press, 1885.

A Southern Episcopalian family tries to
regain its wealth and self-respect after the
Civil War. An orphaned niece, fervently
Catholic, converts them and others.

1848. ⸻. <u>A Far Away Princess</u>. New York:
Devin-Adair, 1900.

A wealthy New York Protestant family is
"charmed" into conversion by the French
Catholic wife of their artist son. She is
an actress and her personal sanctity
surprises them. Catholicism is depicted as
a powerful conservative force, a restraint
upon the social and moral change that
aristocrats in the 1890s feared.

1849. ⸻. <u>His Victory</u>. Notre Dame, IN: Ave
Maria Press, 1887.

A defense of Catholic marriage.

1850. ⸻. <u>Light of Vision</u>. Notre Dame, IN:
Ave Maria Press, 1911.

An unhappily married woman becomes a
Catholic and later renounces the world.

1851. ⸻. <u>Secret Bequest</u>. Notre Dame, IN:
Ave Maria Press, 1915.

To qualify for a fortune, a would-be
heiress must convert a Catholic cousin and
boyfriend to Protestantism. She converts to
Catholicism instead and renounces the
bequest.

1852.   ————. Vera's Charge. Notre Dame, IN:
Ave Maria Press, 1907.

A critique of divorce and an apology for
Catholic marriage.

1853. Remy (Renault-Roulier, Gilbert). The
Messenger. Westminster, MD: Newman,
1954.

A young priest undertakes a mission behind
the Iron Curtain.

1854. Reynolds, Gerald A. The Red Circle. New
York: P.J. Kenedy, 1915.

The Boxer Rebellion persecutes Christians.

1855. Rider, J.W. Jersey Tomatoes. New York:
Arbor House, 1986.

A Jersey City private eye, an ex-Jesuit
seminarian, is importuned to find who killed
a devoutly Catholic woman. Her death had
been reported as suicide but the deceased's
atheist daughter suspects foul play.

1856. Riley, Frank. The Kocska Formula. Los
Angeles: Sherborne Press, 1971.

A sleazy novel featuring a Los Angeles
priest who repeatedly violates celibacy and
becomes a kind of spy.

1857. Rio, Michel. Parrot's Perch. New York:
Harcourt, 1986.

A priest recovering from torture in Latin
America repudiates the faith and commits
suicide.

1858. Rios, Teresa. An Angel Grows Up. New York:
Duell, 1957.

Life in a convent school on Long Island.
A gifted, lonely Puerto Rican girl refuses
to conform; an understanding nun helps her.

1859. ————. The Fifteenth Pelican. New York:
        Doubleday, 1965.

Fantasy about a flying nun.

1860. Rivabella, Omar. Requiem for a Woman's
        Soul. New York: Random House, 1986.

A priest discovers the diary of a woman
brutalized by a South American regime, and
he comes to identify with her suffering.

1861. Rivers, Caryl. Girls Forever Brave and
        True. New York: St. Martin's, 1986.

A kind of sequel to Virgins, with the main
characters living active lives in Washington
in the 1960s. One of the girls encounters
her former lover, now a priest. They have
an affair and marry.

1862. ————. Virgins. New York: St. Martin's,
        1984.

Growing up Catholic and female in a
Maryland suburb in the 1950s. A hilarious
satire.

1863. Roark, Garland. The Witch of Manga Reva.
        New York: Doubleday, 1962.

A French priest is the central character
in this novel about the 19th century South
Sea Islands.

1864. Roberts, Keith. Pavane. New York:
        Doubleday, 1986.

What if England had remained a Roman
Catholic country at the time of the Reformation? A kind of alternative historical
fiction or allegory.

1865. Roberts, Marta. Tumbleweeds. New York:
        Putnam, 1940.

A Mexican woman's religious faith helps
her cope with the bewildering complexities
of life in California.

1866. Robertson, Esther. The World Well Lost.
       New York: Benziger, 1898.

A nun helps a woman overcome a life of
sorrow and pain.

1867. Robichaud, Gerard. The Apple of His Eye.
       New York: Doubleday, 1965.

A recently orphaned teenager learns the
art of survival in a small French Catholic
town in Maine in the 1920s. Part of the
plot revolves around the concept of making
restitution for sins committed and
confessed.

1868. ———. Papa Martel. New York: Doubleday,
       1961.

A loving portrait of a French Catholic
family in Maine.

1869. Robinson, Henry Morton. The Cardinal. New
       York: Simon & Schuster, 1950.

A realistic and full-blooded portrait of a
man's rise from Irish Boston to Cardinal.

1870. ———. The Perfect Round. New York:
       Harcourt, 1945.

A returned soldier tries to recover his
lost Catholic faith.

1871. Roche, Lise. The Fool's Heart. New York:
       Viking, 1970.

Conflict between nonbelievers and a devout
priest in a French town during wartime.

1872. Roche, Paul. O Pale Galilean. London:
       Harvill, 1954.

A plea for humanistic Christianity,
written in the form of a fantasy.

1873. ———. <u>Vessel of Dishonor</u>. New York:
Sheed & Ward, 1962.

As a seminarian and later a priest, a
handsome young English Catholic struggles
between his love for the church and God and
for sexual love. He finally chooses
Vanessa, the one girl he had ever truly
loved. He leaves the priesthood and they
marry, happily. The novel ends as they
anticipate the birth of a child.

1874. Rochlin, Doris. <u>Frobisch's Angel</u>. New
York: Taplinger, 1987.

A sparkling serio-comic novel about a
Jewish accountant from Washington who has a
vision in a Rome hotel room. He is visited
by an angel and receives a clairvoyant
prediction of the death of the Pope. The
hero consults a priest-friend when he
returns home.

1875. Roddan, John T. <u>John O'Brien, the Orphan of
Boston</u>. Boston: Donahue, 1850.

A young Irishman encounters all kinds of
Protestant sects, which are satirized
unmercifully.

1876. Rohrbach, Peter Thomas. <u>Bold Encounter</u>.
Milwaukee: Bruce, 1960.

The life of St. John of the Cross.

1877. ———. <u>The Disillusioned</u>. New York:
Doubleday, 1968.

Quiet despair marks the lives of disillusioned clergy who suffer from an
authoritarian bishop. The author depicts a
rich parish as spiritually dead, with death
and corruption reaching the highest echelons
of the church.

1878. ———. <u>A Gentle Fury</u>. New York:
Doubleday, 1959.

A youthful priest is suddenly thrust into

a life that is completely foreign to his
background, training and experience.

1879. Roland, Nicholas. <u>Natural Causes</u>.
       Nashville: Aurora, 1971.

A Maronite monk emulates the hermits of
the East.

1880. Rolvaag, Ole. <u>Their Father's God</u>. New
       York: Harper, 1931.

A family disintegrates because of
religious differences between a Catholic
wife, an agnostic husband, and a Lutheran
mother-in-law.

1881. Romaniello, John. <u>The Bird of Sorrow</u>. New
       York: P.J. Kenedy, 1957.

A Maryknoll priest's ordeal in Red China.

1882. Romanis, Robert. <u>The Holy Foot</u>. New York:
       Dutton, 1954.

Credulous people look for a long lost
relic of St. Stephen.

1883. Rooney, Frank. <u>Shadow of God</u>. New York:
       Harcourt, 1967.

During World War II five nuns are captured
and forced into prostitution.

1884. Ross, Henry Martin. <u>In God's Good Time</u>.
       New York: Benziger, 1907.

The son of a non-practicing Catholic
father and a Protestant mother converts and
becomes a priest. Conversions are frequent.

1885. ———. <u>The Test of Courage</u>. New York:
       Benziger, 1908.

Religion improves family life.

1886. ———. <u>That Man's Daughter</u>. New York:
       Benziger, 1905.

Love, religion and self-sacrifice.

1887. Ross-Williamson, Hugh. The Florentine
       Woman. London: Joseph, 1970.

The French Wars of Religion.

1888. Rossi, Jean Baptiste. Awakening. New York:
       Harper, 1952.

A nun has a love affair with an adolescent
boy.

1889. Rossiter, Leonard. Bernardin, My Love. New
       York: Doubleday, 1962.

A love story during the days of the
Albigensians.

1890. Roth, Arthur J. The Shame of Our Wounds.
       New York: Crowell, 1961.

A boy leaves a Catholic orphanage during
the Depression and seeks a father figure.

1891. ————. A Terrible Beauty. New York:
       Farrar, Straus, 1950.

An idealistic man joins the IRA but cannot
reconcile their activities with his faith.

1892. Ruber, Johannes. Bach and the Heavenly
       Choir. New York: World, 1957.

A fantasy about a violin-playing Pope who
intends to canonize the great Lutheran
musician, J.S. Bach. His plan outrages the
conservatives at the Vatican.

1893. Russell, Jennifer. The Threshing Floor.
       New York: Paulist, 1987.

In 14th century England many remain faithful to Christ and his church in a time of
suffering.

1894. Russell, Ray. The Case Against Satan. New
       York: Obolensky, 1962.

A priest assigned to perform the rite of
exorcism on a young girl experiences doubts
about his faith.

1895. Ryan, Edwin. <u>One Clear Call</u>. New York:
       Macmillan, 1962.

An octogenerian priest on Brooklyn's
waterfront is summoned to his bishop and
spends the day reflecting on his many years
as a priest.

1896. Ryan, John Victor. <u>The Brighter Vision</u>.
       New York: McMullen, 1951.

Episodes in the early career of a priest.

1897. Rye, Anthony. <u>Giant's Arrow</u>. London:
       Gollancz, 1956.

1898. Sadlier, Anna. <u>Gerald de Lacy's Daughter</u>.
       New York: P.J. Kenedy, 1957.

A romance of old New York after the
accession of William of Orange made life
precarious for Catholics.

1899. ————. <u>New Lights</u>. New York: Sadlier,
       1885.

Irish Catholics struggle to preserve their
faith in the 17th century.

1900. ————. <u>The Pilkington Heir</u>. New York:
       Benziger, 1903.

A tangled tale of lost fortune.

1901. ————. <u>The Red Inn of St. Lyphar</u>. New
       York: Benziger, 1904.

Devoutly Catholic peasants in the Vendee
region of France rise up against their anti-
religious persecutors.

1902. ————. <u>The Silence of Sebastian</u>. Notre
       Dame, IN: Ave Maria Press, 1913.

"A Catholic novel with well-sustained
mystery." (<u>America</u>)

1903.   ————.   The True Story of Master Gerard.
        New York: Benziger, 1900.

1904.   Sadlier, Mary Anne.   Aunt Honor's Keepsake.
        New York: Sadlier, 1866.

        The brutal reform schools of New York
        discriminate against Catholics by forbidding
        prayer, religious services or family
        visitations.   The hero in this story remains
        loyal to his religion and helps to convert
        many others.

1905.   ————.   Bessy Conway. New York: Sadlier,
        1865.

        An Irish girl finds temptations in America
        and so returns to Ireland.

1906.   ————.   The Blakes and the Flanagans.   New
        York: Sadlier, 1855.

        The Flanagans are loyal Catholics who send
        their children to church schools.   Their
        children remain faithful to the church.   The
        Blakes, eager to get ahead, choose public
        schools and colleges, where their children
        fall away.

1907.   ————.   Confessions of an Apostate.   New
        York: Sadlier, 1864.

        An Irish Catholic becomes a Protestant in
        order to be admitted to polite American
        society.   After he is reconverted at a
        Catholic mission, his family rejects him and
        a mob threatens to burn his house.

1908.   ————.   Con O'Regan. New York: Sadlier,
        1864.

        An Irish immigrant suffers hostility in
        New England but settles happily on an Iowa
        farm where there is no prejudice.

1909.   ————.   The Fate of Father Sheehy.   New
        York: Sadlier, 1863.

        A priest pretends to be a beggar to ward
        off Orangemen, but is betrayed and executed.

1910.   ———. <u>MacCarthy More!</u> New York: P.J.
         Kenedy, 1868.

    An Irish-Catholic family struggles to
retain its religion and property during the
persecutions.

1911.   ———. <u>Old and New</u>. New York: Sadlier,
         1862.

    An Irish family becomes worldly and loses
their faith.

1912.   ———. <u>Willy Burke</u>. Boston: Donahue,
         1850.

    In an Irish family one brother leaves the
church because he wants to become successful. Willy remains loyal and wins the
respect of his employer, who converts and
leaves his money to Willy.

1913.   Saint-Pierre, Michel de. <u>The New Aristo-
         crats</u>. Boston: Houghton, Mifflin, 1963.

    Conflict in a French Catholic school. The
author implies that the new intellectuals
think they are an elite, a harbinger of a
new civilization.

1914.   Salzer, Patricia M. <u>The Montagues of Casa
         Grande</u>. New York: Pageant Press, 1953.

    Lives and fortunes of early Catholic
settlers in New Mexico.

1915.   Sanchez-Silva, Jose Maria. <u>Marcelino</u>.
         Westminster, MD: Newman, 1955.

    A baby is left at a monastery where he is
adopted and raised by monks.

1916.   Sandys, Nicholas. <u>Starset and Sunrise</u>. New
         York: Sheed & Ward, 1951.

    An actress, who has had numerous love
affairs, prepares to play the role of a
saint. Learning that she is dying of an
incurable disease, she returns to Catholicism.

1917. Sanford, Mary Bouchier. <u>The Romance of a
       Jesuit Mission</u>. New York: Baker &
       Taylor, 1897.

1918. ———. <u>Trail of the Iroquois</u>. St. Louis:
       Herder, 1925.

       Two novels about the Jesuit missionaries
       in early New York and Canada.

1919. Sansom, Clive. <u>Passion Play</u>. New York:
       Day, 1952.

       In a small Bavarian village, an outsider
       upsets a local girl and a priest.

1920. Santos, Jesus Fernandez. <u>Extramuros</u>.
       New York: Columbia University Press,
       1984.

       A nightmarish story of two lesbian nuns in
       15th century Spain who forge a miracle to
       save their convent from draught and pesti-
       lence. One of the sisters pretends she has
       received the stigmata, and her fame brings
       riches to the convent. She becomes the
       prioress but is exposed and punished.

1921. Saramago, Jose. <u>Baltasar and Blimunda</u>. New
       York: Harcourt, 1987.

       In 18th century Portugal the royal court
       decrees the building of a convent to rival
       St. Peter's Basilica. An unbalanced priest
       devises a magic flying machine in this
       magical novel.

1922. Saul, John. <u>Punish the Sinners</u>. New York:
       Dell, 1978.

       Supernatural evil grips a Catholic high
       school for girls in a sleepy Washington
       State town.

1923. Savage, Marmion W. <u>My Uncle, the Curate</u>.
       New York: Harper, 1849.

       Irish politics and religion in the 1830s.

1924. Saviane, Giorgio. The Finger in the Candle
       Flame. London: Allen, 1964.

1925. Scarfoglio, Carlo. The True Cross. London:
       Gollancz, 1956.

       Religious fervor during the Crusades.

1926. Scarlett, Will. False Gods. New York:
       Benziger, 1929.

       A young San Francisco reporter loses his
       faith but is brought back to it by his
       girlfriend.

1927. Scheibl, Herbert J. Fool's Pilgrimage. St.
       Louis: Herder, 1929.

       A shallow romance with a dash of religion.

1928. Schiff, Barry and Hal Fishman. The Vatican
       Target. New York: St. Martin's, 1978.

       Palestinian terrorists hijack a plane
       carrying the Pope.

1929. Schmidt, Elsa. In Father Gabriel's Garden.
       New York: Benziger, 1915.

       A priest uses legends of flowers to
       cultivate virtues in his First Communion
       class.

1930. Schmitt, Gladys. The Godforgotten. New
       York: Harcourt, 1972.

       A monk fights boredom and sins of the
       flesh.

1931. Schofield, William G. The Deer Cry. New
       York: Longmans, 1949.

       Life and times of St. Patrick.

1932. Schoonover, Lawrence L. The Chancellor.
       Boston: Little, Brown, 1961.

       Portrait of a 15th century cardinal.

1933.   Schulberg, Budd. <u>Waterfront</u>. New York:
        Random House, 19<u>5</u>5.

        A tough-guy priest fights for justice
        against all odds in this classic novel of
        men on the docks.

1934.   Schwab, Charles J. <u>Man in a Wheel Chair</u>.
        New York: Exposit<u>i</u>on, 1961.

        A man overcomes polio and converts to
        Catholicism.

1935.   Sciascia, Leonardo. <u>One Way or Another</u>.
        New York: Harper, <u>1977</u>.

        An enigmatic priest runs a hermitage-
        hotel, where mystery, corruption and
        violence abide.

1936.   Scott, Barbara. <u>Look to Beyond</u>. London:
        Hutchinson, 195<u>1</u>.

        A Scottish Presbyterian minister becomes a
        Catholic, a priest, and a missionary to a
        leper colony.

1937.   ————. <u>The Road Back</u>. London: Hutchin-
        son, 19<u>5</u>2.

        A man whose brother becomes a priest finds
        salvation.

1938.   Scott, Martin J. <u>Mother Machree</u>.
        New York: Macmi<u>ll</u>an, <u>1922</u>.

        A boy with an angelic voice devotes his
        life to the church.

1939.   ————. <u>Upstream</u>. New York: P.J. Kenedy,
        1929.

        A poor but musically talented boy remains
        close to his widowed mother and to his Faith
        despite temptation.

1940.   Scott, Natalie Anderson. <u>The Story of Mrs.
        Murphy</u>. New York: Dutt<u>on</u>, 1947.

A grim but moving story of a Catholic
man's inexorable descent into alcoholism,
despair and death.

1941. Scott-Moncrieff, George. Death's Bright
       Shadow. London: Wingate, 1948.

       Catholics wrestle with complicated
       problems of conscience.

1942. Scotti, R.A. The Devil's Own. New York:
       Donald Fine, 1985.

       Corruption at the Vatican Bank.

1943. ———. The Kiss of Judas. New York:
       Donald Fine, 1985.

       Terrorists plan to kidnap the Pope.

1944. Sedgebury, Edwina. Realization. New York:
       Benziger, 1934.

       A Catholic orphan boy is adopted by a good
       Protestant woman who strives in vain to rear
       him in her own faith. Instead, he chooses
       the priesthood.

1945. Seifert, Elizabeth. Dusty Spring. New
       York: Dodd, Mead, 1946.

       Both Catholics and Protestants ruin each
       other's lives because of worldliness and
       bigotry.

1946. Seipolt, Adalbert. Rum, Rome and Rebellion.
       New York: Sheed & Ward, 1963.

       A humorous novel about a pilgrimage of
       Germans to Rome. Every zany thing imagin-
       able happens. Published in England as All
       Roads Lead to Rome.

1947. Selwin-Tait, Monica. Three Ships Come
       Sailing. New York: Benziger, 1931.

       Three pleasure-loving women are converted.

1948. ———. Uncharted Spaces. New York:
       Longmans, 1933.

> The only son of an Episcopalian Dean
> decides to become a Roman Catholic on the
> eve of his ordination to the Episcopal
> church - a decision causing consternation
> and disbelief among his family and friends.

1949. ———. Winding Ways. Notre Dame, IN: Ave
Maria Press, 1939.

> Love triumphs over bigotry.

1950. Servin, Michel. Deo Gratias. New York:
St. Martin's, 1965.

> A wonderful satire about a devout French
> Catholic who steals from the alms boxes in
> the churches of Paris to relieve his
> financial distress. He becomes an expert
> con artist and is soon wealthy. But he also
> becomes one of Holy Mother Church's great
> benefactors.

1951. Seton, Anya. Devil Water. Boston:
Houghton, Mifflin, 1962.

> An English Catholic is executed in 1746
> for his loyalty to the Stuart cause.

1952. Sewell, Elizabeth. Now Bless Thyself. New
York: Doubleday, 1962.

> An English Catholic poet observes faculty
> and student life at an American state
> university and at a nearby Catholic men's
> college.

1953. Shaw, Charles. Heaven Knows, Mr. Allison.
New York: Crown, 1952.

> A nun and a marine are the sole survivors
> on a Pacific island occupied by the
> Japanese. He falls in love with her but she
> resists.

1954. Shaw, Richard. The Christmas Mary Had
Twins. New York: Stein & Day, 1983.

> A priest's life is enriched by a woman's
> forbidden love.

1955.   Shaw, Russell B. Church and State. Hunting-
        ton, IN: Our Sunday Visitor, 1979.

        Sex, Catholicism and Presidential politics
        sometime in the American future.

1956.   ————. The Dark Disciple. New York:
        Doubleday, 1961.

        A zealous Catholic tries to convert every-
        one to his faith at the secular college
        where he teaches. He soon begins to confuse
        his own objectives with those of genuine
        faith and causes great evil. "It is a
        worthy tale of the terrors which religious
        fanaticism can unloose in any area of modern
        American life." (Christian Century)

1957.   ————. Renewal. San Francisco: Ignatius
        Press, 1986.

        The editor of a diocesan newspaper is
        caught up in the turmoil that comes when a
        reformed-minded liberal bishop tries to
        reshape the church.

1958.   Shea, Robert. All Things Are Lights. New
        York: Ballantine, 1986.

        A knight is involved in the Crusades and
        the Cathar Wars.

1959.   Sheed, Wilfred. The Hack. New York:
        Macmillan, 1963.

        A witty and insightful look at the trials
        and tribulations of a Catholic inspirational
        writer who is about to crack up as Christmas
        approaches.

1960.   Sheehan, Edward. The Governor. New York:
        World, 1970.

        A Massachusetts governor is embarrassed by
        the activities of his brother, who is an
        activist priest in hot water with church
        authorities.

1961.   Sheehan, Patrick Augustine (Canon). The
        Blindness of Dr. Gray. New York:
        Longmans, 1909.

An Irish priest is stern, hard-hearted,
and egotistical until he encounters the
sincere faith of an old blind woman.

1962.   ———. *Luke Delmege*. New York: Longmans,
         1900.

Portrait of an academically talented
priest.

1963.   ———. *My New Curate*. New York:
         Longmans, 1899.

An enthusiastic new priest clashes with a
cautious old one. The new priest eventually
wins out.

1964.   ———. *The Triumph of Failure*. New York:
         Longmans, 1899.

A chronicle of a young unbeliever's
journey to the Catholic faith.

1965.   Sheehy, Maurice Stephen. *The Priestly
         Heart*. New York: Farrar, Straus, 1956.

Even as he is dying, a young priest helps
others.

1966.   ———. *Six O'Clock Mass*. New York:
         Farrar, Straus, 1952.

"A much more effective apologia for the
Catholic faith than most theological works."
(*Kirkus*)

1967.   Sheldon, Walter J. *Rites of Murder*. New
         York: St. Martin's, 1984.

A Catholic bishop of Washington, D.C.
emerges as fiction's first episcopal detective in a case involving the murder of a
high-priced call girl, who was a parishioner
of the cathedral.

1968.   Shepherd, Eric. *More Murder in a Nunnery*.
         New York: Sheed & Ward, 1954.

A gardener at a convent school discovers a
body. Sequel to *Murder in a Nunnery*.

1969.   ————. <u>Murder in a Nunnery</u>. New York:
        Sheed & Ward, 1940.

        Nuns, students and police search for an
        elusive killer when murder occurs in a
        convent boarding school.

1970.   Shepherd, Michael. <u>The Road to Gandolfo</u>.
        New York: Dial, 1975.

        Four disreputable characters plan to
        kidnap the Pope and ransom him for 400
        million dollars. An absurd tale in which
        the Pope is an opera-loving buffoon.

1971.   Sheridan, John D. <u>God Made Little Apples</u>.
        New York: Farrar, Straus, 1962.

        A sentimental novel about a simple man who
        cooks for a community of beggar monks in
        Dublin.

1972.   ————. <u>The Rest Is Silence</u>. London:
        Dent, 1955.

        An elderly Irish American revisits the
        beloved place of his early life and also
        goes to Rome for the 1950 Holy Year. "Rome
        is our mother-house, a dream in the hearts
        of our children, a heritage and a promise."

1973.   Shulman, Irving. <u>Good Deeds Must Be
        Punished</u>. New York: Holt, 1956.

        A Catholic student at a West Virginia
        college tries to win the affections of a
        Protestant girl. He finds prejudice and
        bigotry at every corner.

1974.   Shuster, George N. <u>Brother Flo</u>. New York:
        Macmillan, 1938.

        A loveable priest wins the respect of
        students at a men's college.

1975.   Singleton, Betty. <u>A Note of Grace</u>. New
        York: World, 1957.

        A humorous tale of a convent in a small
        English Protestant town.

1976. Skinner, Henrietta. <u>Espiritu Sancto</u>. New
       York: Harper, 1899.

       A devoutly Catholic opera singer and his
       equally virtuous girlfriend both die before
       they can be married. Their tragic deaths
       bring about spiritual regeneration in
       several friends and relatives.

1977. S.M.C. <u>As the Clock Struck Twenty</u>. Notre
       Dame, IN: Ave Maria Press, 1953.

       A priest tries to conquer a disordered
       world through love and sacrifice.

1978. ————. <u>Brother Petroc's Return</u>. Boston:
       Little, Brown, 1937.

       A community of English monks discover a
       grave during their rebuilding of a chapel
       destroyed four centuries before, during the
       Reformation. A long-dead monk arises as if
       from sleep.

1979. ————. <u>The Chronicle of Thomas Frith</u>.
       London: Blackfriars, 1958.

       Dominican monks in Eastern Europe.

1980. ————. <u>The Dark Wheel</u>. New York: P.J.
       Kenedy, 1940.

       Imaginative fantasy about a London
       barrister who witnesses the martyrdom of a
       priest four centuries ago. At the end the
       lawyer is converted.

1981. ————. <u>The Spark in the Reeds</u>. New York:
       P.J. Kenedy, 1940.

       A priest tries to help the poor but fails
       miserably and dies unknown and alone.

1982. ————. <u>Storm Out of Cornwall</u>. New York:
       P.J. Kenedy, 1959.

       Catholics loyal to the Latin Mass fight
       the prayerbook rebellion in 16th century
       Cornwall. The author was Sister Mary
       Catherine, who also wrote under the pen name
       of Francis Brookfield.

1983.   Smith, Betty. A Tree Grows in Brooklyn.
         New York: Harper, 1943.

         Irish Catholic family life.

1984.   Smith, John Holland. To Beg I Am Ashamed.
         Chicago: Scepter, 1962.

         Conversion of an Anglican pastor.
         Published in England as Nine Days to
         Eternity.

1985.   Smith, John Talbot. The Art of Disappear-
         ing. New York: Benziger, 1899.

         After finding his wife unfaithful, a man
         deserts her and moves to another city where
         he converts to Catholicism. He falls in
         love with a Catholic, and under the Pauline
         Privilege, is able to marry her.

1986.   ———. The Black Cardinal. New York:
         Champlain, 1914.

         The papal secretary of state gets involved
         in a complicated marriage question.

1987.   ———. Solitary Island. New York: Young,
         1888.

         A Catholic politician renounces political
         corruption and adopts a life of poverty,
         celibacy and personal discipline. A woman
         friend of his enters a convent but discovers
         it is not the life for her.

1988.   Smith, Martin Cruz. Canto for a Gypsy. New
         York: Putnam, 1972.

         All sorts of people try to steal the Holy
         Crown of St. Stephen when it is displayed at
         St. Patrick's Cathedral.

1989.   Smith, Robert Charles. Three Days to Live.
         New York: Roy, 1968.

         Fortune hunters, killers and three nuns
         are trapped in an underground cavern in
         Brazil - home of vampire bats.

1990. Smith, Mrs. Rufus W. <u>The Novice</u>. La
       Grange, GA: Cox & Ward, 1894.

       A former nun falls in love with her
       employer.

1991. Smithson, Annie. <u>By Strange Paths</u>. Dublin:
       Talbot, 1948.

       A nurse in a London hospital loves an
       Anglican clergyman, but converts to
       Catholicism and marries an Irish national-
       ist. They return to Ireland to find
       happiness.

1992. Soldati, Mario. <u>The Confession</u>. New York:
       Knopf, 1958.

       A teenager struggles against sins of the
       flesh.

1993. Sommers, Lillian E. <u>Jerome Leaster</u>.
       Chicago: Sergel, 1890.

       An agnostic man marries a postulant from a
       convent, but her guilt and remorse drive her
       nearly mad. Their daughter is driven to her
       death by a meddlesome priest. <u>Atlantic</u>
       called it morbid and biased.

1994. Southern, Terry. <u>Blue Movie</u>. New York:
       World, 1970.

       An outrageous satire on religious crusades
       against pornography. During the filming of
       a porno epic, a cardinal and his priests
       steal the prints and negatives. The film
       ends up in the Vatican.

1995. Spark, Muriel. <u>The Abbess of Crewe</u>. New
       York: Viking, 1974.

       A rollicking satire on a Watergate-type
       scandal in a convent.

1996. ————. <u>The Bachelors</u>. Philadelphia:
       Lippincott, 1961.

       A spiritualist is on trial for fraud, and
       his primary accuser is a Catholic who wanted
       to be a priest.

1997.   ————. The Comforters. Philadelphia:
         Lippincott, 1957.

         A satirical look at Catholic life in the
         context of a retelling of the Book of Job.
         The heroine is a slightly dotty writer and
         recent Catholic convert who discovers that
         conversion does not solve all of life's
         difficulties.

1998.   ————. The Mandelbaum Gate. New York:
         Knopf, 1965.

         Barbara, a middle-aged English teacher and
         Catholic convert, is deeply in love with a
         divorced archaeologist. While she is on a
         pilgrimage in Jerusalem, he is in Rome
         trying to get his first marriage annuled.
         While in the Holy City, she explores Jewish
         culture. A fluke, involving a false
         baptismal certificate, allows them to marry
         in the Catholic church.

1999.   ————. Memento Mori. Philadelphia:
         Lippincott, 1959.

         A group of elderly Londoners each receives
         a call saying, "Remember you must die."
         They reflect on the certainty of their
         deaths. The Catholic characters see death
         in terms of eternal life. One Catholic
         mystic reflects, "The more religious people
         are, the more perplexing I find them."

2000.   ————. Robinson. Philadelphia:
         Lippincott, 1958.

         Three survivors of a plane crash are
         rescued by a reclusive resident of a tiny
         island. The recluse is a former seminarian.
         The story's only female character is a
         convert. As in The Comforters, there is an
         investigation of the nature of truth and
         religious belief.

2001.   Speaight, Robert. The Unbroken Heart.
         Detroit: Basilian Press, 1946.

A sensitive intellectual struggles against skepticism.

2002.   Spearman, Frank. The Marriage Verdict. New
York: Scribner, 1923.

A bishop tries to help a woman, a recent convert, to remarry with the blessing of the church.

2003.   ————. Robert Kimberly. New York:
Scribner, 1911.

A Catholic woman divorces her non-Catholic husband but cannot marry her true love because of church disapproval. She dies and her lover becomes a devout Catholic.

2004.   Spellman, Francis (Cardinal). The
Foundling. New York: Scribner, 1951.

A blind soldier finds a baby in St. Patrick's Cathedral and raises him. An immensely popular but exceedingly mediocre story.

2005.   Spillman, Joseph. Victim to the Seal of
Confession. St. Louis: Herder, 1898.

A French priest is jailed for refusing to reveal knowledge of a crime obtained in confession.

2006.   ————. The Wonderful Flower of Woxingdon.
St. Louis: Herder, 1908.

The Babington Conspiracy.

2007.   Spindler, Karl. The Nun. New York:
Dewitt, 1850.

2008.   Stafford, Ann. The Blossoming Rod. London:
Hodder, 1955.

A woman finds health and peace through the intercession of the Virgin Mary.

2009.   ————. Seven Days Grace. London: Hodder,
1957.

A woman has a week before a critical
operation to find the reality of God.

2010.   Stahl, Norman and Don Horan. The Buried
        Man. New York: McGraw-Hill, 1985.

        A popular Polish priest in a Pennsyl-
        vania town is actually a KGB agent.

2011.   Stancourt, Louis. A Flower for Sign. New
        York: Macmillan, 1937.

        Autobiographical conversion novel.

2012.   Stand, Marguerite. Death Came With Flowers.
        London: Hale, 1966.

        A monk is poisoned, and a local doctor
        hires a private detective to find out why.

2013.   Stauffer, Donald Alfred. The Saint and the
        Hunchback. New York: Simon & Schuster,
        1946.

        Compelling fantasy about missionary monks
        in the 7th century.

2014.   Steegmuller, Francis. The Christening
        Party. New York: Farrar, Straus, 1960.

        Catholic family life circa 1906.

2015.   Stenius, Goran. The Bells of Rome. New
        York: P.J. Kenedy, 1961.

        A young Finnish art historian is converted
        while studying in Rome and becomes a priest.
        Because of his talents he is assigned to the
        Vatican archives. But a spiritual crisis
        makes him request a poverty-stricken parish,
        where he dies in his prime.

2016.   Stephan, Ruth. The Flight. New York:
        Knopf, 1956.

2017.   ———. My Crown, My Love. New York:
        Knopf, 1960.

        These two volumes recount the conversion
        and romantic life of Queen Christina of
        Sweden.

2018. Stephenson, Clarine. <u>Undine</u>. New York:
       Broadway, 1911.

       A Catholic woman in Jamaica undergoes a
       startling religious experience associated
       with an unusual portrait of Christ.

2019. Stern, Karl. <u>Through Dooms of Love</u>. New
       York: Farrar, Straus, 1960.

       A refugee and his daughter move toward
       health of the spirit through suffering and
       self-knowledge.

2020. Stevens, Clifford. <u>Flame Out of Dorset</u>.
       New York: Doubleday, 1964.

       A 20th century monk encounters a 13th
       century monk in this fantasy.

2021. Stiles, Hilary. <u>Assault on Innocence</u>.
       Albuquerque: B & K Publishers, 1987.

       Supposedly based on a real incident, this
       is an angry portrait of a priest's abuse of
       teenage boys and its effect on the lives of
       parishioners.

2022. Stoddard, Charles Warren. <u>For the Pleasure
       of His Company</u>. Notre Dame, IN: Ave
       Maria Press, 1897.

       Autobiographical conversion novel.

2023. Stokes, Cedric. <u>The Staffordshire
       Assassins</u>. London: Macdonald, 1945.

       Murder in a monastery.

2024. Stolpe, Sven. <u>Night Music</u>. New York:
       Sheed & Ward, 1960.

       "Religious and psychological novel about
       the workings of grace in human lives."
       (<u>Kirkus</u>)

2025. ————. <u>The Sound of a Distant Horn</u>. New
       York: Sheed & Ward, 1957.

       A gifted priest persecutes a fellow priest
       out of jealousy.

2026.   Stone, Robert.   A Flag for Sunrise.   New
        York: Knopf, 1981.

        A weary alcoholic priest and a radical nun
        are drawn into a Central American revolu-
        tion.

2027.   Storer, Maria.   Sir Christopher Leighton.
        St. Louis: Herder, 1915.

        An English baronet is so obsessed by anti-
        Catholic prejudice that he attempts to
        murder his Catholic nephew and heir.

2028.   Stowe, Harriet Beecher.   Agnes of Sorrento.
        Boston: Ticknor & Fields, 1862.

        Catholic Italy in the days of Savonarola.

2029.   Strong, Jason Rolfe.   The Starlight of the
        Hills.   New York: Pustet, 1923.

        A devout Catholic woman hesitates to marry
        a man who has drifted from the church and
        participates in labor agitation.   After he
        is shot, he returns to the church and to
        her.

2030.   Stuart, Francis.   The Pilgrimage.   London:
        Gollancz, 1955.

        A French bishop shows love and kindness
        toward the illegitimate daughter of his
        housekeeper.

2031.   ————.   Redemption.   New York: Devon-
        Adair, 1950.

        A kindly priest in a small Irish town
        becomes involved in sins of the flesh and
        murder.

2032.   Stuart, Henry Longan.   Weeping Cross.
        Chicago: Regnery, 1954.

        An Irish Catholic cavalier is sentenced to
        prison in Puritan New England in 1652.

2033.   Sugrue, Thomas.   Such is the Kingdom.   New
        York: Holt, 1940.

Irish Catholic family life in a factory
town.

2034. Sullivan, Richard Thomas. Summer After
       Summer. New York: Doubleday, 1942.

       A financially pressed young Catholic
       couple anxiously await the birth of an
       unplanned second child.

2035. Sullivan, Tony. In the Palm House. London:
       Deutsch, 1987.

       A young seminarian is torn between a
       sincere desire for the priesthood and the
       sensual temptations of the everyday world.

2036. Summers, Richard A. The Devil's Highway.
       New York: Nelson, 1937.

       Father Kino's missionary activities in
       Arizona.

2037. Sutton, Bertha Radford. Catherine de
       Gardeville. New York: Macmillan, 1930.

       Conversion of a well-bred English society
       girl.

2038. Sylvester, Harry. Dayspring. New York:
       Appleton, 1945.

       Spiritual regeneration of an archaeologist
       in New Mexico.

2039. ————. Dearly Beloved. New York: Duell,
       1942.

       A Catholic layman confronts racial
       prejudice among his fellow Catholics when he
       tries to help blacks in a Southern Maryland
       town.

2040. ————. A Golden Girl. New York:
       Harcourt, 1950.

       A young Catholic girl is torn between
       Catholic sexual standards and her free-
       wheeling, amoral life style.

2041.   ———.   Moon Gaffney. New York: Holt,
         1947.

         A brilliant, unflattering portrait of the
         New York Irish.

2042.   Synon, Mary. Copper Country. New York:
         P.J. Kenedy, 1931.

         "Thoroughly Catholic romance." (America)

2043.   Tabrah, Ruth M.   Pulaski Place. New York:
         Harper, 1950.

         A Polish Catholic war veteran returns home
         to find prejudice.

2044.   Taggart, Marion Ames.   Cable. New York:
         Benziger, 1923.

         An indifferent Catholic girl almost
         marries a divorced man.

2045.   Tannahill, Reay.   The World, the Flesh and
         the Devil. London: Century, 1985.

         Sex, politics and religion in 15th century
         Scotland.

2046.   Taylor, Elizabeth.   The Wedding Group. New
         York: Viking, 1968.

         A possessive Catholic mother ruins the
         marriage of her journalist son.

2047.   Teilhet, Darwin.   The Road to Glory. New
         York: Funk & Wagnalls, 1956.

         The last three years of Father Serra's
         life among his beloved California missions.

2048.   Templeton, Charles.   Act of God. Boston:
         Little, Brown, 1978.

         A cardinal challenges an archaeologist who
         claims to have found the body of Jesus.

2049.   Tennant, Roger.   The Litany of St. Charles.
         London: Joseph, 1968.

2050. Tenney, Sarah. <u>Marian Elwood</u>. New York: Dunigan, 1859.

A spirited and proud Catholic girl fights to maintain her faith in the household of her hostile uncle. (Second printing of Item 713)

2051. Terrell, Dorothy. <u>Common of Angels</u>. New York: Appleton, 1926.

A complicated love triangle among artists, who alternate between love for themselves and conversion to Catholicism.

2052. Thebaud, Augustus. <u>Louisa Kirkbridge</u>. New York: Collier, 1879.

Irish Catholic immigrants in New York.

2053. Thoby-Marcelin, Philippe. <u>All Men Are Mad</u>. New York: Farrar, Straus, 1970.

A priest tries to eradicate voodoo in Haiti.

2054. Thomas, Frances. <u>Seeing Things</u>. London: Gollancz, 1986.

When an Irish schoolgirl sees the Virgin Mary in a London park, reactions vary widely from skepticism to belief.

2055. Thompson, Clara M. <u>Hawthorndean</u>. Philadelphia: Cunningham, 1873.

Positive virtues of Catholic family life.

2056. Thompson, Dunstan. <u>The Dove with the Bough of Olive</u>. New York: Simon & Schuster, 1954.

Aristocratic Catholic Londoners are torn between worldliness and spiritual values.

2057. Thompson, Sylvia. <u>The Candle's Glory</u>. Boston: Little, Brown, 1953.

A divorced Catholic woman is counseled by a priest as she searches for peace and contentment.

2058. Thruston, Lucy Meacham. <u>Mistress Brent</u>.
       Boston: Little, Brown, 1901.

       Catholic Maryland in 1638.

2059. Thurston, Katherine. <u>The Fly on the Wheel</u>.
       London: Virago, 1987.

       The impact of illicit love on the Irish
       Catholic middle class. Originally published
       in 1908.

2060. Timperley, Rosemary. <u>The Echo-Game</u>.
       London: Hale, 1973.

2061. Tincker, Mary Agnes. <u>Grapes and Thorns</u>.
       New York: Christian Press, 1874.

       A priest is robbed and his mother is
       killed by the robber. The murderer
       confesses his crime but the priest is
       forbidden to reveal his identity. An
       innocent Jewish musician is convicted and
       sentenced to death. Justice triumphs in the
       end and the Jewish character is converted.

2062. ————. <u>House of Yorke</u>. New York:
       Catholic Publication Society, 1872.

       A love triangle set amidst Catholic-
       Protestant antagonisms in Ellsworth, Maine
       during the Know Nothing days.

2063. Torchia, Joseph. <u>The Kryptonite Kid</u>. New
       York: Holt, 1979.

       Two hapless boys suffer through parochial
       school and develop a fantasy world to
       survive.

2064. Tracy, Don. <u>Chesapeake Cavalier</u>. New York:
       Dial, 1949.

       Protestants and Catholics vie for control
       of the Chesapeake Bay in the 17th century.

2065. Tracy, Honor. <u>The First Day of Friday</u>. New
       York: Random House, 1963.

A lazy Irish Protestant landlord, newly impoverished by taxes, tries to fire his incompetent Catholic maid in this eccentric comedy.

2066.   ———. The Straight and Narrow Path. New York: Random House, 1956.

"Catholic readers, especially those of Irish descent, will probably find it highly scandalous." (Time)

2067.   Tremain, Rose. Letter to Sister Benedicta. New York: St. Martin's, 1978.

A woman, facing a crisis as her husband lies paralyzed, writes letters to the nun who taught her in a convent school many years ago. She has moved far from her Catholic upbringing but still yearns for love and hope.

2068.   Trent, Lynda. Wyndfell. New York: Nal/Onyx, 1988.

An English woman must choose between her family and her faith during the bitter religious conflict in 16th century England.

2069.   Trevino, Elizabeth Borton de. Even As You Love. New York: Crowell, 1957.

A young housewife discovers the meaning of love and saves her marriage.

2070.   ———. The Fourth Gift. New York: Doubleday, 1966.

Sympathetic account of the Cristero revolt in Mexico.

2071.   ———. The House on Bitterness Street. New York: Doubleday, 1970.

An aristocratic woman clings to a vital Catholic faith during the persecutions of the Mexican Revolution. She becomes a nun, saying, "I know why I was chosen. I who had been so wicked and self-willed and hateful was chosen, the better to show God's mercy and to reveal his glory."

2072. Trevor, Meriol. <u>Shadows and Images</u>. New
       York: McKay, 1962.

       A conversion novel featuring an Anglican
       clergyman's daughter. Cardinal Newman
       appears as a character.

2073. Trouncer, Margaret. <u>The Reluctant Abbess</u>.
       New York: Sheed & Ward, 1957.

       Biographical novel of the Abbess of Port
       Royal.

2074. ———. <u>The Nun</u>. New York: Sheed & Ward,
       1955.

       The life and trials of St. Margaret Mary
       Alacoque.

2075. Troy, Una. <u>The Graces of Ballykeen</u>. New
       York: Dutton, 1960.

       A witty tale of two nuns who run the
       workhouse in an Irish coastal town.

2076. Undset, Sigrid. <u>The Burning Bush</u>. New
       York: Knopf, 1932.

       A professor's conversion causes estrange-
       ment from his wife. Sequel to <u>The Wild
       Orchid</u>.

2077. ———. <u>Kristin Lavransdatter</u>. New York:
       Knopf, 1935.

       Massive trilogy of medieval Scandinavia.
       Winner of the Nobel Prize for literature.

2078. ———. <u>The Wild Orchid</u>. New York: Knopf,
       1931.

       A young university professor's growing
       interest in Catholicism conflicts with his
       free-thought upbringing.

2079. Valera, Juan. <u>Pepita Jimenez</u>. New York:
       Collier, 1900.

       A seminarian falls in love with a widow
       and marries her.

2080.   Van Greenaway, Peter. The Judas Gospel.
        New York: Atheneum, 1972.

        The Vatican sends an agent to purchase a
        new Dead Sea Scroll purporting to be the
        life of Christ written by Judas.

2081.   Van Rindt, Philippe. The Tetramacus
        Collection. London: Macdonald, 1977.

        A crippled Polish priest discovers proof
        of Vatican-Nazi ties in papers in the
        Vatican library. He steals the papers and
        many people try to recover them.

2082.   Van Zile, E.S. With Sword and Crucifix.
        New York: Harper, 1900.

        LaSalle and the French missionaries.

2083.   Vaughan, Agnes Carr. Bury Me in Ravenna.
        New York: Doubleday, 1962.

        Catholic life in 5th century Rome.

2084.   Verdick, Mary. A Place of Honor. New York:
        Doubleday, 1961.

        The investigation of an apparent suicide
        casts suspicion on an ex-seminarian.

2085.   Vidal, Nichole. The Right Hand. London:
        Deutsch, 1968.

        A Maronite priest and his wife live in
        great poverty.

2086.   Vitello, John A. Sicola, the Papal Bull.
        Huntington, IN: Our Sunday Visitor, 1979.

        Satire on modern liberal Catholicism.

2087.   Vollmoeller, Karl. The Last Miracle. New
        York: Duell, 1949.

        Beatification of a German nun.

2088.   Voynich, E.L. The Gadfly. New York: Holt,
        1897.

In 19th century Italy an atheist revolutionary meets his father, a famous cardinal.

2089. Vukelich, George. Fisherman's Beach. New
        York: St. Martin's, 1962.

        Franco-American family saga.

2090. Waddell, Helen. Peter Abelard. New York:
        Holt, 1933.

        The best of the Abelard-Heloise novels.

2091. Wallace, Irving. The Miracle. New York:
        Dutton, 1984.

        A stunning thriller about Lourdes filled
        with excellent characters and the possibi-
        lity of genuine miracles.

2092. Wallace, M.A. Well! Well! New York:
        Sadlier, 1863.

        An immigrant serving girl outwits her
        Protestant employers and brings about
        several conversions.

2093. Wallace, Mary. The Ruby Cross. New York:
        Benziger, 1917.

        A man deserts his wife and child after
        inheriting a fortune but comes to repentance
        and conversion.

2094. Walsh, Edmund A. The Woodcarver of Tyrol.
        New York: Harper, 1935.

        A woodcarver dies before completing a
        Pieta. His wife sets up a wayside shrine
        and completes the figure in her own way.

2095. Walsh, Jill Paton. Lapsing. New York: St.
        Martin's, 1987.

        An Oxford student is in love with the
        Catholic chaplain and has an affair with
        him. She eventually marries a dour Catholic
        but continues to love the priest and
        renounces her faith.

2096. Walsh, Louis J. The Guileless Saxon.
Dublin: Gill, 1917.

Clever satire on English prejudice against
Irish Catholics.

2097. Walsh, Thomas. The Eye of the Needle. New
York: Simon & Schuster, 1961.

A priest knows too much about the murder
of his brother's wife, but he refuses to
talk so that he does not implicate an
innocent man. He then becomes the main
suspect.

2098. Walsh, William Thomas. Out of the
Whirlwind. New York: McBride, 1935.

Passion and murder among Polish and
Lithuanian Catholics in a New England
industrial town. "It is an American
counterpart of the French Catholic novels
best represented by Mauriac." (New York
Times)

2099. Walworth, Mansfield. The Mission of Death.
New York: Sadlier, 1854.

The suffering of Catholics under the New
York Penal Laws.

2100. Ward, Mrs. Humphry. Helbeck of Bannisdale.
New York: Macmillan, 1898.

Religious differences between a fanatical
Catholic and a spirited skeptic destroy any
chance of romantic happiness.

2101. Ward, Josephine Mary (Mrs. Wilfrid). Horace
Blake. New York: Putnam, 1914.

Penetrating psychological study of a
dramatist who returns to the Catholic faith
on his deathbed after a lifetime of
rebellion against it.

2102. ————. Job Secretary. New York:
Longmans, 1911.

A married novelist falls in love with his married secretary, but both return to their mates.

2103.   ————.   The Light Behind the Bars.   New York: Lane, 1903.

An ambitious Catholic in British political life finds he must make too many compromises.

2104.   ————.   One Poor Scruple.   New York: Longmans, 1899.

A young English woman is tempted to marry a divorced man but refuses at the end.

2105.   ————.   Out of Due Time.   New York: Longmans, 1906.

The theme is the church's attitude toward the scientific spirit of the modern world.

2106.   ————.   Tudor Sunset.   New York: Longmans, 1932.

Vividly conceived and historically accurate depiction of the trials of Catholics in Elizabethan England.

2107.   Ward, Leo Richard.   Holding Up the Hills. New York: Sheed & Ward, 1941.

Irish Catholics struggle to maintain old customs in Iowa.

2108.   Warner, Marina.   In a Dark Wood.   New York: Knopf, 1977.

A scholarly priest falls in love with an attractive musicologist. His faith is also disturbed after interviewing a Sicilian girl who claims to have seen the Virgin Mary.

2109.   Warner, Rex.   The Converts.   Boston: Little, Brown, 1967.

St. Augustine.

2110.   Warner, Sylvia Townsend. The Corner That
        Held Them. New York: Viking, 1948.

        Life in a 14th century priory.

2111.   Watson, Peter. Crusade. London: Hutchin-
        son, 1987.

        An American Pope sells Vatican art
        treasures to raise money for disaster
        victims, but this leads to controversy.

2112.   Waugh, Auberon. The Foxglove Saga. New
        York: Simon & Schuster, 1961.

        Satire on moral decay in a Catholic prep
        school.

2113.   Waugh, Evelyn. Brideshead Revisited.
        Boston: Little, Brown, 1946.

        A masterfully told story of a doomed
        family of English aristocrats. "The worse I
        am, the more I need God."

2114.   ———. Helena. New York: Doubleday,
        1950.

        Life of St. Helena and her search for the
        True Cross.

2115.   ———. The Ordeal of Gilbert Pinfold.
        Boston: Little, Brown, 1957.

        Portrait of a cranky colonel whose private
        demons almost overwhelm him. He is clearly
        Catholic but finds little solace in his
        faith.

2116.   ———. Sword of Honour. Boston: Little,
        Brown, 1966.

        A one-volume work including Men at Arms,
        Officers and Gentlemen and Unconditional
        Surrender, this comprises the Guy Crouchback
        trilogy. Crouchback is an upperclass
        officer in World War II who grows increas-
        ingly disaffected by the war. Catholic
        doctrine and ritual serve important
        functions in shaping his life and character.

2117.   Weatherby, William J.   One of our Priests is
        Missing. New York: Doubleday, 1968.

        An English priest grows disillusioned by
        problems in his parish. "This moving book
        sheds light on the role of the priest."
        (Library Journal)

2118.   Webb, Henry B.L.   Dew in April. New York:
        Kendall, 1935.

        Love story set in a convent.

2119.   Webb, Jack.   The Bad Blonde. New York:
        Rinehart, 1956.

        Father Shanley, an astute parish priest in
        a tough Los Angeles neighborhood, teams up
        with a Jesish cop, Sammy Golden, to bring
        criminals to justice. In this case he
        fights a dope ring.

2120.   ———.   The Big Sin. New York: Rinehart,
        1952.

        Ignoring strong evidence, Shanley refuses
        to believe that a gorgeous Catholic showgirl,
        a parishioner of his, committed suicide.

2121.   ———.   The Brass Halo. New York:
        Rinehart, 1957.

        A nightclub singer disappears after a
        man's body is found on her dressing room
        floor.

2122.   ———.   The Broken Doll. New York:
        Rinehart, 1955.

        An heiress is kidnapped.

2123.   ———.   The Damned Lovely. New York:
        Rinehart, 1954.

        The murder of a rabbi.

2124.   ———.   The Deadly Sex. New York:
        Rinehart, 1959.

        Murder in the jukebox business.

2125. ———. The Delicate Darling. New York: Rinehart, 1959.

A vanishing poet, foreign intrigue and murder.

2126. ———. The Gilded Witch. Evanston, IL: Regency, 1963.

Robbery, murder and a touch of satanism.

2127. ———. The Naked Angel. New York: Rinehart, 1953.

A man is murdered before the First Station of the Cross as he is saying penance for his sins.

2128. Weeks, Joseph. All Our Yesterdays. New York: Rinehart, 1955.

A Catholic man uses religion as an excuse not to marry the rich Protestant girl he has made pregnant.

2129. Wells, Evelyn. A City for St. Francis. New York: Doubleday, 1967.

The California missions.

2130. Werfel, Franz. Embezzled Heaven. New York: Viking, 1940.

A shrewd peasant woman tries to guarantee her entrance into heaven by paying for her worthless nephew's priestly training. When she discovers she has been tricked, she goes to Rome to see the Pope.

2131. ———. The Song of Bernadette. New York: Viking, 1942.

Immensely popular retelling of the appearance of the Virgin Mary to Bernadette.

2132. West, Morris L. The Clowns of God. New York: Morrow, 1981.

Sometime in the future the Pope abdicates
under duress. He is sent to a monastery
because the cardinals think he is crazy. He
claims to have had a personal revelation of
the Second Coming of Christ. "A stunning
accomplishment." (<u>Library Journal</u>)

2133.   ————. <u>The Devil's Advocate</u>. New York:
         Morrow, 1959.

A priest is assigned by the Vatican to
investigate the case of an Italian layman
being considered for canonization. This
brilliant novel's profound theology is
explored by James M. Connolly in the May 28,
1960 issue of <u>America</u>.

2134.   ————. <u>The Shoes of the Fisherman</u>. New
         York: Morrow, 1963.

A compassionate, visionary Russian Pope
brings a new world-view to the Vatican.

2135.   Westlake, Donald E. <u>Brother's Keepers</u>. New
         York: M. Evans, 1975.

A humorous tale of Park Avenue monks who
try to preserve their way of life.

2136.   ————. <u>Good Behavior</u>. New York:
         Mysterious Press, 1986.

A burglar trapped in a convent after a
failed robbery makes a deal with the nuns.
He will rescue a sister abducted by her
father and they will not turn him in to the
police.

2137.   Whalen, Louise Margaret. <u>Father Ladden,
         Curate</u>. New York: Magnificat Press,
         1920.

A young priest is enthusiastic and filled
with joy.

2138.   Whalen, Will W. <u>Celibate Father</u>. St.
         Louis: Herder, 1927.

A kind priest cares for his orphaned
nieces.

2139. ———. Ex-Nun. St. Louis: Herder, 1927.

A nun is forced to relinquish her vows because of an hereditary legal problem.

2140. ———. The Priest Who Vanished. Ozone Park, NY: Catholic Literary Guild, 1942.

"Catholic fiction hits a new low with the publication of this pseudo-detective story." (Commonweal)

2141. ———. What Priests Never Tell. St. Louis: Herder, 1927.

A priest tries to reconcile a squabbling married couple in this comedy.

2142. White, Antonia. Beyond the Glass. New York: Regnery, 1955.

"One of the best Catholic novels." (Ave Maria)

2143. ———. Frost in May. New York: Viking, 1933.

A brilliant study of convent school life, showing how a mean-spirited Mother Superior tries to break the will of an individualistic school girl.

2144. ———. The Lost Traveller. New York: Viking, 1950.

The emotional life of an adolescent girl and her convert parents.

2145. White, Helen Constance. Bird of Fire. New York: Macmillan, 1959.

St. Francis of Assisi.

2146. ———. Dust on the King's Highway. New York: Macmillan, 1947.

The building of the Franciscan missions in California.

2147.   ———. The Four Rivers of Paradise. New
        York: Macmillan, 1955.

        Fall of the Roman Empire as seen through
        the eyes of a young Christian.

2148.   ———. Not Built With Hands. New York:
        Macmillan, 1935.

        Church-state struggles in the 11th
        century.

2149.   ———. To the End of the World. New York:
        Macmillan, 1939.

        A devoted priest tries to maintain his
        ministry during the French Revolution's
        Reign of Terror.

2150.   ———. A Watch in the Night. New York:
        Macmillan, 1933.

        Sympathetic portrait of the Middle Ages.
        The novel is based on the life of Jacopone
        da Todi, a lawyer and poet who joined the
        Franciscans after his wife's death and went
        about helping the poor and unfortunate.

2151.   White, Olive Bernardine. The King's Good
        Servant. New York: Macmillan, 1936.

        St. Thomas More.

2152.   ———. Late Harvest. New York:
        Macmillan, 1940.

        "Rarely is the Catholic side of religious
        upheavals in Elizabethan England presented
        so justly as here." (Christian Century)

2153.   White, Patrick. Riders in the Chariot. New
        York: Viking, 1961.

        Three Australian Jews are converted for
        reasons of convenience, not conviction.

2154.   White, Terence de Vere. The Distance and
        the Dark. London: Gollancz, 1973.

A Protestant farmer in a heavily Catholic
area of Ireland is increasingly disturbed by
the Troubles in the North.

2155.   Wibberley, Leonard. The Last Stand of
        Father Felix. New York: Morrow, 1974.

        Portrait of a courageous, eccentric
        missionary priest.

2156.   ———. Stranger at Killnock. New York:
        Putnam, 1961.

        On the isolated Atlantic coast of Ireland,
        a Christ-like stranger appears.

2157.   Wilby, Noel Macdonald. A Merry Eternity: A
        Romance of Sir Thomas More's Household.
        New York: Benziger, 1934.

2158.   Wilder, Thornton Niven. The Bridge at San
        Luis Rey. New York: Boni, 1927.

        A Franciscan monk sees five people plunged
        to their death when a bridge collapses. He
        views the accident as the judgment of God
        and probes into the lives of the victims.

2159.   ———. The Cabala. New York: Boni, 1926.

        Church-state intrigue in Rome.

2160.   Williamson, Thames Ross. Christine Roux.
        New York: Current Books, 1945.

        A pious novice is turned out of her
        convent when the French government abolishes
        religious orders. She tries to adjust to
        secular life in Paris.

2161.   Wilmot-Buxton, Ethel Macy. Adventures
        Perilous. London: Sands, 1928.

        The life, labors and persecution of Father
        John Gerard, a priest who fled England
        during the persecutions.

2162.   ———. Gildersleeves. St. Louis: Herder,
        1921.

Conversion of an English schoolteacher.

2163.   Wilson, John Rowan. The Double Blind. New
        York: Doubleday, 1960.

        On a South Atlantic island the local
        priest opposes a bacteriologist's experiment
        with a new vaccine.

2164.   Wise, Evelyn Voss. The Light of Stars.
        Milwaukee: Bruce, 1946.

        A warm-hearted, caring priest loves his
        Baltimore parishioners.

2165.   ————. The Long Tomorrow. New York:
        Appleton, 1938.

        A priest in a Minnesota prairie town
        serves as doctor, friend and advisor to all
        the people.

2166.   ————. Mary Darlin'. New York: Appleton,
        1943.

        A courageous nurse becomes a nun.

2167.   Wiseman, Nicholas (Cardinal). Fabiola; or,
        The Church of the Catacombs. London:
        Burns & Oates, 1854.

        A best-selling story of the conversion of
        a pagan woman.

2168.   Wright, June. Make-Up for Murder. London:
        1966.

        Mother Paul solves a murder in the
        theatre world.

2169.   Wylie, Elinor H. The Venetian Glass Nephew.
        New York: Doran, 1925.

        A subtle, delicate and witty fantasy about
        an 18th century cardinal.

2170.   Wylie, I.A.R. Candles for Therese. New
        York: Random House, 1951.

An embittered artist seeks vengeance on those who betrayed his brother in Nazi occupied France. An innkeeper's daughter and a wise nun urge him to forgive.

2171. Wynne, May. Henry of Navarre. New York: Putnam, 1904.

2172. Wynne, May. The Silent Captain. London: Paul, 1914.

2173. ———. A Trap for Navarre. London: Hodder, 1922.

Three tales of the Religious Wars in France.

2174. Yanez, Agustin. The Edge of the Storm. Austin, TX: University of Texas Press, 1963.

Three Mexican priests try to resist change but are engulfed by it.

2175. Yarbro, Chelsea Quinn. A Mortal Glamour. New York: Bantam, 1985.

Demon possession and hallucination in a French convent.

2176. Yeo, Margaret. A King of Shadows. New York: Macmillan, 1929.

Religious conflict in Scotland.

2177. ———. Salt. New York: Sheed & Ward, 1932.

St. Ignatius Loyola and St. Philip Neri.

2178. ———. Uncertain Glory. New York: Sheed & Ward, 1931.

The secret son of Charles II is debarred by his Catholic faith from succeeding to the throne.

2179. Yoseloff, Martin. The Girl in the Spike-Heeled Shoes. New York: Dutton, 1949.

A priest tries to save a girl from a life of sin.

2180. Young, Joseph A. Old St. Mary's New
        Assistant. New York: Benziger, 1930.

        A whimsical look at the early years of a
        priest's ministry.

2181. ————. Shepherds on the Move. New York:
        Benziger, 1932.

2182. Zermatten, Maurice. The Fountain of
        Arethusa. New York: Doubleday, 1960.

        A French priest struggles with an evil man
        who uses the seal of the confessional to
        falsely implicate the priest in a murder.
        "An unusual spiritual and arresting novel."
        (New York Times).

2183. Ziegler, Isabelle. The Nine Days of Father
        Serra. New York: Longmans, 1951.

        Father Serra makes a novena to St. Joseph
        before deciding God wants him to establish
        a network of missions.

2184. Zola, Emile. The Abbe's Temptation. New
        York: Peterson, 1879.

        A French village priest falls passionately
        and hopelessly in love with a young woman,
        but their idyllic romance cannot last. He
        returns to the altar, and his lover dies.
        "Through the whole romance runs the deep
        undertone of the most fervent type of Roman
        Catholic faith and piety." (Boston Literary
        World)

2185. ————. The Sin of Father Mouret. New
        York: Peterson, 1875.

        A myth-like story of a devout priest who
        falls in love.

Addenda:

2186. Baring, Maurice. <u>Passing By</u>. London:
Heinemann, 1921.

A young man's social and spiritual
struggles culminate in his conversion.

2187. Freind, Stephen F. <u>God's Children</u>. New
York: Morrow, 1987.

Three Villanova graduates follow different
paths. One becomes a priest. One goes into
the Mafia. The other becomes a prominent
Pennsylvania politician who gets embroiled
in the abortion controversy.

2188. McGahern, John. <u>The Leavetaking</u>. Boston:
Little, Brown, 1974.

A teacher in a Catholic school in Ireland
finds that his sexual awakening and his
eventual marriage outside the church
require him to leave his position. Eventually he must leave Ireland itself.

2189. Rothman, Anne and Ken Hicks. <u>Theft of the
Shroud</u>. New York: Dell, 1984.

A journalist tries to discover who stole
the most sacred relic in the world.

2190. Echewa, T. Obinkaram. <u>The Land's Lord</u>.
Westport, CT: Lawrence Hill, 1976.

A French army deserter becomes a
missionary in Africa.

2191. McDonough, Tom. <u>Virgin with Child</u>. New
York: Viking, 1981.

A Brooklyn priest falls in love with a
nun.

2192. Perriam, Wendy. <u>After Purple</u>. New York:
St. Martin's Press, 1982.

A symbolic tale of sex, violence and
religion.

THE 100 BEST CATHOLIC NOVELS

Almedingen, Edith Martha. _The Winter in the Heart_.

Ayscough, John. _Mariquita_.

Baring, Maurice. _Cat's Cradle_.

————. _In My End Is My Beginning_.

Benson, Robert Hugh. _Lord of the World_.

Bernanos, Georges. _The Diary of a Country Priest_.

Bloy, Leon. _The Woman Who Was Poor_.

Bowen, Robert O. _The Weight of the Cross_.

Braine, John. _The Jealous God_.

Byrne, Beverly. _Women's Rites_.

Callaghan, Morley. _Such Is My Beloved_.

Carroll, James. _Prince of Peace_.

Cather, Willa. _Death Comes for the Archbishop_.

————. _Shadows on the Rock_.

Coccioli, Carlo. _The White Stone_.

Connolly, Miles. _Mr. Blue_.

Cooper, Elizabeth Ann. _No Little Thing_.

Corvo, Baron. _Hadrian VII_.

Crone, Anne. _Bridie Steen_.

Cronin, A.J. _The Keys of the Kingdom_.

Cullinan, Elizabeth. House of Gold.

Currier, Isabel. The Young and the Immortal.

Davis, Dorothy Salisbury. A Gentle Murderer.

Delafield, E.M. Turn Back the Leaves.

Descalzo, Martin. God's Frontier.

DuMaurier, Angela. The Road to Leenane.

Dunne, John Gregory. True Confessions.

Eliot, Ethel Cook. Her Soul to Keep.

Endo, Shusaku. Wonderful Fool.

Fielding, Gabriel. Eight Days.

Fogazzaro, Antonio. The Saint.

Fremantle, Anne. By Grace of Love.

Fuentes, Carlos. The Good Conscience.

Galvez, Manuel. Holy Wednesday.

Garvin, Viola. Child of Light.

Gilford, Charles B. Quest for Innocence.

Gironella, Jose Maria. The Cypresses Believe in God.

Godden, Rumer. In This House of Brede.

Gordon, Caroline. The Malefactors.

Gordon, Mary. Final Payments.

Green, Julian. Each In His Darkness.

Greene, Graham. Brighton Rock.

————. The End of the Affair.

————. The Heart of the Matter.

————. The Power and the Glory.

Hanley, Gerald. Without Love.

Hassler, Jon. A Green Journey.

Hemon, Louis. Maria Chapdelaine.

Higgins, Jack. A Prayer for the Dying.

Hobbes, John Oliver. Robert Orange.

————. The School for Saints.

Holton, Leonard (Leonard Wibberley). The Saint
    Maker.

Horgan, Paul. Things As They Are.

Houselander, Caryll. The Dry Wood.

Kaye-Smith, Sheila. Superstition Corner.

Kent, Michael. The Mass of Brother Michel.

Lappin, Peter. The Land of Cain.

Madden, Deirdre. Hidden Symptoms.

Mahoney, Sister Irene. An Accidental Grace.

Mannin, Ethel. Late Have I Loved Thee.

Manzoni, Alessandro. The Betrothed.

Marshall, Bruce. The Fair Bride.

————. The World, the Flesh, and Father Smith.

Martin du Gard, Roger. Jean Barois.

Mauriac, Francois. Viper's Tangle.

————. Woman of the Pharisees.

Miller, Walter M., Jr. A Canticle for Leibowitz.

Molloy, Robert. Pride's Way.

Montaurier, Jean. A Passage Through Fire.

Moore, Brian. Catholics.

————. Cold Heaven.

Moore, George. Evelyn Innes.

————. Sister Teresa.

Novak, Michael. The Tiber Was Silver.

O'Brien, Kate. The Land of Spices.

O'Connor, Edwin. The Edge of Sadness.

Oliver, John Rathbone. Rock and Sand.

Percy, Walker. Love in the Ruins.

Plagemann, Bentz. The Heart of Silence.

Powers, J.F. Morte d'Urban.

Prescott, H.F.M. The Man on a Donkey.

Reed, Kit. At War As Children.

Shaw, Russell B. The Dark Disciple.

Sheed, Wilfred. The Hack.

Spark, Muriel. The Comforters.

————. The Mandelbaum Gate.

Steegmuller, Francis. The Christening Party.

Sylvester, Harry. Dearly Beloved.

————. Moon Gaffney.

Undset, Sigrid. Kristin Lavransdatter.

Walsh, Thomas. The Eye of the Needle.

Waugh, Evelyn. Brideshead Revisited.

Werfel, Franz. Embezzled Heaven.

West, Morris L. The Clowns of God.

————. The Devil's Advocate.

————. The Shoes of the Fisherman.

White, Antonia. Frost in May.

Wilder, Thornton. The Bridge at San Luis Rey.

Wylie, I.A.R. Candles for Therese.

Zermatten, Maurice. The Fountain of Arethusa.

SUBJECT INDEX

Abelard & Heloise 1611, 1653, 1684, 2089
Abortion 842, 1009, 2187
Adultery 624, 655, 658, 790, 915, 1839
Africa 618, 787, 829, 997, 1061, 1183, 1185, 1267,
  1325, 1537, 1753, 1826, 2155, 2190
Albania 1403
Alcoholism 1940
Allegory – see Fantasy
Anthony, St. 586
Anti-Catholicism 494, 503, 520, 523, 536, 541-542,
  555-556, 595-597, 600, 605, 609, 647, 664, 667,
  677-678, 737, 743, 751-755, 758, 850, 865,
  867-869, 880, 886-888, 901, 934, 941-942, 1099,
  1100, 1115, 1126, 1158-1159, 1164, 1233, 1241,
  1302, 1362, 1366, 1412, 1420, 1423, 1441, 1472,
  1483, 1570, 1612, 1614, 1679-1680, 1691, 1739,
  1746, 1806, 1901, 1904-1910, 1993, 2027, 2062,
  2068, 2070-2071, 2099, 2106, 2161, 2178
Apparition – see Visions
Aquinas, St. Thomas 771, 931
Archbishop – see Bishops
Argentina 1109
Arizona 563, 2036
Atheism 657, 793, 858, 878, 1060, 1127, 1358,
  1367, 1441, 1476, 1490, 1542, 1580, 1814, 1855,
  1871, 1880, 2088
Augustine, St. 932, 2109
Australia 497, 841, 1089, 1375-1376, 1406, 1572,
  1662, 1749, 2153
Austria 1192, 1511, 2094, 2130

Becket, St. Thomas 985, 1624, 1672
Benedict, St. 926
Bernard, St. 861, 1836
Birth Control 514, 548-549, 631, 660, 1469, 1518,
  1700
Bishops 625, 631, 777, 879, 1038, 1042, 1242,
  1258, 1283, 1309, 1499, 1518, 1522, 1587, 1606,
  1677, 1895, 1967, 2002, 2030

289

Brazil   745, 873, 1468, 1989

California   670-671, 891, 920, 989, 1110, 1122,
    1235, 1365, 1648, 1698, 1726, 1734-1735, 1799,
    1856, 1865, 1926, 2119-2127
California Missions   525, 773, 1064, 1194, 1284,
    1347, 1408, 1429, 2047, 2129, 2146, 2183
Canada   720, 884, 889, 903, 956, 1041, 1224, 1491,
    1646, 1667, 1917-1918   (See also Quebec)
Cardinals   517, 1062, 1073, 1085, 1169, 1227, 1269,
    1301, 1525, 1572, 1649, 1671, 1711, 1780-1781,
    1826, 1869, 1932, 1986, 1988, 2048, 2088, 2169
Catherine of Siena, St.   930, 1195
Catholic Colleges   490, 638, 651, 994, 1036-1037,
    1276, 1377, 1407, 1581, 1589, 1735, 1782, 1843,
    1952, 1974, 2186
Catholic Hospitals   1317, 1319, 1393, 1627
Catholic Schools   507, 512, 649, 684, 786, 965,
    1206, 1273, 1359, 1401, 1427, 1535, 1547, 1913,
    1922, 2063, 2112, 2188
Catholic-Jewish Relations   521, 571, 744, 834, 974,
    1041, 1096, 1103, 1118, 1142, 1181, 1211, 1349,
    1421, 1440, 1450, 1502, 1566, 1621, 1742, 1764,
    1874, 2061, 2123, 2153
Catholic-Muslim Relations   656, 882
Catholic-Protestant Relations   497, 499, 501,
    526-528, 541-542, 546-548, 564, 612, 628, 642,
    677, 694, 703, 722, 743, 751-758, 796, 863, 865,
    867-869, 919, 991, 1044, 1056, 1065, 1104, 1108,
    1123, 1205, 1207, 1221, 1241, 1255, 1265-1266,
    1378, 1424, 1446-1447, 1458-1461, 1479, 1482,
    1491-1493, 1563, 1615, 1650, 1661, 1670, 1683,
    1728, 1730, 1875, 1892, 1944-1945, 1948, 1973,
    1975, 2128, 2154
Central America   689, 2026
China   562, 866, 1084, 1854, 1881
Christmas   668, 681, 764, 852, 993, 1027, 1105,
    1303-4, 1454-55, 1734, 1775, 1954
Colombia   1306
Colorado   564
Communism   665, 853, 1186, 1196-1201, 1363, 1403,
    1411, 1549, 1596, 1649, 1759, 1831-32, 1853
Connecticut   570, 2014, 2033
Convent Schools   593, 884, 903, 935, 1093, 1128,
    1224, 1234, 1318, 1365, 1439, 1634, 1658, 1736,
    1760, 1800, 1858, 1968-69, 2143
Convents - see Nuns

Converts and Conversion   491-93, 528, 530, 533,
   546, 568, 570, 575-77, 597, 601, 604, 606, 620,
   626-27, 647, 689, 710-11, 716-17, 725, 734-36,
   752-54, 772, 799, 800, 802-3, 805-7, 811, 813,
   817, 819, 821, 835, 878, 894, 913, 916-18,
   960-61, 967, 980-82, 1006, 1014, 1021, 1025,
   1039, 1046, 1061, 1102-03, 1113, 1130, 1143,
   1146-47, 1208, 1227, 1238-40, 1243, 1263, 1268,
   1282, 1308, 1328-29, 1339-40, 1344, 1349, 1353,
   1358, 1367, 1402, 1404, 1413, 1425, 1432, 1439,
   1448, 1461, 1475, 1484, 1499, 1511, 1532-34,
   1542, 1608, 1615, 1628, 1639, 1646, 1655, 1665,
   1681-82, 1752, 1760, 1764, 1791-93, 1798, 1814,
   1818, 1838, 1842, 1845-48, 1850-51, 1884, 1898,
   1912, 1916, 1926, 1934, 1936-37, 1947-48, 1956,
   1964, 1984-85, 1991, 1997-98, 2000, 2003, 2011,
   2015-17, 2022, 2037, 2061, 2072, 2076, 2078,
   2092-93, 2101, 2109, 2143-44, 2153, 2162, 2167
Crusades   861, 983, 988, 1116, 1409-10, 1737, 1925,
   1958
Cuba   1283
Czech-Americans   962, 1740
Czechoslovakia   1474, 1759

Damien, Father   727
Detective Stories - see Murder Mysteries
Diocesan Newspapers   623, 1957
Divorce   560, 672, 722, 804, 808, 814, 855, 859,
   864, 1058, 1077, 1380-83, 1699, 1758, 1852, 2003,
   2044, 2057, 2104

Edward, St.   984
England   494-95, 500, 509-10, 520, 535-6, 552-56,
   567, 583, 594-601, 603-08, 620, 643-44, 678,
   680-83, 719, 737, 739, 742, 764, 791, 799, 850,
   872, 877, 886, 888, 907, 906-18, 934, 941-42,
   944, 1006, 1093, 1095, 1099-1102, 1119, 1128,
   1141, 1151, 1164-65, 1182, 1213, 1215, 1217,
   1221-22, 1230, 1233, 1271, 1279-80, 1302, 1311,
   1345, 1353, 1362, 1366-67, 1369, 1401, 1419-20,
   1423, 1458, 1469-72, 1484, 1490, 1492-93, 1503,
   1506, 1517-18, 1539-41, 1579, 1610, 1612, 1614,
   1624, 1633-34, 1659-61, 1672, 1691, 1739,
   1750-52, 1760, 1766-79, 1798, 1802, 1806, 1812,
   1834, 1839, 1864, 1893, 1951, 1968-69, 1975,
   1977-82, 1995-97, 1999, 2006, 2012, 2023, 2027,
   2035, 2037, 2046, 2054, 2056, 2068, 2072, 2095,
   2100-2106, 2110, 2112-13, 2115-17, 2142-44,
   2151-51, 2157, 2161-62, 2178

Exorcism   630, 637, 905, 1894

Family Life   1015, 1027, 1035, 1105, 1129, 1287,
   1613, 1698, 1865, 1885-86, 1983, 2014, 2034,
   2055
Fantasy Novels   598, 602, 635, 838, 850, 1059,
   1086, 1096, 1161, 1180, 1262, 1323, 1379, 1414,
   1416, 1433, 1448, 1455, 1505, 1543, 1625, 1632,
   1793, 1859, 1864, 1872, 1892, 1921, 1977-78,
   1980, 2013, 2020, 2169
Fatima   946, 1291
Finland   505
Florida   970-71, 1283
France   558, 575-82, 613-17, 619, 640, 697, 779-81,
   788, 870, 880, 900, 906, 969, 970-71, 1032, 1086,
   1090, 1138, 1140, 1166, 1179-80, 1191, 1204,
   1208, 1212, 1234, 1275, 1301, 1307, 1312,
   1320-21, 1332, 1337-41, 1379, 1384, 1405, 1441,
   1447, 1450, 1462-63, 1485-87, 1501-02, 1504,
   1526, 1542, 1552-61, 1617, 1625, 1644, 1665,
   1718, 1736, 1782-83, 1817, 1836, 1839, 1846,
   1871, 1887, 1889, 1901, 1913, 1932, 1950, 2005,
   2030, 2073-74, 2090-91, 2118, 2131, 2149, 2160,
   2170, 2171-73, 2175, 2182, 2184-85, 2192.
Francis de Sales, St.   585
Francis of Assisi, St.   666, 928, 1368, 2145
Franco-Americans   975, 1436-38, 1797, 1867-68, 2089

Galileo   1237
Georgia   1738
German-Americans   955, 959
Germany   566, 645-46, 714, 796, 1160, 1385, 1510,
   1919, 2087
Gordon Riots   1233
Goretti, Maria   937
Growing Up Catholic   512, 684, 732-33, 851, 881,
   1112, 1305, 1795-97, 1861
Gunpowder Plot   494, 609

Haiti   685, 2053
Helena, St.   2114
Hidalgo, Father   1150
Historical Novels   488, 494, 502-03, 509-10, 520,
   523, 525, 529, 534, 536, 540, 551, 555-56, 559,
   572, 583-86, 595-97, 600, 605, 607, 609, 633,
   664, 666-67, 669, 673-75, 687-88, 703, 707,
   718-19, 739, 741, 764, 771, 775, 777, 791-92,

Historical Novels (continued) 796, 846, 861, 877,
    882-83, 886, 888, 895, 906, 911, 926-34, 942,
    991, 1001, 1004-05, 1064, 1085, 1099, 1115, 1116,
    1126, 1139, 1150, 1155, 1158-59, 1192-93, 1195,
    1204, 1211, 1233, 1237, 1255, 1264, 1269,
    1301-02, 1312, 1347, 1353, 1356, 1362, 1366,
    1368, 1378, 1387, 1408-10, 1419-20, 1423, 1440,
    1458, 1472, 1480, 1492-93, 1504, 1513, 1517,
    1544, 1567, 1609-11, 1612, 1614, 1624, 1630,
    1653, 1663-66, 1672, 1675, 1679-81, 1684, 1687,
    1691, 1721-22, 1725, 1737, 1739, 1746, 1755-56,
    1766-79, 1806, 1812, 1836, 1876, 1887, 1889,
    1898, 1899, 1920, 1925, 1931-32, 1951, 1958,
    1982, 2006, 2016-17, 2032, 2045, 2058, 2064,
    2068, 2070, 2073-74, 2077, 2082-83, 2090, 2106,
    2109-10, 2114, 2145-52, 2157, 2161, 2171-73,
    2175-78
Holland 1476, 1930
Holy Year 809, 1274, 1972
Homosexuality 507, 592, 908, 1501, 1503, 1786,
    1796, 1920, 1992, 2021
Horror Novels 852, 905, 1216, 1258, 1355, 1757,
    1922, 2175
Huguenots 488, 741, 970-71, 1139, 1301, 1312,
    1447, 2171-73
Humorous Novels 545, 619, 646, 649, 680-83,
    718-19, 732-33, 748, 751, 836-38, 890, 893, 939,
    948, 1036-37, 1091, 1122, 1131, 1136, 1195-1201,
    1354, 1371, 1402, 1520-22, 1528, 1644, 1656,
    1748, 1761-62, 1808-10, 1861, 1874, 1882, 1946,
    1950, 1959, 1994-95, 2063, 2065-66, 2075, 2086,
    2096, 2112, 2135-36, 2141
Hungary 517, 1363, 1411, 1832, 1834

Illinois 512, 790, 1038, 1048-54, 1114, 1167-78,
    1586-87, 1590-92, 1594-95, 1598, 1600-02, 1747,
    1808-10, 1821-24, 2055
India 626, 864, 913, 1278, 1281
Indians - see Native Americans
Iowa 1908, 2047
Ireland 542-43, 584, 642, 674, 677, 684, 701-04,
    748, 770, 842, 844, 863, 874, 898, 992, 1007,
    1055, 1065, 1092, 1115, 1125-26, 1129, 1203,
    1205-06, 1209, 1242, 1255, 1257, 1359-61,
    1389-90, 1430, 1478, 1483, 1494-95, 1511, 1573,
    1581, 1604-05, 1647, 1650, 1654, 1656, 1661,
    1706, 1712, 1715, 1717, 1719-20, 1722, 1801,
    1804, 1816, 1820, 1899, 1909-10, 1923, 1931,
    1971, 2031, 2059, 2065-66, 2075, 2154, 2156, 2188

Irish-Americans   652, 696, 768, 840, 851, 875, 881,
    885, 901, 910, 922-23, 947, 952, 954, 1048-54,
    1067, 1069, 1071, 1167-78, 1244, 1257, 1333-35,
    1402, 1412, 1514, 1582, 1584-85, 1663, 1723,
    1738, 1819, 1972, 1983, 2033, 2041, 2052, 2107
Irish Republican Army (IRA)   765, 768, 827, 910,
    1257, 1271, 1891
Israel   1998
Italian-Americans   936, 938, 1110, 1507, 1815
Italy   518, 550, 586, 610, 621, 666, 669, 706, 709,
    744, 746, 763, 784, 809-10, 821, 831-33, 909,
    928, 1004-05, 1042, 1082, 1085, 1107, 1195, 1201,
    1227-29, 1243, 1251, 1269, 1288, 1368, 1466,
    1480, 1484, 1513, 1534, 1544, 1567, 1670-71,
    1696, 1703, 1742, 1748, 1790, 1838, 1874, 1935,
    1992, 2028, 2088, 2159, 2161, 2169,

Jamaica   824, 2018
Japan   1028-31, 1620, 1675
Jean de Brebeuf   1755
Jogues, Isaac   782
John of the Cross, St.   1876

Kansas   1582, 1825
Kentucky   1415, 1464-65, 2029
Know-Nothings   743, 751, 901, 2062

Labor Problems   1315, 1498, 2029
Lepers   727, 783, 1010, 1013
Loss of Faith   1048-55, 1068-69, 1074, 1103, 1221,
    1369, 1661, 1765, 1784, 2067
Louisiana   848, 1318, 1538, 1663-64, 1666
Lourdes   662, 1275, 2091, 2192
Loyola, St. Ignatius   927, 2177

Maine   1867-68, 2062
Malta   1641
Marquette, Fr.   846
Marriage   582, 654-55, 658, 668, 761, 815, 817,
    955, 1278, 1380-83, 1516, 1550, 1677, 1693, 1700,
    1713, 1728, 1839, 1845, 1849, 1852, 1985, 1998,
    2002-03, 2069, 2102.
Martyrs   508, 797, 1028-29, 1135, 1187
Maryland   959, 1158, 1378, 1803, 1861, 2039, 2058,
    2064, 2164

Massachusetts 774, 776, 853, 893, 905, 922-23,
  993-94, 1104, 1333-35, 1451, 1570, 1576, 1710-11,
  1796, 1869, 1875, 1960
Mexican-Americans 1865
Mexico 833, 1023, 1150, 1155, 1187, 1245, 1412,
  1456-67, 1687, 1697, 1732, 1794, 2069-71, 2174
Michigan 1075, 1207, 1350, 1391-99, 1445, 2042,
  2128
Mindszenty, Cardinal 517
Minnesota 548, 1241, 1277, 1880, 2165-66
Miracles 1057, 1063, 1107, 1275, 1304, 1445, 1511,
  1551, 1606, 2091
Missionaries 618, 633, 675, 787, 864, 866, 997,
  1010, 1012-13, 1043, 1045, 1084, 1101, 1193,
  1388, 1721, 1917-18, 2036, 2082, 2155, 2190
Missouri 641
Mixed Marriages 497, 499, 546-48, 612, 653, 738,
  802, 823, 912, 996, 1058, 1207, 1236, 1265, 1329,
  1386, 1431, 1502, 1621, 1637, 1674, 1690, 1714,
  1724-25, 1742, 1788, 1880, 1889
Monasteries - see Monks
Monica, St. 578
Monks 500, 502, 510, 515, 566-67, 600, 663, 709,
  719, 729, 764, 828, 853, 872, 889, 911, 926, 939,
  968, 976-78, 982, 1004-05, 1118, 1138, 1153,
  1163, 1191, 1193, 1215, 1216, 1243, 1261, 1267,
  1339, 1341, 1379, 1385, 1401, 1407, 1426,
  1453-54, 1464, 1467, 1520, 1541, 1564, 1616,
  1632, 1647, 1727, 1747, 1766-79, 1799, 1802,
  1835, 1841, 1844, 1879, 1915, 1930, 1971, 1979,
  2012-13, 2020, 2023, 2135
More, St. Thomas 583, 687, 2151, 2157
Murder Mysteries 495, 500, 511, 535, 567, 625,
  629, 634, 641, 670-71, 679, 691, 720, 749, 774,
  776, 779-81, 828, 876, 889, 899, 920, 963, 972,
  989, 1005, 1019, 1020, 1038, 1079-80, 1093, 1114,
  1128, 1131, 1153, 1166, 1171-73, 1182, 1277,
  1288, 1290-1300, 1317-19, 1322, 1346, 1351-52,
  1374, 1375, 1391-99, 1401, 1473, 1569, 1586-87,
  1590-92, 1594-95, 1598, 1600-02, 1606-07, 1620,
  1633-34, 1744, 1747, 1766-79, 1786, 1798,
  1821-24, 1844, 1855, 1967-69, 2012, 2023, 2097,
  2119-27, 2168

Native Americans 956, 1330, 1347
Nazism 645, 714, 900, 1385, 1418, 1474
Nebraska 511
Nevada 789
New Hampshire 958

New Jersey   1276, 1959
New Mexico   633, 777, 792, 1304, 1313, 1741, 1914,
   2038
New York   521, 524, 612, 690, 743, 766-67, 901-02,
   963, 990, 1069, 1105, 1159, 1234, 1407, 1427,
   1436-38, 1498-99, 1500, 1507, 1596, 1613, 1657,
   1731, 1746, 1789, 1815, 1848, 1858, 1890, 1895,
   1898, 1904, 1917-18, 1933, 1983, 1988, 2041,
   2052, 2099, 2135-36, 2191
North Carolina   588, 960, 1461, 1531
Northern Ireland   501, 526, 541, 557, 696, 765,
   785, 1044, 1104, 1108, 1123, 1218, 1225, 1248,
   1424, 1446, 1459-60, 1496, 1563, 1603, 1635,
   1651, 1714, 1891
Norway   2076-78
Novices   518, 900, 1336, 1790, 1814, 1990
Nuns 495, 498, 503, 532, 539, 544, 551, 563, 568,
   579, 588, 629, 634, 639, 649-50, 670-71, 686,
   721, 724, 726, 766-67, 779-81, 784, 786, 791,
   812, 850, 862, 876, 877-89, 940-41, 960, 972,
   986, 997, 1013, 1016, 1070, 1079, 1084, 1091,
   1093, 1131, 1140-41, 1145, 1154, 1178, 1253,
   1259, 1272, 1278, 1303, 1307, 1317-19, 1325-26,
   1332, 1336, 1337, 1374, 1384, 1405, 1428, 1441,
   1451, 1455, 1490, 1500, 1503-04, 1512, 1529-30,
   1535, 1570, 1579, 1633, 1640, 1655, 1658, 1707,
   1715, 1717-18, 1734-35, 1744, 1753, 1790, 1811,
   1814, 1821-24, 1859, 1866, 1883, 1888, 1920,
   1953, 1968-69, 1975, 1989, 1995, 2007, 2026,
   2071, 2075, 2087, 2110, 2118, 2136, 2139, 2168,
   2170, 2175

Ohio   839, 1352, 1589, 1597

Papacy - see Vatican
Paraguay   675, 987
Passion Play   1919
Patrick, St.   584, 1931
Pennsylvania   1348, 1514, 1584-85, 1803, 2010,
   2187
Persia   1193
Peru   968, 2040, 2158
Philippines   1010, 1012-13, 1033
Pilgrimages   1946
Poland   503
Polish-Americans   2043, 2098
Popes - see Vatican

Popish Plot   520, 523, 536, 605, 942, 1302, 1362
Portugal   675, 987
Priests   496, 505, 507, 511, 516, 543, 558, 572-73,
   578, 581, 589, 592, 613, 615, 617-18, 622,
   637-38, 659, 679-83, 688, 690, 691, 697, 699,
   708, 727, 731, 742, 744-45, 747, 752, 759,
   769-70,774, 776, 783, 786, 788-89, 829, 831, 833,
   839, 846, 848-49, 852, 854, 858, 873, 891,
   896-97, 899, 902, 905, 924, 938, 963-66, 987,
   989, 990, 994, 1003, 1007-08, 1017, 1019, 1020,
   1029, 1032, 1039, 1041, 1043, 1075, 1082, 1087,
   1096, 1101, 1106, 1109, 1114, 1125, 1144, 1150,
   1151, 1166, 1168-74, 1177, 1186-87, 1188,
   1196-1201, 1203, 1209, 1210, 1212, 1213, 1225-26,
   1245-47, 1254, 1259-60, 1271, 1279-80, 1290,
   1300, 1306, 1310-11, 1320-21, 1330, 1333, 1346,
   1350, 1352, 1363, 1369, 1370, 1377, 1384,
   1391-99, 1411, 1435, 1443, 1452, 1456-57,
   1462-63, 1465-66, 1473, 1477-78, 1483, 1486-88,
   1495, 1511, 1515, 1517, 1521, 1526, 1535, 1557,
   1560, 1562, 1571, 1597, 1604, 1608-09, 1623,
   1626, 1720, 1726, 1731-32, 1748, 1750, 1783,
   1785, 1791, 1803-04, 1807, 1820, 1845, 1853,
   1856-57, 1860-63, 1869, 1871, 1877-78, 1881,
   1895-96, 1909, 1917-18, 1921, 1923, 1929, 1933,
   1935-37, 1960-63, 1965-66, 1974, 1977, 1981,
   2005, 2010, 2015, 2025-26, 2031, 2036, 2053,
   2057, 2061, 2097, 2119-2127, 2137-41, 2149, 2155,
   2161, 2163-65, 2174, 2179-83
Priests, Problems of Sex, Love, Marriage   565, 587,
   685, 689, 845, 871, 892, 909, 992, 1095, 1137,
   1354, 1356, 1364, 1372, 1451, 1519, 1568, 1789,
   1840, 1873, 1854, 2021, 2095, 2108, 2184-85, 2191

Quebec   561, 632, 778, 1057, 1152, 1189, 1202,
   1250, 1444, 1515, 1529, 1730

Relics   1002, 1038, 1154, 1286, 1763, 1882, 1988,
   2189
Rhode Island   1797
Richelieu, Cardinal   1338, 1504
Russia   505, 665, 1106

St. Patrick's Cathedral   489, 910, 1988, 2004
Satire - see Humor
Scotland   630, 793, 865, 868-69, 991, 1223, 1374,
   1387, 1521, 1525, 1528, 1574-75, 2045

Seal of Confession   774, 857, 860, 1254, 2005,
    2061, 2182
Seminaries   592, 864, 908, 1008, 1208, 1309,
    1372-73, 1375-76, 1390, 1444, 1552-53, 1678,
    1703, 1733, 1784, 2035, 2079
Serra, Fr. - see California Missions
Seton, St. Elizabeth   999, 1249
South Carolina   699, 1188, 1636-38, 1716, 1788
South Dakota   1317
Soviet Union - see Russia
Spain   536, 636, 883, 908, 911, 921, 1034, 1062-63,
    1186, 1211, 1220, 1264, 1551, 1743, 1764, 1813,
    1876, 1915, 1920, 2079
Spanish Civil War   508, 519, 1095, 1135, 1477,
    1519, 1583
Spy Novels   695, 698, 723, 829, 853, 1098, 1106,
    1134, 1156, 1220, 1270, 1403, 1522, 1545, 1596,
    1763, 1825-31, 1856, 2010
Stigmata   706, 728, 873, 1445, 1794, 1815, 1920
Suspense - see Murder Mysteries
Sweden   2016-17, 2024-25
Switzerland   585, 867

Tennessee   1147
Texas   532, 622, 890, 1096, 1569
Therese, St.   826, 2170
Thompson, Francis   705
Torres, Camillo   1306

Vatican   534, 619, 635, 648, 689, 698, 746, 749,
    827, 850, 945, 1082, 1106-07, 1110, 1117, 1124,
    1134, 1136, 1156, 1193, 1217, 1219, 1230, 1251,
    1270, 1274, 1289, 1398, 1418, 1440, 1443,
    1508-09, 1676, 1701-03, 1747, 1763, 1780-81,
    1793, 1798, 1825-31, 1869, 1892, 1928, 1942-43,
    1946, 1970, 1972, 1986, 1994, 2015-17, 2080-81,
    2111, 2130, 2132-34
Vermont   1322
Vietnam   1226
Virginia   573
Virgin Mary   561, 946, 1023, 1160, 1277, 1507,
    1551, 1638, 1648, 1687, 1708, 1749, 2008, 2054,
    2091, 2108, 2131
Visions   561, 630, 748, 1023, 1277, 1507, 1548,
    1638, 1648, 1657, 1687, 1708, 1749, 2054, 2091,
    2108, 2131, 2170
Voodoo   865, 2053

Washington, DC   631, 637–38, 1862, 1874, 1967
Washington State   879, 1922
Wisconsin   919, 1819

TITLE INDEX OF NOVELS

Abbe Constantin 1212
Abbe Pierre 1320
Abbe Pierre's People
 1321
Abbe's Temptation 2184
Abbess of Crewe 1995
Abbey of Evolayne 1845
Abbot's House 1024
Abbotscourt 527
Abiding City 639, 1217
Accidental Grace 1500
Accuser 520
Act of God 2048
Acts of Darkness 871
Adam Johnstone's Son
 855
Adelaide, Queen of Italy
 1480
Advent of Dying 1734
Adventures of Torqua
 1284
Adventures Perilous
 2161
After Me, the Deluge
 1086
After Purple 2192
Agnes Hilton 1282
Agnes of God 1070
Agnes of Sorrento 2028
Alabado 1408
Alban 1328
Alice O'Connor's
 Surrender 760
All About Brother Bird
 1799
All Good Men 1071
All Men Are Mad 2053
All of It 1209
All Our Yesterdays 2128

All Roads Lead to Rome
 1946
All Things Are Lights
 1958
Altar of Sacrifice 799
Always a Catholic 732
Ambition's Contest 1039
Amedeo 550
American Son 1494
Anchorhold 940
And Down the Days 647
And Then There Was Nun
 1821
And Then They Die 1569
Angel Grows Up 1858
Angel of the Delta 1663
Angels in the Dust 1409
Angel's Metal 490
Angel's Mirth 1021
Angels of September
 1167
Anguish of Father Rafti
 1096
Ann Decides 1369
Anne 1240
Anne's Head 641
Anointed 1211
Anteroom 1706
Antonio 1727
Apology for Roses 700
Apostate 488, 896
Appassionata 1336
Apple of His Eye 1867
Archbishop 631
Archbishop and the Lady
 870
Archbishop's Pocketbook
 1258

Arm and the Darkness
    741
Armine   1846
Art of Disappearing
    1985
Arthur Lee   1785
Article Thirty Two   1728
As a White Candle   1814
As the Clock Struck
    Twenty   1977
Ascent Into Hell   1168
Ash Wednesday   1631
Ashes to Ashes   1427
Assault on Innocence
    2021
Assault With Intent
    1391
Assisi Murders   1288
At the Sign of the Silver
    Cup   523
At War As Children   1842
Aunt Honor's Keepsake
    1904
Average Man   594
Awakened   1724
Awakening   654, 878,
    1888

Bach and the Heavenly
    Choir   1892
Bachelors   1996
Bad Blonde   2119
Ball and the Cross   793
Baltasar and Blimunda
    1921
Ban of Maplethorpe   916
Barbara Blomberg   1001
Barbara's Marriage and
    the Bishop   1677
Barnaby Rudge   934
Barrier   575
Basket Case   1586
Bavarian Story   1510
Be Not Angry   1626
Beautiful Lady   540
Bells of Rome   2015
Bells of St. Mary's
    1535

Beloved Intruder   998
Beneath Another Sun
    1474
Bernardin, My Love   1889
Bess of Cobb's Hall   941
Bessy Conway   1905
Betrothed   1513
Better Part of Valour
    1088
Better Sons   1035
Beyond the Glass   2142
Beyond These Voices   995
Bickerton   751
Big Sin   2120
Bird of Fire   2145
Bird of Sorrow   1881
Bishop   1518
Bishop as Pawn   1587
Bishop Finds a Way   879
Bishop Must Move   625
Bishop of Havana   1283
Bitter Orange   1218
Black and White   794
Black Banners   1413
Black Cardinal   1986
Black City   785
Black Robe   1646
Black Soil   951
Blackbirds of Mulhouse
    1502
Blackrobe   846
Blakes and the Flanagans
    1906
Bless Me Father   680
Blessed Are the Meek
    1410
Blind Agnese   734
Blind Side   829
Blindness of Dr. Gray
    1961
Blond and Brunette   1329
Blossoming Rod   2008
Blue Movie   1994
Bold Encounter   1876
Both Your Houses   557
Boys   1645
Bramble Bush   1622
Brass Halo   2121
Bread and Roses   1110

Brendan 718
Bride Adorned 1670
Bride for New Orleans
  1664
Brideshead Revisited
  2113
Bridge at San Luis Rey
  2158
Bridie Steen 863
Brighter Vision 1896
Brighton Rock 1182
Brigit 1692
British Museum is Falling
  Down 1469
Broken Doll 2122
Broken Paths 1380
Broken Rosary 1351
Broken Vows 790
Bronze Christ 1675
Brother Anselmo 1138
Brother Flo 1974
Brother Petroc's Return
  1978
Brother's Keepers 2135
Brother's Sacrifice
  1019
Brown House at Duffield
  1439
Buddha Tree 1688
Bump on Brannigan's Head
  836
Burden Light 1370
Burden of God 1515
Burden of Honor 1040
Buried Man 2010
Burning Bush 2076
Burnt Out Case 1183
Bury Me in Ravenna 2083
Button, Button 963
By Grace of Love 1095
By Nature Equal 1034
By Strange Paths 1991
By What Authority? 595

C 552
Cabala 2159
Cable 2044
Call 1565

Call for a Miracle 1389
Call My Brother Back
  1603
Called and the Chosen
  544
Callista 1681
Camphor 1111
Can These Things Be?
  1275
Candle at Dusk 502
Candle to St. Anthony
  1673
Candles for Therese
  2170
Candle's Glory 2057
Candlestick Makers 660
Canticle for Leibowitz
  1632
Canto for a Gypsy 1988
Captive Cardinal 517
Cardinal 1869
Cardinal and his
  Conscience 1301
Cardinal of the Medici
  1269
Cardinal Sins 1169
Cardinal's Mistress
  1671
Cardinal's Snuff Box
  1227
Carina 800
Carmelite 1193
Carpenter Years 834
Carrack Sailed Away
  1045
Casa Braccio 856
Case Against Satan 1894
Case of Conscience 801
Cat and Mouse 1160
Catalina 1551
Cathedral 910, 1339
Cathedral In the Sun
  1064
Catherine de Gardeville
  2037
Catherine Sidney 1314
Catholic 1796
Catholic Education 592
Catholic Girls 1843

Catholics   1647
Cat's Cradle   553
Celebration   904
Celibate Father   2138
Celibates   1364
Certain Slant of Light
   651
Certain Widow   922
Chameleons   701
Chancellor   1932
Change of Gods   1742
Change of Scene   874
Chaplain of St.
   Catherines   1259
Charles Elwood   711
Chesapeake Cavalier
   064
Child of Julian Flynn
   992
Child of Light   1113
Child of Mary   1847
Child of the Ball   496
Children of Darkness
   1686
Children of Eve   802
Children of Tempest
   1659
Choice   894
Chosen   1008
Christ In Concrete   936
Christening Party   2014
Christine Roux   2160
Christmas Mary Had Twins
   1954
Christopher and Cressida
   761
Christopher Humble   1362
Chronicle of Thomas Frith
   1979
Chronicles of Mount
   Benedict   893
Chronicles of the Little
   Sisters   1512
Church and State   1955
Circus Rider's Daughter
   686
Citadel of God   926
Cities of the Flesh
   1725

City for St. Francis
   2129
City of Light   1492
Clang Birds   1451
Clemencia's Crisis   1235
Cloister and the Hearth
   1841
Cloudy Summits   803
Clown   645
Clowns of God   2132
Coaina, the Rose of the
   Algonquins   956
Cockpit   673
Cold Coming   1374
Cold Heaven   1648
Color of Blood   1649
Come Back to Erin   1719
Come Rack! Come Rope!
   596
Come Sunrise   730
Comforters   1997
Coming Harvest   576
Coming of the Monster
   976
Coming Storm   1315
Common of Angels   2051
Company of Women   1148
Compassionate People
   1307
Comrade Don Camillo
   1196
Con O'Regan   1908
Concerning the Eccen-
   tricities of Cardinal
   Pirelli   1062
Concrete Judasbird   1547
Confession   1992
Confession of a Novice
   1790
Confessional   1270
Confessions of an
   Apostate   1907
Connolly's Life   1588
Conquest of California
   1194
Conscience   957
Constance Sherwood   1099
Consuela Bright   1349
Convent Girl   1658

Convent on Styx   1633
Conventionalists   597
Conversion   1764
Convert   546, 1025
Converts   2109
Copper Country   2042
Corleone   857
Corner of Paradise   1290
Corner That Held Them
  2110
Corpse on the Bridge
  567
Count Bohemond   983
Crazy Doctor   1476
Cripple of Nuremberg
  796
Cross and the Shamrock
  1818
Cross and the Sword
  1429
Crossroads   1120
Crown of Thorns   759
Crusade   2111
Cry for Tomorrow   526
Cry of Dolores   1150
Crying Game   693
Cunning of the Dove   984
Cupid on the Stairs
  1754
Cure of St. Philippe
  1189
Cypresses Believe in God
  1135

Damnation of Theron Ware
  1094
Damned Lovely   2123
Damsel Who Dared   1344
Dan England and the
  Noonday Devil   837
Danish Gambit   729
Daphne Adeane   554
Dark Disciple   1956
Dark Enemy   1009
Dark Extremity   1057
Dark Rosaleen   642
Dark Was the Wilderness
  1721

Dark Wheel   1980
Darkling Plain   724
Davidee Birot   577
Dawn of All   598
Days Beyond Recall   952
Days of a Hireling   715
Days of Eternity   1137
Dayspring   2038
Dead Altars   1639
Dead Man's Ransom   1766
Deadline for a Critic
  1392
Deadly Sex   2124
Dearly Beloved   2039
Death Came With Flowers
  2012
Death Comes for the
  Archbishop   777
Death of Abbe Didier
  1166
Death Wears a Red Hat
  1394
Deathbed   1393
Death's Bright Shadow
  1941
Deep Heart   805
Deer Cry   1931
Defenders of the Faith
  1264
Degree Nisi   804
Delicate Darling   2125
Deliver Us From Evil
  489
Deliver Us From Wolves
  1291
Delorme in Deep Water
  1462
Delusson Family   975
Denounced   542
Deo Gratias   1950
Desmonde   864
Destiny   1081
Devil at Four O'Clock
  783
Devil Flower   1033
Devil in Kansas   1825
Devil Rides Outside
  1191

Devil Takes the Chair
  750
Devil to Play 1292
Devil Water 1951
Devil's Advocate 2133
Devil's Brew 1833
Devil's Cross 1737
Devil's Food 1157
Devil's Highway 2036
Devil's Novice 1767
Devils of Loudun 1337
Devil's Own 1942
Dew in April 2118
Diary of a Country Priest
  613
Dimitrios and Irene 882
Disappearance of John
  Longworthy 1014
Disillusioned 1877
Disorderly House 1428
Distance and the Dark
  2154
Distant Drum 1076
Divine Adventure 1564
Divorce 672
Do Black Patent-Leather
  Shoes Really Reflect
  Up? 1808
Dobachi 528
Dr. Dumont 1132
Dodecahedron 1505
Don Camillo and His Flock
  1197
Don Camillo Meets the
  Flower Children 1199
Don Camillo Takes the
  Devil by the Tail
  1200
Don Camillo's Dilemma
  1198
Don Gastone and the
  Ladies 1748
Door in the Grimming
  1192
Double Blind 2163
Doubleman 1406
Dove with the Bough of
  Olive 2056
Drift 1221

Dry Mass 1540
Dry Wood 1311
Dun Ferry Risin' 1656
Dust on the King's
  Highway 2146
Dusty Spring 1945
Dynamite Factory 1616

Each In His Darkness
  1179
Earthly Bread 1623
East River 521
Echo-Game 2060
Ecstasy of Owen Muir
  1425
Edge of Doom 691
Edge of Sadness 1710
Edge of the Storm 2174
Eight Days 1061
Eighth Sacrament 876
Elizabeth Eden 627
Eliza's Galiardo 1144
Elstones 806
Embattled 519
Ember Days 652
Embezzled Heaven 2130
Empty Shrine 561
En Route 1340
Encounter 1803
End of a Mission 646
End of the Affair 1184
Episode on Beacon Hill
  1104
Espiritu Sancto 1976
Estranged Face 997
Ethelreda 739
Eunice 807
Evelyn Innes 1652
Even As You Love 2069
Evening In Spring 919
Ever Singing Die Oh! Die
  634
Eve's Apple 842
Excellent Mystery 1768
Ex-Nun 2139
Exorcist 637
Extramuros 1920
Extremists 1446

Eye of the Needle 2097

Fabiola 2167
Fabiola's Sisters 797
Face of a Madonna 515
Face to the Sun 1583
Fair Bride 1519
Faith and the Flame
1312
Faith Desmond's Last
Stand 1357
Faith, the Root 1075
Faithful 786, 1405
Fallen Away 547
False Gods 1926
Family 1797
Family That Overtook
Christ 1836
Far Away Princess 1848
Far Dwelling 898
Farragan's Retreat 1584
Fate of Father Sheehy
1909
Father 744
Father and Son 1048
Father Before Christmas
681
Father Bernard's Parish
1731
Father Coldstream 987
Father Connell 543
Father Darcy 1517
Father Drummond and His
Orphans 1007
Father Felix 752
Father Hillary's Holiday
1520
Father Hone and the
Television Set 1310
Father in a Fix 682
Father John 1350
Father Jonathan 1575
Father Juniper and the
General 1697
Father Justin 1087
Father Ladden, Curate
2137

Father Larkin's Mission
in Jonesville 1685
Father Malachy's Miracle
1521
Father O'Brien and His
Girls 789
Father Rowland 1791
Father Tim 1125
Father Under Fire 683
Father's Day 1377
Faustula 529
Favorite 1504
Fear at my Heart 1231
Feast of Lupercal 1650
Felice 903
Fernando 530
Fidelity 1497
Fiery Cross 1387
Fifteenth Pelican 1859
Fifth of November 609
Final Payments 1149
Fine Play 808
Finger in the Candle
Flame 1924
Fire in Stubble 1739
Fire in the Bush 618
Fire In the Rain 964
Fires in Smithfield
1458
First Day of Friday
2065
First Rebellion 1417
Fisherman's Beach 2089
Fishers of Men 1617
Five Devils of Kilmainham
1573
Five for Sorrow, Ten for
Joy 1140
Flag for Sunrise 2026
Flame of the Forest 626
Flame Out of Dorset
2020
Flemmings 958
Flesh and Blood 1552
Flesh Is Not Life 570
Flight 2016
Flight of the Eagle
1722

Fling Out the Banner
   1683
Florence Danby   917
Florentine Woman   1887
Flower for Sign   2011
Flower of Asia   913
Flowers by Request   1293
Flutter in the Dovecote
   1522
Fly on the Wheel   2059
Fogarty and Co   1069
Follow Me Ever   728
Fool's Heart   1871
Fool's Pilgrimage   1927
Footprints Beneath the
   Snow   655
For the Pleasure of His
   Company   2022
For the Religion   970
Forest   1330
Forest of Feathers   1485
Fortune's Football   1614
Found Wanting   1541
Foundling   2004
Fountain of Arethusa
   2182
Four Rivers of Paradise
   2147
Four Ways of Computing
   Midnight   1784
Four Winds   1244
Fourth Down Death   1277
Fourth Gift   2070
Foxglove Saga   2112
Franciscan   633
Fray Mario   968
Friar Observant   707
Frobisch's Angel   1874
Frog in the Bottom of the
   Well   1548
From Out Magdala   661
Frost in May   2143
Full of Grace   1253
Furys   1222
Future Is Forever   1449

Gadfly   2088
Gail Talbot   1026

Galloway Heather   1574
Gallows and the Cross
   1363
Game of Kings   991
Garden of Allah   1267
Gardens of Omar   656
Garish Day   624
Gate of Heaven   1589
Gates of Olivet   662
Gemini   1372
Gentian Hill   1151
Gentle Fury   1878
Gentle Martyrdom of
   Brother Bertram   939
Gentle Murderer   899
Gentleman Riches   663
Gerald de Lacy's Daughter
   1898
Geraldine   491
Getting a Way with Murder
   1590
Giant's Arrow   1897
Gilded Witch   2126
Gildersleeves   2162
Girl in the Spike-Heeled
   Shoes   2179
Girls Forever Brave and
   True   1861
Give Beauty Back   835
Glen Mary: A Catholic
   Novel   1577
God and the Others   851
God Game   1170
God Hunters   1373
God Made Little Apples
   1971
God of Love   1072, 1567
God Speed the Night   900
Godforgotten   1930
Godhead   1642
Godric   719
God's Children   2187
God's Frontier   921
God's Way, Man's Way
   710
Going Home   1532
Gold or God   757
Golden Apples of the Sun
   1705

Golden Days 1679
Golden Girl 2040
Golden Heritage 1667
Golden Rose 1278
Golden Thread 927
Golgotha Falls 905
Gone Tomorrow 953
Good Behavior 2136
Good Conscience 1097
Good Deeds Must Be
  Punished 1973
Good Looking Woman 1749
Good Shepherd 1073
Governess 1628
Governor 1960
Grace Morton 1615
Graces of Ballykeen
  2075
Grand Man 844
Grand Opening 1241
Grandmother and the
  Priests 742
Grantley Manor 1100
Grapes and Thorns 2061
Grass Widow 1591
Greater Love 1729
Greatest of These 1495
Green Grassy Slopes 541
Green Journey 1242
Green Lion 1206
Green Years 865
Gremore 1436
Grey Eminence 1338
Grist 1464
Guileless Saxon 2096
Guy Fawkes 494

Hack 1959
Hadrian VII 850
Halo For Satan 1038
Hamiltons 611
Hand of God 962
Hanging of the Angels
  1568
Happiness of Father Happe
  1213
Happy Are the Clean in
  Heart 1171

Happy Are the Meek 1172
Happy Are Those Who
  Search for Justice
  1173
Harry Layden 753
Hawthorndean 2055
Heart in Pilgrimage 999
Heart of a Man 1498
Heart of Silence 1794
Heart of the Matter
  1185
Heathen Valley 1461
Heaven and Hell 831
Heaven Knows, Mr. Allison
  1953
Heavenly Ladder 1484
Helbeck of Bannisdale
  2100
Helena 2114
Hell Catholic 1274
Hell to Answer 1481
Heloise and Abelard
  1653
Henry and Cato 1660
Henry of Navarre 2171
Her Death of Cold 1592
Her Father's Share 1805
Her Soul To Keep 1022
Hermit of Etyon Forest
  1769
Heroic Dust 906
Hidden Symptoms 1496
High Road 1381
Higher Court 891
Hills Were Liars 1323
His Eminence 1085
His Eminence, Death
  1826
His Father's Way 949
His Victory 1849
Holding Up the Hills
  2107
Holy Foot 1882
Holy Pictures 684
Holy Sinner 1509
Holy Wars 689
Holy Wednesday 1109
Home and the Homeless
  735

Honour Without Renown
  1342
Horace Blake   2101
Hounds of the Vatican
  1289
House   657
House of Cards   885
House of Exile   853
House of Gold   875
House of Shanahan   954
House of the Misty Orchid
  1745
House of Yorke   2062
House on Bitterness
  Street   2071
House on the Sands   648
House Possessed   630
Household Saints   1815
How Far Can You Go   1471
How George Edwards
  Scrapped Religion
  1068
How Will It End?   1263
Hungry Grass   1804
Hunter of the Blood
  1545
Hylton's Wife   1693

I Have Friends in Heaven
  784
I Hear In My Heart   766
I Will Not Serve   1501
Ice for the Eskimo   1786
If I Were You   1180
In a Dark Wood   2108
In Father Gabriel's
  Garden   1929
In God's Good Time   1884
In Monavalla   690
In My End Is My Beginning
  555
In Quest of Splendour
  1444
In the Jersey Hills
  1276
In the Lean Years   886
In the Name of the Father
  512, 1831

In the Palm House   2035
In the Service of the
  King   1345
In This House of Brede
  1141
In This Thy Day   1604
Indian Cottage, A
  Unitarian Story   1792
Indulgence   1067
Initiation   599
Instead of Ashes   1190
Into the Labyrinth   1795
Inviolable   722
Iron in the Valleys
  1750
Isidro   525
Island Priest   1817
Isle of Youth   1482
Issue of the Bishop's
  Blood   1606
It Happened in Rome   809
Italian Adventure   810

Jack-in-the-Box   1355
Jacqueline   531
Jealous God   694
Jean Barois   1542
Jerome Leaster   1993
Jersey Tomatoes   1855
Jesuit   1106, 1493
Jesuit of Today   1608
Jesus Man   776
Job Secretary   2102
Jock, Jack and the
  Corporal   1539
John Bull and the Papists
  1006
John Maxwell's Marriage
  1205
John O'Brien, the Orphan
  of Boston   1875
Jose   1743
Joy   614
Joyful Beggar   928
Judas Figures   1456
Judas Gospel   2080
Judgement Day   1049
Judith's Marriage   1308

Kappillan of Malta   1641
Katherine   1533
Keys of St. Peter   1780
Keys of the Kingdom   866
Khufra Run   1154
Kill and Tell   1395
Killing a Mouse on Sunday   1813
Killing for Christ   1219
Killing Orders   1747
Kind Hearts and Coronets   1236
King of Shadows   2176
King's Achievements   600
King's Good Servant   2151
King's Highway   664
King's Legacy   1056
King's Mountain   1694
King's Persons   1181
Kiss of Judas   1943
Knight of God   1806
Knights of Malta   1781
Kocska Formula   1856
Kristin Lavransdatter   2077
Kryptonite Kid   2063

Lace Curtain   612
Ladies of Soissons   877
Ladies of St. Hedwigs   503
Lady and the Sun   946
Lady from Toledo   792
Lady of Fort St. John   782
Lady of Lyte   1302
Lady Paramount   1228
Lady Trent's Daughter   811
Ladybird   1101
Lake   1654
Lalor's Maples   840
Lamb   1553
L'Amour Profane   1384
Lamp of Destiny   812
Land of Cain   1424
Land of Delight   674
Land of Spices   1707

Land's Lord   2190
Lapsing   2095
Lark's Creek   1404
Last Catholic in America   1809
Last Crescendo   977
Last Crusader   929
Last Hurrah   1711
Last Lap   1581
Last Magic   1676
Last Miracle   2087
Last Rites for the Vulture   1827
Last Stand of Father Felix   2155
Last Time I Saw Hell   1828
Late Harvest   2152
Late Have I Loved Thee   1511
Laughter from Downstairs   1740
Lay Siege of Heaven   930
Leave of Absence   1593
Leavetaking   2188
Left Hand of God   562
Left Hander   950
Legacy of Gabriel Martel   1704
Legion   638
Leper of Saint Giles   1770
Less Than the Angels   955
Let No Man Put Asunder   1516
Let Us Consider One Another   1431
Let Us Prey   1822
Let's Talk of Graves, of Worms, and Epitaphs   1798
Letter to Sister Benedicta   2067
Life of John William Walshe   762
Life Returns to Die   1256
Life With Its Sorrow...   524

Lifetime on Clouds   1662
Liffey Lane   1430
Light Behind the Bars
   2103
Light in Silence   1407
Light of Stars   2164
Light of Vision   1850
Light on the Lagoon   813
Light Over Fatima   1708
Lighten Our Darkness
   1369
Like Unto a Merchant
   1162
Lillies of the Field
   563
Lily of the Mohawks   775
Limbo   920
Lines of Life   1554
Linked Lives   967
Linz Testament   1763
Listener   972
Litany of St. Charles
   2049
Little Girl Under a
   Mosquito Net   1421
Little Green Truck   1252
Little Raw on Monday
   Mornings   847
Little Saint of God   880
Little Ships   1698
Little Squire Jim   1531
Little Valley of God
   832
Little World of Don
   Camillo   1201
Lively Arts of Sister
   Gervase   649
Lizzie Maitland   798
Lois   1268
Loneliness?   601
Lonely Passion of Judith
   Hearne   1651
Long Probation   1121
Long Shadow   1755
Long Tomorrow   2165
Longest Night   1447
Look to Beyond   1936
Lord of the Dance   1174

Lord of the World   602
Lord On Our Side   1459
Loretto   1629
Loss and Gain   1682
Loss of Patients   1594
Lost Rosary   1723
Lost Sheep   658
Lost Traveller   2144
Louisa Kirkbridge   2052
Love in the Ruins   1761
Love Is a Bridge   1077
Love Is My Vocation   826
Loved and the Unloved
   1555
Loyalist   559
Lucinie   1753
Lucky Prisoner   1139
Luke Delmege   1962
Lying Three   1595

Mabel Stanhope   1736
MacCarthy More!   1910
Mademoiselle Lavalliere
   1665
Madonna Red   768
Magnificat   578
Maiden's Heritage   935
Make-Up for Murder   2168
Malefactors   1146
Maltaverne   1556
Man Born Again   583
Man Cleansed By God   584
Man in a Wheel Chair
   1934
Man in the Wheat Field
   1433
Man of Good Zeal   585
Man Of His Age   971
Man on a Donkey   1812
Man on a Pillar   1130
Man Who Captivated New
   York   1453
Man Who Sold Christmas
   1454
Mandelbaum Gate   1998
Mango on the Mango Tree
   1546

Manor Farm 643
Manuscripts of Pauline
  Archange 632
Many Shall Come 772
Marble Faun 1243
Marcelino 1915
Margaret Brent,
  Adventurer 1158
Maria Chapdelaine 1250
Marian Elwood 713, 2050
Marion Howard 506
Mariquita 532
Mark 965
Marriage of Elizabeth
  Whitacker 1265
Marriage of Reason 1015
Marriage Verdict 2002
Married Man 1839
Martie, the Unconquered
  1699
Marx the First 1523
Mary Darlin' 2166
Mary Doherty 1714
Marzio's Crucifix 858
Mask of Innocence 1557
Mass 1098
Mass of Brother Michel
  1379
Massingers 912
Masterful Monk 978
Matter of Conscience
  610
McElroy 1709
Melchior of Boston 993
Memento Mori 1999
Memories of a Non-Jewish
  Childhood 733
Men of No Property 901
Merchant Prince and His
  Heir 493
Merry Eternity 2157
Merry Miracle 1625
Messenger 1853
Mezzogiorno 533
Michael 979
Michel, Michel 1450
Midas Coffin 1829
Miguel of the Bright
  Mountain 1741

Mill Town Pastor 839
Mind Over Murder 1396
Miners Hill 1733
Minor Miracle 1657
Minstrel's Leap 629
Miracle 2091
Miracle at Cardenrigg
  1223
Miracle at Lemaire 1486
Miracle at St. Brunos
  764
Miracle for Caroline
  1059
Miracle for Mexico 1687
Miracle of Pelham Bay
  Park 1507
Miracle of the Bells
  1348
Miracles 1249
Miracles of the Red Altar
  Cloth 1327
Mirror for Toby 1214
Mirror of Hell 1294
Mission Boy 787
Mission of Death 2099
Mister Billy Buttons
  1437
Mr. Blue 838
Mr. Coleman, Gent 942
Mistress Brent 2058
Mrs. Foley, God Bless
  Her 1402
Mrs. Gerald's Niece
  1102
Mitre and Crook 1309
Mixed Marriage 548, 738
Mobrays and the
  Harringtons 1619
Modern Prometheus 621
Modernist 1316
Mollie's Mistake 653
Molokai 727
Monk 1216
Monk Dawson 1840
Monk of Hambleton 1467
Monk of the Aventine
  1004
Monk's Hood 1771
Monk's Pardon 911

Monogamist 1105
Monsieur Henri 1204
Monsignor 1333
Monsignor Connolly of
   St. Gregory's Parish
   1571
Monsignor Quixote 1186
Monsignore 1443
Montagues of Casa Grande
   1914
Montarges Legacy 1618
Moon Gaffney 2041
Mora Carmody 754
Morbid Taste for Bones
   1772
More Excellent Way 887
More Murder in a Nunnery
   1968
Mortal Glamour 2175
Morte D'Urban 1807
Moscow 1979 1414
Mostly Fools 1834
Mother 909, 1700
Mother Machree 1938
Mount Benedict 1570
Moviegoer 1762
Mulberry Leaf 1530
Multitude of Sins 872,
   1636
Murder at St. Dennis
   1317
Murder at the Flood 498
Murder Before Matins
   1844
Murder in a Nunnery
   1969
Murder in the Sacristy
   1473
Murder Takes the Veil
   1318
My Brother Tom 497
My Brothers, Remember
   Monica 1578
My Crown, My Love 2017
My Days of Anger 1050
My Fellow Devils 1239
My Friend Prospero 1229
My Lady Rosia 1195

My Life for My Sheep
   985
My New Curate 1963
My Time and What I've
   Done With It 725
My Uncle and the Cure
   697
My Uncle, the Curate
   1923
Myrtle Among Thorns
   1058
Mystery of the Priest's
   Parlour 1346

Naked Angel 2127
Naked I Leave 1702
Name of the Rose 1005
Natural Causes 1879
Necromancers 603
Net Is Cast 1837
Never Forgotten 736
New Antigone 568
New Aristocrats 1913
New Lights 1899
Niche Over the Door
   1232
Night is Darkest 615
Night Music 2024
Night of Decision 1159
Night of Spring 1695
Nightmovers 990
Nine Days of Father Serra
   2183
Nine Days to Eternity
   1984
Nine Times Nine 670
Ninety and Nine 1411
No Country for Young Men
   1717
No Empty Hands 914
No Lasting Home 923
No Little Thing 845
No Mate for the Magpie
   1635
No True Life 1083
None Other Gods 604
Noonday Devil 1596

Norway Man 1712
Not a Blessed Thing
  1823
Not All of Your
  Laughter... 499
Not All Saints 1837
Not Built With Hands
  2148
Not For This World Only
  1689
Note of Grace 1975
Nothing Is Impossible
  545
Noughts and Crosses
  1266
Novena for Murder 1735
Novice 518, 1990
Now and Forever 1358
Now Bless Thyself 1952
Now With the Morning Star
  1385
Nun 579, 2007, 2074
Nun in the Closet 1131
Nun of the Above 1824
Nunnery 791
Nuns and Soldiers 1661
Nun's Story 1325
Nuplex Red 1830
Nurse with Wings 1529
Nursery Crimes 1128

O Distant Star 947
O Pale Galilean 1872
Oblate 1341
Occasion of Sin 624a
Oddsfish! 605
Old and New 1911
Old Order Changes 1506
Old Parish 1334
Old St. Mary's New
  Assistant 2180
O'Loughin of Clare 1126
Once a Catholic 733
One Clear Call 1895
One Corpse Too Many
  1773
One of our Priests is
  Missing 2117

One Poor Scruple 2104
One Red Rose for
  Christmas 1303
One Way or Another 1935
Open Mind 616
Orange and Green 1255
Orchids 721
Ordained 1435
Ordeal By Silence 509
Ordeal of Gilbert Pinfold
  2115
Oriental Pearl 959
Orthodox 1118
Other Island 828
Other Miss Lisle 1537
Others Will Come 1246
Our Hearts Are Restless
  538
Out in the Sunset 1582
Out of Due Time 2105
Out of the Depths 1295
Out of the Whirlwind
  2098
Outlander 1202
Outward and Visible Signs
  1122

Pack Rat 1371
Pact with Satan 1296
Padre Must Die 622
Padre of the Plains
  1388
Pageant of Life 980
Papa Martel 1868
Papers of a Pariah 606
Pardon and Peace 758
Parish and the Hill 881
Park 1161
Parrot's Perch 1857
Parting of the Ways 1133
Passage Through Fire
  1643
Passing By 2186
Passion in Rome 746
Passion of Gabrielle 685
Passion Play 1919
Passionate Heart 587
Pastor Halloft 1260

Pathway to Heaven   659
Patience of a Saint
   1175
Pauline Seward   716
Pavane   1864
Peace Comes to Sainte
   Monique   1463
Penance of Brother Alaric
   1153
Penance Was Death   1607
Pendulum   1475
Penitent   937
Penitentes of San Rafael
   1313
Pentecost Project   698
Pepita Jimenez   2079
Pere Antoine   1666
Pere Jean   1609
Pere Monniere's Ward
   1438
Perfect Round   1870
Peter Abelard   2090
Peter the Priest   1356
Peter the Second   1524
Peter's Pence   827
Picturegoers   1470
Pilgrim at Sea   1416
Pilgrim Came Late   1816
Pilgrim of Hate   1774
Pilgrimage   702, 2030
Pilgrims on the Earth
   1514
Pilgrim's Regress   1448
Pilkington Heir   1900
Pimpernel 60   1403
Pious Agent   695
Pistols and Pedagogues
   1036
Place at Whitton   1375
Place of Coolness   709
Place of Honor   2084
Place of Jackals   1226
Play by Play   1142
Play in the Sand   1207
Plot   536
Plough and the Harrow
   1349
Pocketful of Rye   867

Pope from the Ghetto
   1440
Pope Must Die   1701
Pope of the Sea   635
Portrait of the Artist as
   a Young Man   1359
Potter's House   814
Pound Foolish   1637
Poverty and the Baronet's
   Family   620
Power and the Glory
   1187
Pray Love, Remember   767
Prayer for the Dying
   1271
Prelate   1251
Prelude and Spring   593
Price of Chips   1248
Price You Pay   915
Pride of Summer   703
Pride's Way   1638
Priest   587, 774, 1210,
   1225, 1597
Priest Among the Pigeons
   1748
Priest and a Girl   892
Priest and the Man   1684
Priest Who Vanished
   2140
Priestly Heart   1965
Priestly Murders   1114
Priest's Secret   1562
Priest's Wife   1354
Prince of Peace   769
Principato   1585
Prism   1426
Prisoner's Years   815
Problem in Angels   1297
Profit and Loss   1819
Prophet of the Ruined
   Abbey 1820
Pulaski Place   2043
Punish the Sinners   1922
Pyx   720

Quarup   745
Queen's Tragedy   607

Quest 1422
Quest for Innocence
1127
Question of Choice 510
Quiet as a Nun 1093
Quiet Light 931

Rabbits in the Hay 1419
Rafael 773
Ralphton, the Young
Carolinian of 1776 699
Ramona 1347
Raven in the Foregate
1775
Real Presence 573
Realization 1944
Rebellion 1758
Recent Martyr 1538
Red and the Green 1661a
Red Ascent 1678
Red Circle 1854
Red Inn of St. Lyphar
1901
Red Sky at Night 1549
Redemption 580, 2031
Refugee 1089
Relic 1002, 1286
Religious Body 495
Reluctant Abbess 2073
Remember No More 513
Renewal 1957
Requiem for a Spy 1134
Requiem for a Woman's
Soul 1860
Rest House 816
Rest in Pieces 1598
Rest Is Silence 1972
Restless Flame 932
Revenge in the Convent
679
Rich Inheritance 1691
Rich Young Man 586
Riders in the Chariot
2153
Right Hand 2085
Rings of Love 1566
Rise of Father Roland
966

Rite of Spring 1176
Rites of Murder 1967
Road Back 1937
Road Less Traveled 589
Road Through the Woods
1092
Road to Gandolfo 1970
Road to Glory 2047
Road to Hell 1644
Road to Leenane 986
Road to Somewhere 943
Rob of the Bowl 1378
Robert Kimberly 2003
Robert Orange 1279
Robert Peckham 556
Robinson 2000
Rock and Sand 1730
Rocket to the Morgue
671
Roman Collar Detective
1352
Romance of a Jesuit
1208
Romance of a Jesuit
Mission 1917
Romance of a Spanish Nun
539
Romance of the Recusants
1472
Romanesque 1599
Romans, Countrymen,
Lovers 1074
Rome and the Abbey 492
Rosary Murders 1397
Rose of Alhambra 883
Rose of Yesterday 859
Rose on the Summit 1800
Rose Rent 1776
Rosemary 1331
Roses for Mexico 1023
Rox Hall Illuminated
1760
Royal Road 1415
Ruby Cross 2093
Rue Notre Dame 1783
Ruined for Life 795
Rum, Rome and Rebellion
1946
Run With the Killer 511

Running Nun   1079

Sabaria   1832
Sabrina   1801
Sacred Hill   558
Safe Lodging   1233
Saint   1082
Saint and the Hunchback
  2013
St. Dingan's Bones   748
St. Francis   1368
Saint Maker   1298
St. Patrick's Battalion
  1412
Saint Peter's Fair   1777
St. Peter's Finger   1634
Saint Peter's Plot   1418
Saint Udo   1544
Saintmaker's Christmas
  Eve   1304
Saints   1624
Saints Are Sinister
  1080
Saints in Hell   788
Saint's Theatre   1063
Salt   2177
Samurai   1028
San Celestino   534
Sanctity   1744
Sanctuary Sparrow   1778
Satan and Cardinal
  Campbell   1525
Satan's Daughter   1326
Savage City   1746
Savages and Saints   1726
Saving Grace   1136
Says Mrs. Crowley, Says
  She   1335
Scarlet Sword   572
Scenes and Characters
  from a Comedy of Life
  755
Schism   1156
School for Saints   1280
Season's Greetings   1027
Second Husband   628
Second Vespers   1600
Secret Bequest   1851

Secret of the Doubting
  Saint   1299
Seed Upon the Wind   1627
Seeing Things   2054
Seek the Fair Land   1483
Seldom Without Love   890
Seminarian   908
Serpent's Circle   1230
Serpent's Delight   1749
Set All Afire   933
Seven Days Grace   2009
Seven Reductions   675
Seventeen Come Sunday
  1112
Seventh Sacrament   889
Seventh Station   1601
Shackles of the Free
  522
Shadow of Death   1398
Shadow of Eversleigh
  1423
Shadow of God   1883
Shadow of the Cathedral
  636
Shadow on the Earth   981
Shadowed Faith   623
Shadows and Images   2072
Shadows of the Images
  564
Shadows on the Rock   778
Shame of Our Wounds
  1890
Shandy McGuire   677
Shannon's Way   868
Shepherd of the North
  1499
Shepherd of Weepingwold
  944
Shepherds on the Move
  2181
Sherborne   918
Shield of Silence   1254
Shiksa   571
Shining Tides   708
Shoes of the Fisherman
  2134
Shroud   852
Sicola, the Papal Bull
  2086

Sidney Carrington's
  Contumacy 1432
Signs and Wonders 692
Silence 1029
Silence of History 1051
Silence of Sebastian
  1902
Silent Captain 2172
Silver Answer 1281
Silver Fountains 1487
Silver Glade 1668
Silver Trumpets Calling
  665
Sin of Father Amaro
  1003
Sin of Father Mouret
  2185
Sing to the Sun 666
Singer, Not the Song
  1457
Sinner of St. Ambrose
  1838
Sir Christopher Leighton
  2027
Sister Clare 726, 1640
Sister Innocent and the
  Wayward Miracle 1455
Sister of Charity 960
Sister Philomene 1145
Sister Simon's Murder
  Case 1319
Sister Teresa 1655
Sister Teresita and the
  Spirit 1091
Sisters by Rite 1460
Six O'Clock Mass 1966
Six Wounds 873
Skerrett 1720
Slammer 1188
Sleep of the Pigeon
  1090
Slippy McGee 1716
Small Miracle 1107
Snares of the Enemy
  1401
So Falls the Elm Tree
  650
Soeur Angele and the
  Bellringer's Niece
  779

Soeur Angele and the
  Embarrassed Ladies
  780
Soeur Angele and the
  Ghosts of Chambord
  781
Soggarth Aroon 1203
Solitaries of Sambuca
  763
Solitary Island 1987
Son of Marietta 1042
Song at the Scaffold
  1441
Song of Bernadette 2131
Song of Sixpence 869
Soul of a Priest 1466
Souls and Bodies 1471
Sound of a Distant Horn
  2025
Sound of Anthems 501
Spaewife 678
Spark in the Reeds 1981
Speak the Sin Softly
  740
Special Friendships
  1782
Spider Love 1273
Spirit and the Clay
  1477
Spirit Wrapper 712
Spitballs and Holy Water
  948
Spoiled Priest 849
Staffordshire Assassins
  2023
Stage of Fools 687
Star Gazer 1237
Star Inn 1353
Star of Satan 617
Star Trail to Bethlehem
  668
Starforth 667
Starlight of the Hills
  2029
Stars In My Heaven 1382
Starset and Sunrise
  1916
State of Corruption
  1117

State of Grace   1789
Stealing Heaven   1611
Stephen's Light   504
Stillborn   1018
Stillness, The Dancing
  1765
Stones Cry Out   1306
Stones for Bread   1465
Storm Out of Cornwall
  1982
Stormalong   841
Story of Mrs. Murphy
  1940
Story of Sir Charles
  Vereker   1115
Straight and Narrow Path
  2066
Straight Cut Ditch   507
Strange Case of Miss
  Annie Spragg   706
Strange Children   1147
Strange Loop   1811
Strange September of 1950
  1543
Strange Way Home   1041
Stranger   770
Stranger at Killnock
  2156
Strangers   1621
Strangers of Rome   818
Student of Blenheim
  Forest   961
Subject to Authority
  819
Success of Patrick
  Desmond   1016
Such Is My Beloved   747
Such is the Kingdom
  2033
Sudden Death   1399
Summer After Summer
  2034
Summer of Desire   1143
Superstition Corner
  1366
Sweet Citadel   817
Sweet Morn of Judas Day
  1468

Sword of Honour   2116
Swordblade of Michael
  1215

Take Two Popes   749
Takers of the City   1245
Taquisara   860
Tell Me, Stranger   1078
Tempest of the Heart
  1163
Temptation of Norah
  Leecroft   1690
Tenebrae   1478
Tents of Wickedness
  1234
Teresa   537
Terrible Beauty   1891
Test   1400
Test of Courage   1885
Tetramacus Collection
  2081
That Man's Daughter
  1886
That Romanist   1479
Theft of the Shroud
  2189
Their Father's God   1880
There Is No Peace   1285
There Was an Ancient
  House   1390
Therese   1558
These Two Hands   1010
Thicker Than Water   1602
Thin Gold Ring   1674
Things As They Are   1305
This Bread   717
This Dark Monarchy   1434
This is Kate   1224
This Is My Land   1360
This Land Fulfilled   688
This Night Called Day
  1011
This Side of Paradise
  1066
This, My Son   581
Thomas   1672
Thorn Birds   1572

Thornberry Abbey 1752
Those of His Own
   Household 582
Three Cheers for the
   Paraclete 1376
Three Circles of Light
   938
Three Daughters of the
   United Kingdom 1343
Three Days to Live 1989
Three O'Clock Dinner
   1788
Three Priests 924
Three Ships Come Sailing
   1947
Three Wishes of Jamie
   McRuin 1738
Threshing Floor 854,
   1893
Through Dooms of Love
   2019
Through the Valley of
   Death 500
Thunder on St. Paul's Day
   1420
Thy Brother's Wife 1177
Thy People, My People
   1012
Thy Tears Might Cease
   1055
Thy Wedded Husband 1713
Tiara 1508
Tiber Was Silver 1703
Tighe Lifford 756
Tight White Collar 1452
Time Cannot Dim 771
Tippy Locklin 1613
To Beg I Am Ashamed
   1984
To Drain the Sea 945
To Every Man a Penny
   1526
To Live Alone 1365
To Love and To Dream
   974
To the End of the World
   2149
Told by Brother Giles
   1261

Touch 1445
Touch of Jonah 1300
Tower of Ivory 1084
Towers of St. Nicholas
   1164
Town Landing 1046
Town on the Hill 1696
Trail of Blood 1802
Trail of the Iroquois
   1918
Training of Silas 925
Traitor's Moon 1680
Trap for Navarre 2173
Travellers 1060
Tree Grows in Brooklyn
   1983
Tree of Dark Reflection
   1103
Tremaynes and the
   Masterful Monk 982
Trembling Earth 830
Tremor of Intent 723
Tressider's Sister 820
Trial of Margaret
   Brereton 996
Tribe of Women 574
Triumph of Failure 1964
Trouble of One House
   1129
Trouble With Turlow
   1037
Troubles 1563
Truce of God 1630
True Confessions 989
True Cross 1925
True Story of Master
   Gerard 1903
Trumpet of God 988
Truth In the Night 1605
Tudor Pilgrimage 591
Tudor Sunset 2106
Tudor Underground 1612
Tumbleweeds 1865
Turn Back the Leaves
   907
Turn of the Tide 1165
Twilight Rendezvous
   1579
Two Nuns 1332

Two Schools: A Moral Tale
    1324
Two Solitudes   1491
Two Standards   569
Tyler's Lass   644

Unbidden Guest   843
Unbroken Heart   2001
Uncertain Glory   2178
Uncharted Spaces   1948
Unconquerable   1759
Under the Rose   888
Undine   2018
Unfrocked   897
Unholy Communion   1322
Unholy Sanctuary   1272
Unoriginal Sinner and the
    Ice Cream God   1810
Untimely Guest   535
Unworthy Pact   1119
Upper Hand   848
Upstream   1939
Urban the Ninth   1527
Ursula Finch   821

Valley of Sound   516
Valley Under the Cross
    714
Vatican   1536
Vatican Cellars   1124
Vatican Roulette   1469
Vatican Target   1928
Veil of Veronica   1442
Venetian Glass Nephew
    2169
Vera's Charge   1852
Very Rich Hours   1576
Vessel of Dishonor   1873
Via Crucis   861
Via Dolorosa   1580
Vicar of Christ   1669
Victim to the Seal of
    Confession   2005
Victory   1247
View from the Parsonage
    1367
Villa by the Sea   822

Vine and the Olive   549
Vintage   1361
Viola Hudson   823
Violent Season   1152
Violent Take It By Storm
    1488
Viper's Tangle   1559
Virgin   1757
Virgin and Martyr   1178
Virgin in the Ice   1779
Virgin of San Gil   1732
Virgin Territory   1503
Virgin with Child   2191
Virgins   1862
Visit of Brother Ives
    1835
Vocation of Edward Conway
    1017
Vocations   1715
Voices from the Moon
    973
Volcano   1030

Wages of Zen   1620
Waking of Willie Ryan
    704
Wall for San Sebastian
    1043
Walls Came Tumbling Down
    1020
Wandering Osprey   1489
Was It Worth While   588
Watch in the Night   2150
Water in the Wine   514
Water is Wide   1123
Waterfront   1933
We Are Besieged   1065
We Are Utopia   508
We Who Died Last Night
    1787
Wedding Bells of
    Glendalough   994
Wedding Group   2046
Weeping Cross   2032
Weight of the Cross   676
Welcome   824
Well! Well!   2092
What Priests Never Tell
    2141

When Love Is Strong 1383

Where Is the Pope? 619

Where the Dark Streets Go 902

White Fire 1013

White-Handed Saint 1751

White Hawthorn 669

White Ladies of Worcester 551

White Lion 590

White Sister 862

White Stone 833

White Wampum 1756

Whole Difference 1386

Whom God Hath Joined 1534

Whore Mother 1257

Whose Name Is Legion 825

Wide House 743

Wild Orchid 2078

Wild Times 737

Willitoft 1610

Willy Burke 1912

Winding Ways 1949

Wine and the Music 565

Wine of Satan 1116

Wings of Hope 1550

Winnowing 608

Winter in the Heart 505

Winter of Discontent 560

Wisdom of Father Pecquet 1032

Witch of Manga Reva 1863

With Crooked Lines 1238

With Friends Like That 1044

With Love, Peter 1287

With O'Leary in the Grave 765

With Sword and Crucifix 2082

Without Love 1220

Woman and the Priest 969

Woman in the House 566

Woman of the Pharisees 1560

Woman Who Was Poor 640

Women in the Wall 1718

Women's Rites 731

Wonderful Flower of Woxingdon 2006

Wonderful Fool 1031

Woodcarver of Tyrol 2094

Wooden Statue 1490

World D 1262

World I Never Made 1052

World, the Flesh and Father Smith 1528

World, the Flesh and the Devil 2045

World Well Lost 1866

World Without End, Amen 696

Wounded Face 1047

Wrath of God 1155

Wreath for the Innocents 1000

Wreath of Song 705

Young and the Immortal 884

Young Lonigan 1053

Young Man in Chains 1561

Young Manhood of Studs Lonigan 1054

You're Welcome to Ulster 1108

Zenosius 1793